D0387530

(602) 577-3281

Michael Horton's provocative challenge to the church reaffirms our primary mission as servants of God: to proclaim the Gospel of Jesus Christ as the salvation of the world. How he does this, however, is to strip away the moral, political, and cultural veneer that has encrusted our faith and to dare us to articulate the eternal truths of our historic creeds to a world (and church) freshly tossed about by windy doctrines.

> Terence Lindvall, Ph.D.
> President, Regent University

Michael Horton's *Beyond Culture Wars* cuts through much non-sense and half-sense to the heart of what it means to be a Christian—in America, or anywhere else. The book poses exactly the right challenges for modern evangelicals—to look at the "crisis" of America as a spiritual crisis and to think of our task in the world as missions rather than warfare. . . . This book is sobering, thought provoking, and courageous.

> Mark Noll
> McManus Professor of Christian Thought
> Wheaton College

This book is persuasively argued by a committed and thoughtful evangelical advocate who is bluntly realistic about the depth of problems evangelicals confront in the postmodern world. This is a brilliant exercise in evangelical reflection on the culture that is following the death of modernity.

> Dr. Thomas C. Oden
> (From the foreword)

BEYOND CULTURE WARS

MICHAEL S HORTON

MOODY PRESS

CHICAGO

© 1994 by
MICHAEL S. HORTON

All rights reserved. No part of this book may be reproduced in any form without permission in writing from the publisher, except in the case of brief quotations embodied in critical articles or reviews.

Sting, "If I Ever Lose My Faith in You,"
copyright © 1992 Magnetic Publishing, Ltd.
Published by Blue Turtle Music / Illegal Songs, Inc.
in the United States and Canada.
All rights reserved.
Used by permission.

All Scripture quotations, unless indicated, are taken from the *Holy Bible: New International Version*®. NIV®. Copyright © 1973, 1978, 1984 International Bible Society. Used by permission of Zondervan Publishing House. All rights reserved.

Quotations from the Lord's Prayer are taken from the King James Version.

The use of selected references from various versions of the Bible in this publication does not necessarily imply publisher endorsement of the versions in their entirety.

ISBN: 0-8024-0893-1

1 3 5 7 9 10 8 6 4 2

Printed in the United States of America

*To the memory of J. Gresham Machen,
casualty of fads, vindicated by time*

BOOKS BY MICHAEL HORTON

WRITTEN

The Law of Perfect Freedom

EDITED

Power Religion
The Agony of Deceit

CONTENTS

FOREWORD

$\mathbf{M}$ichael Scott Horton, like many Christians, has become disheartened by the ways the church has been exploited by ideologies of either the radical right or left. Christians right and left have bought into the polarization of excessively politicized Christianity while forgetting or soft-peddling the very Gospel and active life of faith that would make Christianity more relevant to public life. Since the Enlightenment, Christianity has increasingly colluded in allowing itself to become consigned by the culture either to the private domain of gaining self-esteem or to the instrumental task of eliciting a morality necessary to sustain democracy. Horton shows how the familiar polarized politicizers of both wings have misunderstood the Gospel and its relation to culture and public policy.

I write as one who agrees enough with Mike Horton on the central issue that I think it worthwhile to contend with him on a few miscellaneous minor points: Even though his hyper-Augustinian obsession with Western and Reformed writers needs the corrective of the pre-Pelagian, pre-Augustinian Eastern Orthodox tradition (especially on the interface of grace and freedom), he still is a thoughtful critic. Even though he inexactly imagines that it is pietists and revivalists who have kept the Enlightenment alive, he nonetheless nails pietism and revivalism in many plausible ways. Even though his polemic against holiness revivalism is exaggerated, I agree with his deeper intention of bringing a greater world-affirming rationality to evangelical reflection.

His position, while appealing to the recovery of rational argument, often sounds as thoughtfully paradoxical as that described by H. R. Niebuhr as *Christ and Culture in Paradox*. He rightly opposes identification of religion with political ideologies, but he insists upon the civic implications of the Gospel rightly preached and lived. He has an aggressive attitude toward culture transformation, but he opposes simplistic politicizations of Christianity.

Horton's is a strongly confessional theology, admiring most those historic forms of Christianity that have stuck rigorously to the proclamation of the Gospel, the distinction between Law and Gospel, and the interactive differentiation between the two cities; and which thereby had greater effect on social transformation than if they had made desperate attempts to manipulate political power. His position is akin to those of Aleksandr Solzhenitsyn, Francis Schaeffer, Carl Henry, and more recent critics David Wells, John Leith, Os Guinness, and Alister McGrath. His major historical models are the Western Christian writers: Justin, Tertullian, Augustine, Luther, and Machen, but above all Calvin. His historical interpretation corresponds in many ways with those offered by Henry Chadwick, Donald Bloesch, Mark Noll, Nathan Hatch, and George Marsden. He is prepared to use public opinion analysis by George Gallup and George Barna to show that values of evangelical Christians and non-believers differ embarrassingly little.

Among those against whom he is struggling are not only sentimentalists of the left but also the emotivists, radical right moralists, and single issue policy activists who use abortion as the litmus test of orthodoxy. He takes on directly the supposed evangelical agenda of those who think the public policy battle is less theological than moral and who have allowed the destiny of the Gospel to be tied to a vulnerable political ideology. He is pointed in his critique of tendencies to accommodate church growth to social stratification and to reduce the Gospel to privatized good feelings. He is also critical of premillennialism's tendency to write off the existing world: He exposes those who await the end of the world eagerly, ready to call down fire upon the earth, who like Jonah would prefer to watch Nineveh collapse.

He is correct that evangelicals (with few exceptions) are theologically ill-equipped to battle intelligently and constructively to penetrate postmodern culture. He is aware that many evangelicals have already given up on academia, public schools, art, and culture, except for aggressive attacks on secular humanism.

This book is persuasively argued by a committed and thoughtful evangelical advocate who is bluntly realistic about the depth of problems evangelicals confront in the postmodern world. This is a brilliant exercise in evangelical reflection on the culture that is following the death of modernity. I find Horton's admonitions to me to be penetrating ones that I must take seriously. I think Horton is correct that the theological center must be recovered if moral actions are to be real. Thank you, Michael, for an absorbing and stimulating, and at times inspiring, read.

THOMAS C. ODEN

I do not write this book as a social and political liberal who simply wants to redirect the evangelical cause to his own agenda; rather, it is the whole enterprise I want to call into question as we rethink our calling as Christians at the close of the twentieth century.

The book, therefore, is not going to take sides in the "culture war"—not because I do not have an interest in such things, but because the church is no longer pursuing its authentic mission, generally speaking, and ministers are supposed to ring the bell when that happens.

This book is a call to the church to reassess its mission, its message, and its agenda as we make our way into the twenty-first century.

Michael S. Horton

ACKNOWLEDGMENTS

Special thanks is due to the staff at Christians United for Reformation (CURE) for assisting me in having the time to prepare this material. Especially remembered in this regard is my associate, Sara McReynolds. Also, Kim Riddlebarger, Shane Rosenthal, Alan Maben, and Jim and Jo Horton have contributed tremendously to my freedom to write the book.

David Walsh's book, *After Ideology*, was a significant help in refining my own views and challenging me to think more deeply about some of the issues discussed in this volume. Os Guinness, Ken Myers, Darryl Hart, J. I. Packer, James Boice, Kim Riddlebarger, Dan Bryant, and Eric Gregory assisted me with their reviews of the first draft, and for that I am grateful.

Thanks also to Moody Press, and Jim Bell and Carol Harding, in particular.

PART ONE:

Defining
the
Issues

1

WHAT'S WRONG WITH CULTURE WARS?

Will we "be prepared to give an answer to everyone who asks [us] to give the reason for the hope that [we] have"? Or will we continue to be so caught up in moral and political solutions to this deep spiritual crisis that we end up, ironically, actually deepening the crisis?

O N MONDAY, JULY 17, 1993, Randall Terry, founder of Operation Rescue, told those who had gathered for his press conference that the recent devastating floods in the midwestern United States were divine judgment on Americans for electing Bill Clinton to the U.S. presidency. Flanked by loyal supporters among the Christian Right, Terry questioned whether those who had voted for Clinton could be true Christians. On August 16, *USA Today* reported that a minister in Alabama had sent an ad to newspapers showing a man pointing a gun at a doctor's head, with the caption, "Justifiable Homicide." The minister told the international newspaper, "If 100 doctors need to die to save over 1 million babies a year, I see it as a fair trade." At the same time, then nominee for Surgeon General, Joycelyn Elders, was calling her critics among the Religious Right "non-Christians" with "slave-master mentalities" who can't seem to get over their "love affair with the fetus."[1] A *Washington Post* article arguing that opposition to gays in the military was largely orchestrated by the Religious Right concluded, "Their followers are largely poor, uneducated, and easy to command."[2] President Clinton, in a speech to the Yale University Alumni Association, said, "The problem I have [with the Religious Right] is that so many of them seem to believe that their number-one obligation is to make whatever they think is wrong illegal, and then not worry about what kind of affirmative duties we have to one another."[3]

It doesn't take long to pull together scores of examples like these to illustrate what has come to be called "culture wars," as American society becomes increasingly polarized and civil discourse becomes increasingly uncivil.

But it is not the purpose of this book to add another log to the social conflagration; nor is it the scope of this book to attempt to say what has already been said very well by sociologists such as James D. Hunter, David Martin, Peter Berger; public policy specialists such as Richard John Neuhaus; or commentators such as Garry Wills, Allan Bloom, and a host of respected voices. Rather, I write this book as a Protestant minister who is deeply concerned that both liberal and conservative Protestants have largely abandoned the chief mission of the Christian church—the ministry of Word and sacrament—in an effort to be "relevant" and "practical" in an age which has little tolerance of truth for truth's sake.

Furthermore, I am writing this book as an evangelical for an evangelical publisher and, presumably, an evangelical audience. If I were writing for a more general audience, a great deal could be said to the left-leaning mainline churches along the same lines. In fact, I have no doubts that much harsher criticisms could be made of the "more-liberal-than-thou" churchmen and women of modern Protestantism; they have had a longer history of confusing the Gospel with moral and political triumphs. Nevertheless, even if the transgressions are less heinous on the evangelical side, they are not less serious. Because evangelicals claim adherence to the authority of Scripture and the centrality of Christ and redemptive preaching, their slightest departures are far more fatal than the most lumbering strides of those who have already given up the faith to secularism. I do not write this book as a social and political liberal who simply wants to redirect the evangelical cause to his own agenda; rather, it is the whole enterprise I want to call into

16

question as we rethink our calling as Christians at the close of the twentieth century.

The book, therefore, is not going to take sides in the "culture war"—not because I do not have an interest in such things, but because the church is no longer pursuing its authentic mission, generally speaking, and ministers are supposed to ring the bell when that happens. As we shall see in the introductory chapters, the greatest issues of our day do not have to do with whether one is politically left or right of center. The real division is between those, on the one hand, who believe that revelation, salvation, and the kingdom of God come down from heaven as the sovereign intervention of God breaking into human history and, on the other hand, those who assume that we can save ourselves (either as individuals or as a nation) and bring in the kingdom of God by our own works of righteousness. This book is a call to the church to reassess its mission, its message, and its agenda as we make our way into the twenty-first century. It is also an impassioned plea to Christians to reorient their relationship to the culture from soldiers to missionaries.

Polls demonstrate that the American public—not just the radical left, but the mainstream public—"have about had it with the approaches of political religious types." The Religious Right is marginalized, Lou Harris argues. "Opportunity for their cause is now dwindling, and the more they press, the more likely it is that they will trigger a fierce backlash from a solid majority of the American people."[4] Many even who have some sympathies with the cause have grown increasingly cynical about the leadership, with predictable stances from both Jesse Jackson and Jerry Falwell on nearly every conceivable issue, no matter how dubious its moral and spiritual significance may be. In *Inside America*, Louis Harris reports, "Indicative of its [the Religious Right's] demise were Falwell's trips in 1985 to the Philippines, where he applauded the regime of Ferdinand Marcos shortly before it fell, and to South Africa, where he championed the Botha government, called for reinvestment instead of disinvestment by U.S. companies, and denounced as a 'phony' Archbishop Desmond Tutu, the black Anglican leader in that country."[5] Many Americans came to believe that the agenda of those who combined religion and political ideology were merely "rubber-stamping" the policies of the Reagan administration and raising even the most debatable policy positions (such as the Panama Canal give-away and the Strategic Defense Initiative or "Star Wars") to the level of transcendent biblical absolutes. In effect, it created an atmosphere in many churches in which heresy is not so much attacking a particular tenet of historic orthodoxy, but refusing to become a foot-soldier in the army of the Lord and swallow the dogmas of right-wing ideology whole.

Of course, the same could be said of the mainline churches, which often pride themselves on their openness and tolerance, a tolerance which often extends to everyone *except* those who refuse to accept the minutiae of left-wing dogmatism. In both cases, the secular establishment has created the agenda and the religious leaders have been co-opted to give divine sanction even to positions upon which the Bible is absolutely silent. Those who seek to end abortion by encouraging policies aimed at helping unwed mothers are labeled "socialists," while those who seek to end abortion by overturning *Roe v. Wade* directly are forced to wear the scarlet "B" for bigot, as those who are obviously anti-women. If a particular policy is aimed at helping the poor (a clearly biblical priority), those who support it are charged with being "liberal" by conservatives, while those who wonder whether that particular policy might actually hurt the poor over the long-term are suspected by the more progressive types of not really caring. It's not enough to care about life, to care about the poor, and the family, and so on. One must endorse either the secular left or the secular right and fight with the might of Christian soldiers. James D. Hunter observes, "In the final analysis, each side of the cultural divide can only talk past the other."[6] Columbia University professor, Randall Balmer, added, "On television last summer we had to endure Pat Buchanan and Pat Robertson haranguing us about 'family values' at the Republican National Convention. Jesse Jackson's rhetoric strikes many as inflammatory. Michael Kinsley and John Sununu are forever braying at one another and their (usually) hapless adversaries on CNN, and Rush Limbaugh's banter garners huge audiences."[7] At the risk of hyperbole, one wonders today what would be more dangerous in some evangelical gatherings: disagreeing with someone over the doctrine of the Incarnation or disagreeing with Rush Limbaugh.

The sad thing is, the insults are thrown about by Christians at other Christians. Not only does one have to have a particular position which is biblically justified; one must adopt a particular strategy and course of action in order to be truly orthodox. Christians who support the public schools are regarded by some as having sold out to secular humanism, whereas parents who home-school or support the Christian school are sneered as escapists and separatists. Ironically, at a time when outright heresy flourishes even in the evangelical community[8] and many Christians are unable to define the essential elements of the Gospel[9]—all in the interest of tolerance and unity—the Christian community at the end of the twentieth century does not seem to have any trouble forming deep, hostile divisions over which political package and candidate to endorse. Philosopher Alisdair MacIntyre observed that the sure sign that a new dark age is upon us is that "politics is civil war carried on by other means."[10]

> *Just at the point when the culture is most ready to hear our story for the first time in a while, we are caught up in the very crusade mentality that people, conservatives and liberals, resent.*

Weary of the "political correctness" of the left and the right, many Americans are looking for deeper spiritual solutions that transcend party ideologies. What many on both sides of the "culture wars" don't seem to have noticed is that the deeper philosophical currents in society are decidedly anti-ideological. With the collapse of communism and with cynicism about the ability of American democracy (the modern *Pax Romana*) to civilize the world, people are increasingly impatient with ideological rhetoric and political panaceas. Having swung from contempt of the world in the middle ages to believing we could save it in the modern age, postmodern society is weary of both. "More than at any other time in the past five centuries," writes political philosopher David Walsh, "there is a readiness to accept the eschatological mystery, with its tension between the transfigurative process going on within time and a fulfillment beyond time."[11] In other words, people are ready for the *Christian* teaching that, while there can be tremendous gains in social improvement and cultural strides, salvation is not something we believe we can achieve through humanity, brotherhood, or the "isms" of the Left or the Right. The Russian literary dissident, Aleksandr Solzhenitsyn, told a Harvard University audience, "We have placed too much hope in politics and social reforms, only to find out that we were being deprived of our most precious possession: our spiritual life. It is trampled by the party mob in the East, by the commercial one in the West."[12]

Poignantly framing this "postmodern" sentiment is Sting's "If I Ever Lose My Faith in You"[13]:

> You could say I lost my faith in science and progress.
> You could say I lost my belief in the holy church.
> You could say I lost my sense of direction.

The refrain brings Sting back to the woman in his life: "If I ever lose my faith in you, there'd be nothing left for me to do." Again, "Some would say I was a lost man in a lost world. You could say I lost my faith in the people on TV. You could say I'd lost my belief in the politicians. They all seemed like game show hosts to me." The song closes with this verse: "I never saw no miracle of science that didn't go from a blessing to a curse. I never saw no military solution that didn't always end up as something worse, but let me say this first: If I ever lose my faith in you, there'd be nothing left for me to do." The best we can do under such circumstances is enjoy our relationships, until, of course, they begin to disintegrate as well.

Just at the point when the culture is most ready to hear our story for the first time in a while, we are caught up in the very crusade mentality that people, conservatives and liberals, resent. The question is, will we "be prepared to give an answer to everyone who asks [us] to give the reason for the hope that [we] have"? (1 Peter 3:15). Or will we continue to be so caught up in moral and political solutions to this deep spiritual crisis that we end up, ironically, actually deepening the crisis?

CHRISTIANITY AND CULTURE WARS: HOW DID WE GET HERE?

It was not so long ago that evangelicals, and especially fundamentalists, were content to live on the margins of society. In fact, it was almost seen as a sign of faithfulness that Christians were too interested in the Bible, prayer, evangelism, and spiritual growth to be concerned with a world that was going to be destroyed anyway. Of course, this is not how evangelicals have normally thought since the Reformation, but it is the way they were thinking after two devastating and disillusioning world wars. In fact, from the foundations of Puritan New England until World War I, most evangelicals shared with their secular contemporaries an optimism about the future—not because of any belief in the perfectability of human nature, but because of their view of eschatology (where history is going). Postmillennialism, the reigning view, looked forward to the victory of Christ over the nations through world missions, and this was to bear fruit in righteousness, justice, and peace as Christ's kingdom gradually subdued the kingdoms of this world. However, this positive view was radically rethought when "the war to end all wars" didn't, and Protestants found themselves increasingly marginalized by the very forces of progress and enlightenment for which they had been largely responsible. Nearly 70 percent of America's colleges were in the hands of the old Protestant establishment (Congregationalists, Presbyterians, Episcopalians) before 1820.[14] Hospitals, social services, and publishing houses were often church-related.

But all this Protestant hegemony began to unravel as the secularism unleashed in the Enlightenment gradually led the culture to doubt the authority of Scripture and, therefore, of the institutions founded upon that authority. Weakened already by American revivalism and the individualistic spirit it bred, the church itself often led the way in either accommodating modernity or trying to escape it through radical separation. During the mid-1800s, an evangelical movement, largely spawned by anti-Catholic sentiment and fear of foreigners, formed The Know-Nothing party, a political party of some clout in mid-century, and revivalism became increasingly shaped by the fashions of the world, as late nineteenth-century revivals were heavily influenced (and often backed) by the likes of Andrew Carnegie and P. T. Barnum.

The Ideological Shift

A whole series of ideological forces swept the culture rapidly into a megashift that had earlier shaken Europe: away from belief in a sovereign God who not only governs at a distance, through providence, but interrupts history and so-called "immutable" laws of science and reason to speak and to save. Instead of bringing an objective, transcendent, and universally binding Word from God to humanity, the mission of the church was confined by these Enlightenment presuppositions to helping people feel good about themselves and serving the civil ends of producing the morality and virtue necessary to sustain a democracy. Sound familiar? It should. After all, this Enlightenment notion of the role of religion is exactly what the leaders of the Religious Right and Left have been preaching for nearly two decades. And that is not surprising, since both the Religious Left and the Religious Right are heirs of a common evangelical tradition. In the last century, evangelical activism spawned not only abolition and the crusade for women's rights, but the same people who marched in these rallies also crusaded for Prohibition, strict enforcement of morality codes in society, and often expressed fears concerning the immigration of so many Catholics. Political conservatives and liberals find a common heritage, as the Social Gospel was created by the evangelical movement itself. The problem was, those who became identified with the conservative side of the political aisle gradually became identified with the cause of "fundamentalism," even though both groups drew from the same well of the "American Enlightenment" and had little time for theology.

Those who more or less openly accommodated modernity, with its faith in reason, human nature, and progress (all in the name of making evangelical faith "relevant" in the modern world) eventually came into conflict with those who refused to accept a truce with secularism. In the 1920s, the Presbyterian Church expelled the orthodox J. Gresham Machen; the split within that denomination was followed by similar divisions in other Protestant churches, usually with great sorrow on both sides.

It must be noted that the "liberals" in these mainline Protestant wars were not self-consciously out to destroy biblical faith, but rather, they strongly believed that as long as they were "evangelical" in the *practical* sense (pious, interested in missions, revivals, evangelism, determined opponents of the use of alcohol), subscription to the finer points of theology was quite unnecessary. Machen and those who believed that Christianity could not be separated from its doctrines were also strong opponents of the "Protestant establishment," with its confusion of the American Dream and the Christian Gospel; opponents of Prohibition; and advocates of civil liberties. Observers noted the strange irony: Those who were the most concerned with preserving Christianity's distinct message were also the most concerned with civil liberties, whereas those who were less enthusiastic about doctrinal orthodoxy ended up spending their energies instead on trying to preserve their control over their political and social empire.

Among the more revivalistic evangelicals, separation was not so much a doctrinal issue as it was a long-held suspicion of institutions and the world in general. Soon, not only were the Protestant mainline denominations divided into so-called Fundamentalists and Modernists; the fundamentalists themselves divided into those who were world-affirming, cognitively oriented, and rooted in a particular confessional tradition (Machen and company) versus those who were essentially world-denying, emotionally-oriented, anti-intellectual, and more attracted to itinerant revivalists who "spoke to the heart" in ways that jibed with American experience and pragmatism. Eventually, this latter brand of fundamentalism won and has marked the movement ever since.

The Scopes Trial

The Scopes Trial in 1925 challenged a Tennessee law which forbade the teaching of evolution in the public schools. Front-page news in the international press for weeks, fundamentalists saw this as a showdown with secularism and reveled in the publicity. But the trial, which ended up favoring the existing law, left a sour taste in the mouth of the general public. Even sympathetic voices found the fundamentalists a bit "over the top," and the outcome of the trial was a classic example of winning a battle and losing the war. Fundamentalists never recovered from the image they portrayed in the trial as backward, anti-intellectual "know-nothings" who wanted to use force where they were lacking persuasive arguments.

In spite of calls for greater depth, maturity, and sensible social engagement from such leaders as Carl Henry and Harold Ockenga, evangelicalism, a wider category which included fundamentalists of both stripes, began to create its own subculture, seeing itself as evicted from mainstream society. Founding new colleges, seminaries, missionary agencies, and even publishing houses, broadcasting networks and stations, and eventually creating its own style of music, with its own galaxy of stars and entertainers unknown outside the "reservation," evangelicalism fell under Francis Schaeffer's charge of buying into the ethic of "personal peace and affluence." Now Christians could enjoy themselves at their own camps, conferences, and theme parks, and have the entertainment, famous celebrities, and other trappings of worldliness without having to bother with the world.

With this perceived eviction came a marked shift also in eschatology. Optimism about the future ability of believers to bring in the kingdom eroded, and many Americans after the wars were open to a more apocalyptic reading of the end times. Dispensational premillennialism, with its emphasis on the imminence of Christ's return and an intervening rapture, seemed to fit the pessimism of the moment: Why polish the brass on a sinking ship? Jesus is coming soon, so let's just save as many souls as we can. After all, things are going to continue getting worse until Jesus takes us away from this mess. Many evangelicals found comfort in this position, as it seemed to offer an explanation for their having lost the place of dominance in the culture.

Eschatology

All was well. With the exception of calls every now and then from a handful of evangelical thinkers, most were content to occupy themselves until the rapture with . . . discussions about the rapture. But then, in the 1970s, a thinker in the line of that earlier, more world-affirming "fundamentalism" of Machen, Francis Schaeffer, awakened the evangelicals from their other-worldly slumbers and apathy toward this world. A prolific author, Schaeffer addressed issues ranging from the doctrine of creation and its application to environmental protection to abortion and euthanasia. He railed against racism and pollution as well as big government and sexual permissiveness. Setting up shop in a collection of Swiss chalets, Schaeffer thought Reformation insights could be just the alternative to the secularism that evangelical youths, heavily influenced by the sixties counterculture, had experienced. And he was right on the money: Children of the churched and unchurched, from Harvard and Wheaton, doubters and defenders, liberals and conservatives, flocked to L'Abri for answers to the deeper questions.

At first, most evangelicals did not seem too interested in this rather unorthodox-looking cleric who was ranting about the deeper philosophical currents responsible for the symptoms that most conservative Christians saw (and see) as the ultimate concerns. Schaeffer was calling attention to these deeper issues and the mandate to think "Christianly," but the evangelical movement as a whole did not really rally to the call until Schaeffer led the reaction to *Roe v. Wade*, the Supreme Court decision opening the doors to abortion-on-demand. When Schaeffer was calling Christians to *think*, much of his work went unnoticed, but when he began calling them to *act*, the sleeping giant of American activism awakened, rose to its feet, and mobilized. Suddenly, the evangelicals saw how many of them there were. Coinciding with the American Bicentennial, conservative Christians who had just been attending prophecy conferences telling them the world was going to end very soon were attending rallies calling them to take back America from the "secular humanists." That signal year, 1976, was dubbed the "year of the evangelical" by *Newsweek*. Suddenly evangelicals found themselves the focus of media attention with the election of Carter, the publicized "born again" conversion experiences of famous people, and then the election and re-election of Ronald Reagan.

Suddenly—indeed, almost overnight—the tone changed from apathy toward politics and society to near-obsession, as Christian leaders reveled in rhetorical flourishes about the power of the evangelicals. Faith in the power of America coincided with a faith in the power of an alleged moral majority who could take America back through victories in courts and campaigns.

This is how we found things as we entered the nineties, although, once again, evangelicals seem to be on their way back out to the margins of a Republican party that once courted the favor of the new kid on the political block. The euphoria is gone; the proud boasts at rallies and conventions have left many disillusioned and desperate. No longer do the political figures hear from their media wizards that they have to win the evangelicals, so, as Lou Harris warned in 1986, the backlash of American society against the Religious Right has set the stage for the culture wars. More secular and explicitly anti-religious than ever, many of the nation's opinion-leaders (the "new class" of educators, think-tankers, writers, media personalities, and journalists) are not only refusing to "give America back," but they are bent on moving conservatives as far to the fringes as possible.

But we are back to the 1920s, where fundamentalism had two options: either the world-affirming orthodoxy of Machen or the world-denying revivalism of the frontier. When evangelicals followed the latter course, they committed themselves to popular culture rather than high culture, to passing fashion rather than to long-term philosophical, intellectual, and cultural influence. Modern evangelicals simply do not share with their Puritan forebears a love of learning and of this world and its culture—not as a redemptive sphere, but as a part of God's creation. Until this fundamental orientation is altered, evangelicals will forever be resigned to catching whatever shooting star happens to be making its way across the galaxy of popular culture. This is as true for its trying to find lasting solutions to secularism in marketing methods as its almost blind faith in secular solutions in the political arena. Ironically, lacking a theological and philosophical framework of its own, evangelicalism is dependent on secular methods for fighting secularization. And because the movement downplays the significance of philosophical and theological concepts, it rarely seems to know when it is being conformed to the pattern of the world rather than transformed by the renewing of the mind.

WHAT'S WRONG WITH THE CULTURE WAR?

What could possibly be wrong with the church engaging in culture wars over the values of an entire generation? Surely the church has never hesitated to offer its wisdom and council on matters of civic importance, so why should there be any debate over Christian participation in the war for traditional values?

I am not for one moment arguing that Christians ought in principle to abstain from civic affairs; in fact, coming from the Reformed tradition, I am in agreement with John Calvin that public service is one of the highest callings. Furthermore, we live in a participatory democracy, where "every vote counts," and common individuals—regardless of what we might say concerning the erosion of public confidence in the process—have infinitely more say in shaping public policy than in any other period in the West on record. It is a matter of responsible Christian citizenship to vote and to try to influence others by argument and persuasion. Beyond this, one cannot say that government cannot legislate morality, as every law is based on the moral judgment of law-makers and judges.

With this in mind, how can it be wrong for Christians to take up sides in the "culture wars"? First, it is dangerous. I don't mean dangerous in the sense Jesus intended when He warned us that we would have suffering and trials in this world, although some radical activists have been fond of confusing their being arrested for trespassing with suffering for the Gospel. Rarely do we encounter danger because we have proclaimed the Gospel too clearly these days.

> *Seeking to impose a conservative Protestant set of values will only alienate a culture that already lumps evangelicals with Islamic extremists, however unjustly.*

No, it is dangerous in the sense that we are unprepared for it. The recent history of American evangelicalism is hostility toward culture almost *as* culture. In other words, it is as if the very idea of culture were inherently evil, that the kingdoms of this world were so dominated by corruption that secular institutions were to be shunned or ignored while we engaged instead in building up the kingdom of God through "full-time Christian ministry." This hostility came through in the prohibitions against movies, secular literature, worldly amusements and associations, and the suspicion that participation in secular callings and culture was a waste of time when there were so many souls to be saved. But when evangelicals suddenly awoke to see the fruit of secularization all around them, they failed to ask some really difficult questions of the evangelical movement itself, such as how its theology (its doctrines of God, creation, fall, redemption, eschatology, view of the church, etc.) framed its understanding of the world and culture. It also failed to ask why a society with such a high numerical presence of evangelicals seemed to have little trouble tumbling into rank secularism so quickly.

Unless these deeper questions are asked, as will be done throughout this book, evangelical activity in the public square will continue to exhibit the same hostility toward the world in public that many ex-fundamentalists remember experiencing in private as they grew up. The attitude toward the world and toward culture has not changed, just the realm: Before, conservative Christians tried to modify the behavior of their own number by separation from the world, but now many appear bent instead on trying to modify the behavior of the larger society without having to persuade that larger world of its rationale, beyond, "God said it. I believe it. And that settles it." It is as if we have simply adopted the pagans as our children, demanding that they follow our rule of life while in actual fact they are not our children, but unconvinced and unchurched neighbors who are not persuaded that Christianity carries a binding authority to command their lifestyles. Seeking to impose a conservative Protestant set of values will only alienate a culture that already lumps evangelicals with Islamic extremists, however unjustly. Not only will the greater mission of the church—the proclamation of the Gospel and worship of God—be stalled by our preoccupation and the society's backlash; we will actually further the process of secularization by polarizing society and driving moderates into the arms of liberals simply by giving some credibility to the caricatures.

We cannot be hostile or even apathetic toward culture and yet attempt to redirect it. When we are, the results are obvious:

Our involvement is purely negative. We see this in the arts, where the only contribution we make is opposition to morally objectionable art, creating the impression that Christians want not only to keep their children from reading secular literature, going to movies, and being exposed to a wide variety of viewpoints, but that they want to censor the art and literature of the general public. It simply does not matter whether, in the middle of a war, these images that we present of ourselves are real or imagined. It only matters whether they are successful, whether they are convincing to a broad cross-section of the people we should be trying to persuade. And, by every statistical indicator, these images are indeed successful.

> *Just as we have few of our own artists . . . but have instead created our own subculture of artists (with overtly religious themes) and awards ceremonies, so those who are often the most vocal in Washington about public schools have their own kids in Christian schools.*

In the *American Arts Quarterly*, New York art critic James Cooper offered a stinging indictment in the light of the controversial National Endowment of the Arts funding of pornographic art:

Conservatives have not even made the attempt of creating their own culture program during the last 100 years. Nor has the religious community, despite a tradition of glorious art that has produced Gothic cathedrals, the Sistine Chapel, the music of Johann Sebastian Bach and the art of Raphael, Dürer, and Rembrandt. American churches, business corporations, and government and educational institutions have . . . meekly embraced without protest a nihilist, existential, relativist, secular humanist culture they profess to abhor. Later, they wonder why films are made that are as sacrilegious as "The Last Temptation of Christ." . . . The reason for all of this is simple. Those who believe in absolute values such as God and beauty do nothing, and those who believe in existential humanism have captured the culture.[15]

But, too often, evangelical activists see such comments as an opportunity to act with force, through legislation or economic pressure, instead of really grasping the author's point: When you have to resort to such tactics, you are already too late. R. C. Sproul tells of a letter he sent to the best-selling novelist Pat Conroy, author of *The Lords of Discipline,* praising the famous author's work. Soon, he received a reply from this writer who explained that he was raised in a conservative evangelical background, which he has since abandoned, because his work was branded "satanic" by family and friends. The tragic life of Ernest Hemingway, son of evangelical missionary parents, is another in a trail of sad stories about our treatment of real artists among us. No wonder American society, in many cases led these days by those who were reared in and rebelled against this upbringing, is so afraid of the agenda of conservative Christians in the arts.

Similarly, the only time we seem to get involved in public education disputes is to attack teachers, school boards, and the "system" in general. Just as we have few of our own artists with works hanging in the Getty or musicians performing at the Metropolitan or Pulitzer Prize-winning writers, but have instead created our own subculture of artists (with overtly religious themes) and awards ceremonies, so those who are often the most vocal in Washington about public schools have their own kids in Christian schools and recommend the same for every concerned parent. I was reminded of that very fact recently, when I received a form letter from one of the nation's most respected family activists along those very lines. If we have not paid our dues by years of making positive contributions to culture, we simply do not have the cultural clout to pontificate about cultural crises. Those who do not care about the culture are not often taken seriously in wars over who owns it. As with our artists, our thinkers are not prized; nearly every single architect of modernism, including the realm of education, traces his or her roots to an anti-intellectual spiritual heritage. John Dewey, father of American pragmatic education, was raised in a very conservative Christian home and felt obliged to rid the world of this sort of religion. In fact, *The Humanist Manifesto,* which Dewey signed, could not have been created apart from a background in religious conservatism.

One of the most obvious tactical blunders on the conservative side of the culture wars was to identify the enemy as the "cultural elite." What does that make conservatives? The "culturally impaired"? The "backward fundamentalists"? Evangelicals—that is to say, those who descend spiritually from Luther, Calvin, and the Puritans—were the builders of much of the "high culture" we have had in this nation. No one argues with the idea that Boston is the nation's richest intellectual and cultural center, though not the largest. Furthermore, few would argue that the Reformation faith was not the major religious influence. Richard Hofstadter argues that the Puritans, much unlike today's evangelicals, were the greatest body of thinkers and culture-shapers our nation has ever had.[16] As David Wells observes, in the mid-nineteenth century in New England, "the literacy rate was around 95 percent," although today, in what is ostensibly the more "enlightened" period of that region's history, only "40 percent of the adult population is literate" in Boston.[17]

Harvard, Yale, Dartmouth, Princeton, Brown, Rutgers, and a host of other great academic centers were created by orthodox Protestants. Oxford and Cambridge owed their intellectual revival and physical restoration to the Puritans. The Reformation faith produced the spiritual depth of vision one finds in Bach, Handel, Rembrandt, Dürer, Mendelssohn, Cranach, Donne, Milton, Herbert, Bunyan, and countless other geniuses of "high culture." With its emphasis on activity in this world through one's vocation and the divine blessing on all legitimate work, evangelical piety used to be world-embracing. In short, orthodox Protestants (what "evangelical" used to mean) formed the "cultural elite" when they had a robust grasp of theology and gave it up with their rejection of God-centered theology in particular and the pursuit of a coherent theology in general. Now they were in the soul business, and there was little time for distractions of mind and body. Something had to fill the vacuum in the culture. Something—or rather, everything—did. And now we want it all back without having to go to the trouble of paying the price for being "salt" and "light."

This is why the present course is *dangerous*. It can only create alienation and hostility, a backlash that makes it more and more difficult to get the ear of society so that we can persuade unbelievers of the truth of the Gospel and the rest of the biblical revelation, including God's commands for justice and righteousness. It can never achieve its desired results, but can only serve to deepen the crisis.

But this is a pragmatic concern, and therefore, of a secondary nature. There are greater problems with our participation in "culture wars" that are of much greater concern.

CHRISTIANITY IS NOT A CULTURE

Wrapped around the biography of a Jewish rabbi nearly 2,000 years ago, Christianity is the only religion that cannot exist apart from the truth of certain historical events. This same Jesus claimed for Himself nothing short of equality with God, said He was the mediator between God and humanity, the Savior of the world, the long-awaited Messiah anticipated by the prophets, and the Way, the Truth, and the Life, apart from whom no one can come to the heavenly Father. St. Paul defined Christianity in a nutshell: "For what I received I passed on to you, as of first importance: that Christ died for our sins according to the Scriptures, that he was buried, that he was raised on the third day according to the Scriptures, and that he appeared to Peter and then to the Twelve" (1 Corinthians 15:3). Christianity, then, is the faithful record of Christ's person and work for sinners, and the telling and retelling of that record in each generation.

The Gospel has succeeded in a variety of cultures, from the Roman Empire's colonies in the Near East and its great cosmopolitan cities in Asia and the West, to the islands of the South Pacific and the nations of Africa. It has often prospered under oppression and weakened under prosperity. In fact, the advance of the kingdom of God has never depended on the state of the kingdoms of this world, either under totalitarian communism or democratic capitalism. The Gospel has thrived among groups maintaining vastly different values and mores, and has been just as good at reconciling socialists to God as free market entrepreneurs.

In January, 1993, on the day of his inauguration, President Clinton gathered a group of Southern Baptist ministers to pray with him in Little Rock. Some of the leaders assured the Christian press that Clinton was a genuine Bible-believer, since he wept at the singing of the hymns in church. This same day, I was being interviewed on a radio station in the Bible Belt and someone called in and raised that whole issue, ridiculing those pastors for making the integrity of a profession of faith depend on sentiment. The caller cited the response of one leader of the Religious Right who said, "I don't care if he cries when he sings hymns—what's his position on abortion?" I responded, "Doesn't anyone care about the only important question here: What does he believe about Christ?" If one wants to know where Clinton stands on moral, political, and social issues, his position on abortion is decisive. But if one wishes to discern more clearly the President's Christian commitment, the place to look is neither his sentiment nor his politics, but his confession of Christ. "Who do men say that I am?" is still the question Jesus asks.

But Christianity is rarely defined in doctrinal terms today. Rather, it is defined in experiential terms (being born again, having a personal relationship) or political and moral terms, but rarely is it proclaimed as saving truth these days. After all, doctrine is a distraction when there are wars to be won. And neither side in this war seems willing to trade rhetorical salvos for mature reflection. We have substituted the Gospel for moral and ideological tests. Today, the tie that binds is secular ideology, not doctrine.

This is not to say that public policy positions are unimportant. Quite the contrary. Every believer has a responsibility to both the church and the state. Rather, it is to say that in the church the concern is not public policy, but proclamation of the Word and administration of the sacraments. I was deeply impressed with the honesty of Billy Graham in this regard. "It is an error to identify the Gospel with any particular system or culture," he said, adding, "this has been my own danger." He concluded, "When I go to preach the Gospel I go as an ambassador for the Kingdom of God, not America. To tie the Gospel to any political system, secular program, or society is wrong and will only serve to divert the Gospel."[18]

Surely one who got involved in policy debates, Francis Schaeffer nevertheless knew the difference between the Gospel and a particular political or cultural agenda. He warned against alienating a whole generation again, as happened in the sixties, by identifying Christianity with the white, middle-class establishment, and even concluded from that what many missionaries and visitors from other countries would happily applaud: that the presence of the American flag in the front of the church, where symbolism is most important, sends mixed signals:

> In the United States many churches display the American flag. The Christian flag is usually put on one side and the American flag on the other. . . . So if by having the American flag in your church you are indicating to your young people that there are two equal loyalties or two intertwined loyalties, you had better find some way out of it. . . . It must be taught that patriotic loyalty must *not* be identified with Christianity. . . . Equating any other loyalty whether it is political, national, or ethnic with our loyalty to God is sin, and we better get our priorities right now.

Schaeffer then added this warning:

> There is a tremendous pressure to lose the Reformation memory as the years pass and our first task is not to align our message with the middle class establishment only to have our children rebel against our faith because of our politics, but to recover the lost truth of our Reformation heritage.[19]

---

*History offers ample testimonies
to how easily appeals to Christian
truth and its absolute values
have been misused to justify evil.*

I have always wondered why any homosexual would listen to us when we talk about AIDS as the judgment of God, musing at what a lucky thing it is for the rest of us that God does not hand out diseases for gossip, greed, or self-righteousness. But there are other reaches of alienation. Gallup tells us that white evangelicals are more likely than any other group to object to having black or Hispanic neighbors. How can we avoid creating the impression in the media that the opposition, for instance, of many Christians to gays in the military is really based on moral absolutes and not on bigotry, when we are proven bigots where the issue has nothing to do with an immoral lifestyle? We must face the reality that our agenda has more to do with preserving the dominance of white, middle-class values than with the clear ethical commands of Scripture.

But beyond the nature of the agenda, evangelicalism just doesn't seem to be about the "evangel" these days. It's about a culture. It's about preserving traditional values of, for, and by, a certain segment of society.

Christianity is not a culture. At its best, its understanding of God, human nature and identity, the meaning of life and history, the problem of evil and redemption, and so on, can shape a culture for the better. Nevertheless, history offers ample testimonies to how easily appeals to Christian truth and its absolute values have been misused to justify evil. At its best, Christianity can influence even unbelievers who are influenced by it into being more humane neighbors—an interesting fact, when you think of how often moderns refer to the Crusades, but pretend that Christianity had nothing to with democracy, tolerance, and so on. But there will not be a redeemed culture until Christ returns at the end of human history.

A Grand Offense

Offending unbelievers is certainly not something Christians should avoid at all costs. Paul speaks of the "offense of the cross" (Galatians 5:11), and Peter uses Isaiah's words to describe Christ: "A stone that causes men to stumble and a rock that makes them fall" (1 Peter 2:8). Our Lord Himself comforted His disciples with the words, "Blessed are you when people insult you, persecute you and falsely say all kinds of evil against you because of me" (Matthew 5:11). The problem is, the offense these days is not the cross, nor Christ Himself—for this no longer occupies the center of evangelical faith and witness. Rather, we are the rock of offense and we are not being insulted, persecuted, and falsely accused because of Christ, but because of our own follies and quests for political power.

At the National Religious Broadcasters' Convention in 1993, the star of "Murder, She Wrote," Angela Lansbury, was scheduled to address the delegates, but the planners were going to cancel her appearance when they learned that she would be playing a prostitute in an upcoming movie role. That morning, the hosts of a network show could not keep from making the obvious remark: "Wow! A convention of televangelists barring someone from their platform for *playing* immoral roles." All around us, not just on the fringes, but in mainstream evangelical circles, some of the most outspoken defenders of so-called "traditional values" are divorcing, having affairs, and visiting their kids in jail. I know certain Christian leaders who were writing books on marriage and the family while they were in divorce proceedings or adulterous relationships. The books were published as if nothing had happened. Where do we muster the gall to go after the world for being worldly? Gallup and Barna have issued survey after survey demonstrating that the values of evangelicals and non-Christians hardly differ.[20]

Peter counseled believers who were suffering at their jobs, in the schools, and in society generally for being Christians, "Dear friends, do not be surprised at the painful trial you are suffering, as though something strange were happening to you," and added, "If you are insulted because of the name of Christ, you are blessed, for the Spirit of glory and of God rests on you. If you suffer, it should not be as a murderer or thief or any other kind of criminal, *or even as a meddler.* However, if you suffer *as a Christian,* do not be ashamed, but praise God that you bear that name" (1 Peter 4:12–16). The early church was so full of martyrs that many believers developed a "martyr-complex," where they went looking for trouble so they could achieve the dignity of martyrdom. We must always beware, as Peter warns here, of suffering for our own foolishness rather than for the Gospel.

The irony in all of this is that while we ourselves have become the rock of offense, we have removed the offense from the Gospel. We will stand up for the most doubtful positions with unyielding resolve, while the notions of sin and grace, Law and Gospel, repentance and faith, divine wrath and mercy are replaced with more "relevant" themes of pop-psychology. Even the cross itself is no longer the way God dealt with my guilt toward Him and His condemnation toward me, but is rather the way God shows me how much I'm worth and that should keep me from feeling guilty and condemning myself. We are offensive for all the wrong reasons while we remove the offense of the cross. Those who are committed to immoral lifestyles will not give us a hearing for the Gospel—not because of the Gospel itself, but because we have made it clear that we do not stand in the tradition founded by our Lord, the "friend of sinners." We are their enemies, like Jonah who refused to go evangelize Nineveh, a wicked city that had murderously tyrannized Israel, because he knew that God would bring success to His Word and Nineveh would repent. Jonah wanted judgment, fire from heaven, but God wanted to have mercy on the inhabitants. A similar situation erupted when the Samaritans (generally regarded as half-breeds) did not welcome Jesus and His disciples because they were on their way to Jerusalem (enemy territory). Again, the Samaritans were not rejecting the Gospel (they hadn't heard it yet), nor the person of Christ. The Jews and the Samaritans simply lived on opposite sides of the tracks and were not welcome in each other's neighborhoods. Even though the reasons for rejection were cultural rather than doctrinal, James and John ("sons of thunder," by nickname) asked Jesus, "Lord do you want us to call fire down from heaven to destroy them?" "But Jesus turned and rebuked them, and they went to another village" (Luke 9:51–56).

The church's task in this age
is to collect, gather, harvest.
At the last day, God Himself will
separate the wheat from the weeds
and exercise final judgment.

Are we calling down fire from heaven because we don't feel welcome in the new neighborhood? Like Jonah, whose rebuke took the form of a whale, and James and John, whom Jesus rebuked, we might well learn our lesson and reach beyond culture wars to bring the Good News to our enemies rather than judgment. Still another example is given, where Jesus offers a parable. An enemy planted weeds in a man's field, and the wheat and weeds sprouted together. "Do you want us to go and pull them up?" the servants asked the owner. "'No,' he answered, 'because while you are pulling the weeds, you may root up the wheat with them. Let both grow together until the harvest. At that time I will tell the harvesters: First collect the weeds and tie them in bundles to be burned; then gather the wheat and bring it into my barn'" (Matthew 13:24–30). Judgment of the world belongs to God, not to us, and it will come at the end of the age, not now. By seeking to pull up the weeds now, we are only alienating many who might otherwise hear the Gospel and respond in faith and repentance. We risk pulling up the wheat along with the weeds. The church's task in this age is to collect, gather, harvest. At the last day, God Himself will separate the wheat from the weeds and exercise final judgment.

CONCLUSION

Tim LaHaye, active leader of the religious right, outlined the evangelical strategy in the eighties as *The Battle for the Mind.* Secular humanists had taken over, and we had to raise a generation of Christian young people who had Judeo-Christian values. This meant that they would even follow the conservative political agenda on such issues as the Panama Canal giveaway and specific social programs. But there was very little discussion of the real intellectual challenges we face not only in the world, but in the church, where secularization is involved. In fact, LaHaye insisted that this battle is moral, not theological.[21] But that is just where we went wrong, it seems to me. Viewing moral issues as ultimate, instead of as effects of one's deeper theological and philosophical beliefs, we never did engage in a battle for the mind. As anti-intellectual as we have become, in sharp contrast to our heritage as evangelicals, we are ill-prepared to engage in this kind of battle today. Until we begin to see the deeper issues and regroup to learn all over again what we believe and why we believe it, we will continue to mistake symptoms for illnesses, effects for causes, and the fruit for the root. T. S. Eliot argued, "To justify Christianity because it provides a foundation of morality for the general culture, instead of showing the necessity of Christian morality from the truth of Christianity is a very dangerous inversion. It is not enthusiasm but dogma that differentiates a Christian from a pagan society."[22] A church, both conservative and liberal, that is so "enthusiastic" and eschews doctrine as a diversion needs to learn that lesson.

Secularism is a "genie" that will not be put back in its bottle. The result of a vacuum of God-centered Christianity in the culture, the triumph of secularism is simply the effect of a church that has weakened in its understanding, articulation, communication, and living out of the transcendent Word of God.

Perhaps we have learned our lesson out of the disillusionment of the last few years. Carl Henry writes of the Moral Majority, "But its enlistment of conservative Catholics, Jews, Mormons and others soon established a heightened political morality and not theology to be its objective while it placed ethical concerns firmly on the national agenda. Moral Majority achieved none of the legislative specifics it endorsed," while the West slides deeper into paganism.[23] At this hour, where can we turn but to the Lord? Having trusted too much in the idols of nation, pragmatism, ideology, and secular power, whether the carved image is in the shape of a donkey or an elephant, the stage is perhaps set for a return to the main message and mission of the church.

NOTES

1. *Time*, July 19, 1993.
2. *Christianity Today*, 19 July 1993, 15.
3. Reported in Focus on the Family newsletter, January 1994, 4.
4. Louis Harris, *Inside America* (New York: Vintage, 1987), 267–68.
5. Ibid., 263.
6. James D. Hunter, *Culture Wars* (New York/San Francisco: HarperCollins, 1991), 131.
7. Randall Balmer, *Evangelical Studies Bulletin*, Spring, 1993, vol. 10, no. 1, 1.
8. A growing number of self-proclaimed evangelical thinkers and writers are now arguing for notions as foreign to historic Christianity as pantheism, goddess worship, and process philosophy; there is also something of a renaissance of Pelagianism (belief in the inherent goodness of man and freedom of his will) in our generation. In addition, universalism and religious pluralism, the nature of sin and the atonement, and a whole variety of soteriological issues threaten to divide evangelicals in the coming decades (cf. James D. Hunter, *Evangelicals: The Coming Generation* [University of Chicago]; Philip Lee, *Against the Protestant Gnostics* [Oxford University Press]; David Wells, *No Place for Truth* [Eerdmans]). Notice that many of the most incisive critiques of modern evangelicalism's slippage are coming not from fundamentalist publishing houses, and they are well-documented.
9. See the figures in chapters 2 and 3.
10. Alisdair MacIntyre, *After Virtue: A Study in Moral Theory* (South Bend, Ind.: Univ. of Notre Dame, 1984), 20.

11. David Walsh, *After Ideology: Recovering the Spiritual Foundations of Freedom* (New York/San Francisco: HarperCollins, 1990), 187.

12. *Solzhenitsyn at Harvard,* the speech and responses (Washington, D.C.: Ethics and Public Policy Center, 1989), 19.

13. Sting, "If I Ever Lose My Faith in You," copyright © 1992 Magnetic Publishing, Ltd. Published by Blue Turtle Music / Illegal Songs, Inc. in the United States and Canada. All rights reserved. Used by permission.

14. Mark Noll, *The History of Christianity in the United States and Canada* (Grand Rapids: Eerdmans, 1992), 230.

15. Quoted by Pat Buchanan, The *Washington Times,* 22 May 1989.

16. Richard Hofstadter, in his Pulitzer Prize-winning book, *Anti-Intellectualism in American Life* (N.Y.: Vintage, 1964), contrasts the intellectual heritage of Puritanism with the anti-intellectualism of nineteenth and twentieth century Arminian revivalism, demonstrating the profound impact of the latter on shaping the general attitudes toward the intellect in modern America.

17. David Wells, *No Place for Truth* (Grand Rapids: Eerdmans, 1993), 187.

18. Billy Graham, cited in *Modern Reformation,* May/June 1993, 2.

19. Francis Schaeffer, *The Church at the End of the Twentieth Century* (Westchester, Ill.: Crossway, 1985), 79–80.

20. George Gallup and Jim Castelli provide these statistics in *The People's Religion: American Faith in the 90's* (New York: Macmillan, 1989). George Barna and William Paul McKay come to similar conclusions in *Vital Signs: Emerging Social Trends and the Future of American Christianity* (Westchester, Ill.: Crossway, 1984): "Survey data supply ample evidence of the bankruptcy of the commonly held world views of Christians. It is undeniable that as a body, American Christians have fallen prey to materialism, hedonism, secular humanism, and even to a jaded form of Christianity that rejects much of the commitment required of faithful servants. A recent national survey discovered that no fewer than seven out of ten Christians are prone to hedonistic attitudes about life. . . . As a final example, three out of ten Christians agree that 'nothing in life is more important than having fun and being happy'" (140–41). Wade Clark Roof, in *A Generation of Seekers* (New York/San Francisco: HarperCollins, 1993), substantiates the similarities, as does Hunter, in *Evangelicals.*

21. Tim LaHaye, *The Battle for the Mind* (Old Tappan, NJ: Fleming Revell, 1980), 187: "The battle against humanism, however, is not theological; it is moral." LaHaye displays the reductionistic "Christian America" approach that makes it difficult to take the challenges of secularism seriously (and indeed, for secularists to take Christians seriously). For instance, the Panama Canal giveaway under Jimmy Carter is ample evidence that humanism is anti-God and anti-America. "A humanist," therefore, "is just not qualified to be elected to public office by patriotic, America-loving citizens" (78). The origins of "secular humanism" cannot be attributed to any godless sources in America, but instead are explained as foreign corruptions: "During the latter part of the nineteenth century, many of our bright young educators went to Europe to pursue their graduate degrees. They enrolled at the Sorbonne in France, Bonn University in Germany, Edinburgh University in Scotland, Oxford University in England, and many other humanistic graduate schools. In time, these professors returned with their Ph.D.s, bringing with them the skepticism, atheism, rationalism, and existentialism of humanistic Europe" (43). A patriotic but altogether unhistorical read on the situation.

22. T. S. Eliot, *Christianity and Culture* (New York: Harcourt, Brace and Co., 1949), 46.

23. Carl F. H. Henry's opening address, published in *Evangelical Affirmations* (Grand Rapids: Zondervan, 1991), 23.

2

FIXING BLAME OR FIXING PROBLEMS: FIVE MYTHS WE NEED FOR CULTURE WARS

Who are the "secular humanists"? *Beside this question, the world's woes pale in significance.*

THERE WAS ISRAEL, recently liberated from Egypt, bowing down to the God of Israel in the form of a golden calf. Repeatedly God reminded His people that they belonged to Him, not because they were more righteous than the barbarous nations around them, but because He had chosen to have mercy on them for His own name's sake (Deuteronomy 9:1–6). Even though they had been liberated from slavery in Egypt, the children of Israel returned again and again to the old patterns of pagan bondage.

Martin Luther said that human nature is such that, ever since the Garden of Eden, we will always return eventually to some form of paganism. John Calvin added that the human imagination is an "idol factory." This is why the church is always in need of reformation, always open to criticism, always subject to the authoritative judgment of Holy Scripture: *ecclesia reformata semper reformanda,* "the church reformed and always reforming," according to the Word of God. And that disrepair into which the church frequently falls always takes the form of a departure from the clear message of the Gospel. Today, one must wonder once more if the churches —not just the liberal ones, but the conservative evangelical ones as well—are too much a part of Egypt to bring liberation to the captives.

Under the subtitle, "Blame Is Critical," Randall Terry states explicitly what many Christian activists pursue implicitly: "We want the pagan's signature on America's burned churches. Then we will be in a position of strength to lead the country out of moral and social chaos."[1] In an effort to end the blame game in this culture war and wake some of us to the responsibilities the church must face in terms of its own unfaithfulness, in this chapter I want to pose this question: *Who are the "secular humanists"?* Beside this question, the world's woes pale in significance.

OUR TACTICAL MISTAKES IN THE CULTURE WAR

Myth #1: The Problem Is Humanism

One mistake we have made in the so-called "culture war" is fundamental: we have incorrectly defined the enemy as the "cultural elite" in general and "humanists" in particular. First, some definitions are in order. "Humanism" is a terrific word. In fact, part of the demise of Western civilization is the *weakening,* not the *strengthening,* of its humanistic tradition. The term itself derives from the Renaissance effort in the fifteenth through the seventeenth centuries to recover the classical tradition, including the histories, poetry, prose, art, and insights of ancient Greco-Roman civilization. The Protestant Reformation owed much of its origins to this movement, as humanists recovered many of the tools, skills, and primary sources necessary to understand the Bible, which had been corrupted by poor translations and buried under a mountain of commentaries and authoritative interpretations. *Ad fontes,* or "Back to the sources!" was the battle-cry of the Renaissance. The Protestant Reformers, trained in classical humanism, answered the call. Such scholarship led them to the great biblical discoveries which unleashed the Reformation.

When the Puritans rebuilt a decaying Oxford and Cambridge and founded Harvard in the New World, they not only taught the Bible, but they made certain students were educated in the great classics of the Western tradition. Defenders of the humanities (which included history, literature, and philosophy), these believers thought culture was important and enriching, even when produced by pagans. It was important to appreciate one's culture in order to understand the ancient context of the Bible itself, rooted as it was in Near Eastern and Greco-Roman civilization, and to understand the major traditions and interpretations that have shaped the world in which we live and move and have our being down to the present day. To the degree that we ignore these influences, we will naively embrace the reigning philosophical fads without even knowing (or admitting) that this is happening.

> *One wonders how those with little knowledge of or appreciation for their own culture can possibly interact with, much less appreciate, the rich and diverse cultures of the world.*

As J. I. Packer and Thomas Howard argued some years back, Christianity is the true humanism, and biblical Christians ought to be the most ardent defenders of classical humanism. But earlier this century a group of prominent secularists created a document entitled *The Humanist Manifesto*. Included in the star-studded line-up were John Dewey, father of modern American pragmatic education, and influential Supreme Court Justice Oliver Wendell Holmes. There is no doubt that this small but elite band of educators, scientists, artists, jurists, and activists had an enormous hand in shaping the current worldview. But these opinion-leaders were hardly humanists. In fact, it was the educational philosophy of Dewey that had so much to do with the deconstruction of classical education in this country, which came into full flower in the eighties when Stanford caved in to the demand of a generation of students educated in such nonsense: "Hey, hey, ho, ho, Western Civ. has got to go!" The deconstructionists in the university departments across America are no friends to the humanities, dissolving the appreciation for classical culture in the acid of "diversity." A love affair with politics has seduced educators—

even the department heads in the humanities—away from their task of passing down the knowledge of a particular history. One wonders how those with little knowledge of or appreciation for their own culture can possibly interact with, much less appreciate, the rich and diverse cultures of the world.

If Christians are so interested in taking things back, they should take back this label. But to do so with integrity, Christians must demonstrate by paying their dues that they are friends of the academy, culture, science, history, philosophy, education, and the arts. Nobody wins back titles and institutions by force (without guns and tanks), and no one should.

But there is no question that secularists exist and exercise considerable control beyond their numbers. That does not, in itself, make secularists wrong. And this brings us to our second mistake.

Myth #2: The Problem Is the Conspiracy of a "Cultural Elite"

The creation of culture always takes the "trickle-down" approach, and the cultural "elite" have always been the handful of men and women who shaped the values, attitudes, and outlooks of the society. Many evangelicals are so much a part of the popular culture, however, that they think everything, including culture-shaping, takes place (or should take place) according to democratic principles. In other words, if the majority of the American population say they believe in God (whoever he/she/it might be), the idea is that this is what the professors are duty-bound to endorse. But the impression is often given that the "cultural elite" are not evil because of their positions, but, following the conspiratorial mind-set many Christians adopt, they are evil precisely because they are part of a "cultural elite."

The suspicion conservatives have shown toward the movers and shapers of culture is as much a part of modern evangelicalism's attachment to popular, mass culture as it is a legitimate frustration over the specific direction. But this suspicion of culture has not always dominated evangelical thinking. After all, the Reformers and the Puritans, forebears of the modern evangelicals, were the cultural elite of Northern Europe, Britain, and the New World. Though a persecuted minority, the French Calvinists founded the Academy of Painting in Paris, and their English counterparts led the way in science, founding Britain's Royal Society. There was a time in our own country when the leading evangelists were also presidents of Harvard, Yale, and Princeton. Christians did not dominate these institutions because they were actively trying to take over the "power bases" of society; rather, it was because the Reformation worldview, until replaced by the Enlightenment worldview, was the accepted system and paradigm through which every discipline was interpreted.

> *Christians have, throughout church history, gotten tangled up in paganism— often without knowing it.*

Many educators, lamenting the unraveling of the intellectual tradition, have spoken about the "dumbing down" of American society. The Puritan culture of New England created a "cultural elite" who, in turn, created the most literate populace in the modern world. Ask yourself if you would rather have your physician educated by the self-help medical section of B. Dalton's Bookstore or a respected medical school. The cream always rises to the top; by maintaining high standards among the "cultural elite," the idea was that the whole society would be better off. But this gnaws at our populist, democratic sentiment, and evangelicals are so attached to popular, mass culture today that many Christian activists actually think that the media, entertainment, politics, and popular literature are decisive in shaping the worldview of the wider culture. Nevertheless, the leaders of popular culture depend on the "cultural elite" themselves. To win the culture, Christians must pay their dues, make their case, and win their arguments in the libraries and lecture halls, not just on CNN.

The problem is, evangelicals today are more likely to be influenced by popular culture than high culture. This means that they are out of touch with the very world and institutions they want to influence. Hence, wars are fought in the media, in debates about movies, novels, and pop music, not at the source of the cultural fountain. Protests and boycotts may be successful if you are an auto worker trying to get a raise, but they are utterly useless in winning cultural ground. In fact, the resentment they create among even those who are generally sympathetic further alienates the masses they are trying to influence. Even in the process of winning a small victory, such as changing the rating of an "R" movie to "X," evangelicals dig themselves deeper into the hole of isolation, as the general impression is given that because they cannot win arguments, they will try to impose their will by economic and political pressure.

Myth #3: American Culture Is a Judeo-Christian Monolith

Christians have, throughout church history, gotten tangled up in paganism—often without knowing it. Only in retrospect can we see how thoroughly the medieval world and the medieval church were shaped by Greek dualism. Usually, the church simply adopted existing philosophical systems, reinterpreted them in the light of Scripture, and made use of them as points of contact with the wider culture. "Contextualization" is not a recent development, but it is easier for an American missionary to know when he or she is doing this among an unknown people group than it is for us to distinguish between reason and revelation when pagan and biblical language, symbols, and patterns of thought develop slowly side-by-side. The benefit, of course, lies in influencing the culture out of paganism; the danger lies in being seduced by paganism ourselves.

One of the greatest mistakes in the current debates is assuming that Western culture in general or American culture in particular is shaped exclusively by "Judeo-Christian" values. From the very beginning, Western culture has combined elements of pagan thought with Christianity, and the founding of the American republic is no exception. Sounding in retrospect almost like a "flower child" of the 1960s, John Adams chanted, "Let the human mind loose. It must be loose. It will be loose. Superstition and Dogmatism cannot confine it."[2] Adams thought it ridiculous that people like John Quincy would still believe in the Trinity and the deity of Christ. An evangelical parent might complain to the public school board that her son's teacher refers to God as "The Force" or "World Spirit," calling on the founding fathers for support. But she will find little support in 1776, as the infinite-personal God of Scripture was traded in by many of the founding fathers themselves for a Universal Governor and Benign Providence—an equally amorphous idol.

Although evangelicals can, with much legitimacy, call for a return to certain civil values of the founding fathers, they cannot call for Americans to come back to the faith of our fathers, to the Bible of our fathers, and to the biblical principles that our fathers used as a premise for this nation's establishment—unless they think deism (i.e., insipient secularism) is Christian. In trying to win the culture war by appealing to the religious convictions of the founding fathers—even the deistic ones—evangelicals, ironically, end up identifying with the very anti-supernaturalism and secularism that they so lament in its full flower today.

Benjamin Franklin, Tom Paine, Thomas Jefferson, John Adams, and many other founding fathers were not only *not* evangelical believers; they were vocal in their antagonism toward supernatural religion. For Jefferson, religion served a purpose only so long as it remained nothing more than a system of morality—something many Christian activists seem all too willing to pass for Christianity these days. As for the "Judeo" part of "Judeo-Christian," Jefferson said the attributes of the Jewish God were "degrading and injurious" to morality and "not only imperfect, but often irreconcilable with the sound dictates of reason." But the New Testament does not get any better review. Because the disciples were "the most unlettered, and ignorant of men," Jesus' teachings found in the Bible are "mutilated, misstated, and often unintelligible." "I not only write nothing on religion, but rarely permit myself to speak on it, and never but in a reasonable company," Jefferson wrote to a friend, although Jefferson did write his own bible: the moral teachings of Jesus, with the miracles, claims to deity and resurrection, salvation, and the like expunged, referring to these as "impious heresies."[3]

When he built the University of Virginia, Jefferson refused to appoint any faculty members in theology, following the radical rationalism of the Enlightenment in its belief that this discipline got in the way of education and civility. Bitterly attacking the Trinity as "superstition," along with the deity of Christ, Jefferson was hardly viewed as a religious cohort by believers in his day. He saw his new university as a place where students would be freed from such outdated notions. In fact, Jefferson sounds remarkably like a modern crusader of secular education.[4] Nevertheless, the most orthodox trinitarian could support Jefferson's scheme of the separation of church and state, and many did, especially the Baptists in the tradition of Roger Williams.

In correspondence with Jefferson, John Adams frankly expressed his disdain for classical Christianity, particularly its doctrine of miracles, the deity of Christ, the necessity of supernatural redemption, and a final judgment. "My Adoration of the Author of the Universe is too profound and too sincere," he wrote. "The Love of God and his Creation; delight, Joy, Tryumph, Exultation in my own existence, tho but an Atom, a Molecule Organique, in the Universe; are my religion. Howl, Snarl, bite, Ye Calvinistick! Ye Athanasian Divines, if You will. Ye will say, I am no Christian: I say Ye are no Christians: and there the Account is ballanced." Jefferson's reply is equally direct, referring to the legacy of Puritan New England: "I join you therefore in sincere congratulations that this den of the priesthood is at length broken up, and that a protestant popedom is no longer to disgrace the American history and character," concurring with Adams that if by "religion" people meant doctrines—particularly orthodox Christian ones, "'this would be the best of all possible worlds, if there were no religion in it.' But if the moral precepts, innate in man, and made a part of his physical constitution, as necessary for a social being, if the sublime doctrines of philanthropism, and deism taught us by Jesus of Nazareth in which we all agree, constitute true religion, then, without it, this would be, as you again say, 'something not fit to be named, even indeed a Hell.'"[5]

But people read what they want to read, and the secularists today pretend that Jefferson rejected even the civil virtues affirmed by Christianity, while the conservatives pretend that he was a precursor of themselves.

In a work profoundly influential and warmly received by many of the "cultural elite" at our nation's founding, Thomas Paine wrote, "It is better, far better, that we admitted, if it were possible, a thousand devils to roam at large, and preach publicly the doctrines of devils, if there were any such, than that we permitted one such impostor and monster such as Moses, Joshua, Samuel, and the Bible prophets, to come with the pretended word of God in his mouth, and have credit among us." After all, look at all of the wars. "Whence arose they, but from this impious thing called revealed religion, and this monstrous belief that God has spoken to man? The lies of the Bible have been the cause. . . . What is it the Bible teaches us?—rapine, cruelty, and murder. What is it the [New] Testament teaches us?—to believe that the Almighty committed debauchery with a woman engaged to be married; and the belief of this debauchery is called faith."[6] Ethan Allen threw yet another log on the fire with *Reason the Only Oracle of Man* (1784). So much for the "Judeo-Christian" tradition in the hands of Paine, Jefferson, Allen, and Adams!

In many ways, the radical secularism we see all around us today is as much a part of our American history, since the mid-eighteenth century, as the "Judeo-Christian" tradition.

Similar stories could be told of Ben Franklin and other founders. To be sure, there were Patrick Henrys too, men and women of solid evangelical convictions who made common cause with infidels in order to build a free, just, and civil state. Nevertheless, the sad truth is that the period just following the Revolutionary War was decidedly secular. The percentage of church attendance was lower than it has ever been in American history.[7] Things were no better in the South. Thomas Askew and Peter Spellman observe, "David Rice, the first settled minister in Kentucky, states that when he came to the region in 1783 he 'found scarcely one man and but few women who supported a creditable profession of religion. Some were grossly ignorant of the first principles of religion.'"[8] Protestants of all stripes lamented the immorality of the new nation. With the demise of Puritanism, the colonial spirit on the eve of the War of Independence was decidedly mixed. The older Protestant notions of human nature could account for the "checks and balances" in the United States Constitution even while rationalistic individualism was calling enlightened souls to break their chains and become free of the alleged fables of orthodoxy. In short, the founding of America is a mixed bag, with New

England Puritanism and immigrant European Protestantism giving way quite rapidly to a very secular outlook.

Therefore, in many ways, the radical secularism we see all around us today is as much a part of our American history, since the mid-eighteenth century, as the "Judeo-Christian" tradition. But both sides in the culture wars refuse to acknowledge the plain historical facts, fearing that by giving the other party any historical legitimacy they cannot claim the nation wholly for themselves.

By equating Christianity and Western culture, "Christian America" evangelicals not only have a problem with history, but with the essence of faith in the modern world. In the history of our relative faithfulness and unfaithfulness as the people of God, our allegiance to modernity does not speak in our favor. In modernity, I am "god" by appealing to my own reason; there is no revealed truth, only natural revelation; no miracles, only natural laws; no salvation, merely natural, moral improvement. Man is basically good, and evil is not innate to human nature but the result of warped social institutions. And yet, this secularist creed is implied in the belief that through legislation and moral crusades we can save America. It is explicitly stated in the words of one contemporary evangelical theologian who writes, "Sin is indeed 'inherited,' not in a biological sense, as Augustine argued, and certainly not because of the legal imputation of Adam's guilt, as in the federal theology, but historically." In other words, "Man is shaped by the warped social situation into which he is born and in which he grows up to maturity."[9] The popular nineteenth century evangelist Charles Finney, like most revivalists of his day, expressed the same sentiment.[10]

This essentially Pelagian view of the self has dominated American thinking ever since the Enlightenment, whether in the academies of New England or the revival tents of the Western frontier. At the 1983 convention of the National Association of Evangelicals, President Ronald Reagan delivered his "evil empire" speech and met his most ardent supporters, concluding with the line from Thomas Paine, "We have it within our power to begin the world again." This secular, Enlightenment notion of progress through the human spirit pervades American nationalism and is embraced by most evangelicals. Though utterly at odds with the Christian revelation and an unbroken consensus in church history, this fundamental myth of modernity underlies much of the preaching, teaching, and activity of American evangelicals. Although it is being abandoned by cynical pagans, in the wake of its failed experiment—not because it contradicted reason, but because it contradicted experience—this view of human nature has yet to be overthrown in the church, whether conservative or liberal.

Myth #4: The Greatest Challenge Today Is Atheism

First, both liberals and conservatives err in thinking that secularization is a-religious or anti-religious. Secularization is not only religiously guided and directed; specifically, it could not exist in its present form *apart from* Christianity. Liberals naively assume that modern notions of democracy (now devolving into the rule of the mob), liberty (turning into moral anarchy), and justice (rapidly becoming state oppression) were freshly discovered, like penicillin, by those enlightened souls who had emancipated themselves from the dark ages of Christian superstition. In fact, however, they were merely heirs of that very tradition they so bitterly oppose and without which they could not have the material from which to build their own edifice.

But Christian conservatives often naively assume that "Judeo-Christian" means all is well. Just as the blessings of this age cannot be understood apart from this heritage, so too the curses must not be ignored. The "Judeo-Christian tradition" is fallible, even if Scripture is not. Much evil has been done in this name, and the appeal to the "Judeo-Christian tradition" does not exonerate bad ideas. That tradition is a mixture of paganism and revealed religion; it is not only the story of what Moses was doing on top of the mountain (receiving the truth from God), but of what the people were doing down below (worshiping the golden calf). It is a tradition that combines faithfulness and unfaithfulness. It is itself secularized, and we must never treat the "Judeo-Christian tradition" or civilization as if it were a direct product of divine revelation or even scriptural reflection.

Furthermore, the problem with secularism itself needs to be correctly identified. Atheistic secular humanism gets the brunt of evangelical criticism these days, but while atheism may be the logical effect of deism, both are a part of *modernity*, which has replaced the supernatural with naturalism. But this worldview is being rejected by most intellectuals in the West. Even while Jefferson, Paine, Franklin, Voltaire, and others mocked revealed "dogma," they established their own "self-evident" truths. Nothing is self-evident to postmoderns. There is no such thing as "truth," either religious or secular. The products of the Enlightenment, including our founding fathers, were in no doubt that there was a god, although he was a false deity of rationalistic deism. Today, the problem is not deism or atheism, but the very opposite: pantheism. As Chesterton predicted, when we get rid of biblical revelation, it is not that we stop believing in anything, but that we believe in anything and everything. Thus, Nietzsche's vision of a "rain of gods" comes true. According to Gallup, it is now the educated in America who are most likely to believe in astrology and maintain an essentially superstitious, pantheistic, mystical worldview. It is not that *nothing* is true, but that *everything* is true.

Evangelical Christianity has just become one more voting bloc asserting its political rights, along with other special interest groups.

At this point, we are back to the position of the first Christians. They faced an empire that had a place for every conceivable idol, so long as the worship of that idol promised to serve the almighty idol of the state. Much like the belief that it does not matter who is praying in public places, or to whom, as long as this symbol of American civil religion is upheld, the Roman patricians would even have tolerated Christianity. But there was just one problem. The apostles and their followers would not allow Christianity to be one truth among others helping hold the society together. Christ was *Lord* even over Caesar! He was the *only* way to God: that was the "heresy" of the early Christians. It did not matter what they believed in their own particular private religious communities, so long as they did not insist on it as the universal, public truth which ruled out competing truth claims.

But today, we accept the essentially pagan view of civil religion, for the most part. Yale law professor Stephen Carter refers to Frederick Mark Gedicks' definition of "civil religion" as "faintly Protestant platitudes which reaffirm the religious base of American culture despite being largely devoid of theological significance." In fact, Carter argues,

> The platitudes of America's civil religion are expected and accepted —but they are only platitudes. They have no theology, except perhaps, as Wuthnow notes, a theology of "America First." It may be that we are comfortable with them precisely because they demand nothing of us. Not only are they easily ignored by those who happen to have no religious beliefs, but they make virtually no demands on the consciences of those who do. God is thanked for the success of an enterprise recently completed or asked to sanctify one not yet fully begun. God is asked to bless the nation, its people, and its leaders. But nobody, in the civil religion, is asked to do anything for God.[11]

Ironically, we rail against religious pluralism while we push for prayer in the schools, no matter the religion or object of faith. The "unknown god" will do just fine. So, evangelical Christianity has just become one more voting bloc asserting its political rights, along with other special interest groups. Unlike the early Christians, who grounded their mission in specific truth claims, we argue for dominance on the basis of (a) seniority (i.e., the precedent of the founding fathers) and (b) pragmatism (i.e., the moral and civic usefulness of Christian morality). In so doing, we risk not only alienating the unbelievers before they hear the Gospel; we actually end up laying the basis for a rejection of Christianity on the basis that it simply is not the option one chooses to adopt in the marketplace of competing interests. Instead, we should follow the example of those first-century Christians by arguing our case, not as a program of moral improvement or national salvation, but as the truth about God and humanity. This, then, is a spiritual, intellectual, and ecclesial mission, with political consequences being merely derivative.

Once we see that the real problem is idolatry, not atheism, we recognize immediately our affinity with the early Christians and their mission.

Myth #5: Political Solutions Are Ultimate

Thus far, we have sought to demonstrate that the intellectual climate (postmodernity) is in the process of repudiating the modern myth that political solutions are ultimate and that humanity, being basically good, merely needs good social structures in order to accomplish peace, harmony, order, justice, and righteousness. And yet, having lost the older concern with the truth about God and ourselves, as revealed in Scripture (i.e., theology), many modern evangelicals are still confident in the modern disciplines (psychology, the social sciences, and politics) as ultimate solutions. In other words, just as the world is losing its confidence in these authorities and wonders aloud about spiritual solutions, wide sections of the evangelical community are enamored with these newly discovered idols.

Modern intellectuals used to relish referring to the horrors of their "Christian" past, like the Crusades. And yet, after the deaths of literally hundreds of millions in the Enlightenment experiment of building heaven on earth through self-confident rationalism and moralism, postmoderns have lost their confidence in the power of modern science and its relatives, including politics, to solve the deepest conflicts. For the first time in two centuries, intellectuals are now talking about the *spiritual* roots of the crisis.

As many thinkers are pointing out, it was often pietists and revivalists who unwittingly kept the Enlightenment myths going. When the French Revolution devolved into the "Reign of Terror," religious revivals sweeping France restored some of the balance and, of course, gave the impression that the experiment wasn't finished after all. The secularists of modernity realized that they needed religion—not for salvation, but for spiritual ballast. Religion was to provide spiritual incentive for an essentially antispiritual program of rebuilding the Tower of Babel, and often even evangelical religion offered a hand by supporting belief in human goodness, God's existing for our happiness, with generous doses of nationalism. It was not enough to say, "This experiment will work!" What the ambitious project needed was, "God is on our side!"

By reducing the miraculous to "a philosophical result of the right use of means" (Finney), American revivalists obliged the Enlightenment and assisted in a reign of secularism down to the present.

All of this is to say that evangelicals have often (though not always) bought into the program of salvation through Enlightenment programs, and that often included its political mission and the underlying dogmas necessary to sustain it. Revival as dependence on the sovereign God, working by His Spirit through the proclamation of sin and grace is evidenced in the Great Awakening of the mid-eighteenth century, while by the Second Great Awakening, evangelicals, embracing Arminianism, regard revival and conversion in purely naturalistic and mechanical terms.

This is even in evidence today, not only in our evangelism, but in the recent efforts of more thoughtful evangelical leaders in Washington. In his call to arms, *Winning the New Civil War*, Robert Dugan, director of the National Association of Evangelicals' Office of Public Affairs, offers a strategy for "those who want to reshape society through the political process."[12] But has this ever happened? Has society ever been reshaped through the political process? Politics is the place where the ideas that have already shaped society find their legislative applications. One cannot reshape society through politics, it seems to me. Democracy was not legislated by a grass-roots political movement; it was a philosophy of government whose time had come.

Similarly, Marxism only gained power and moved armies after its creed had been embraced by the fertile intellects of revolutionaries. The Russian peasants, cruelly mistreated under the Czar, surely could have gathered the steam to destroy the tyranny of the crown, but the two powers struggling in 1917 were the adherents of representative democracy (first in power) and the Marxist-Leninists, who, of course, ended up in power. The peasants could rise up, but it was the "culture elite"—university trained intellectuals—who moved them in various directions.

Furthermore, in our own context, it is impossible to win significant victories in a democracy where the voting members of society are motivated at their deepest thoughts and instincts by secular convictions. Political triumphs were first intellectual victories; history will bear that out.

At that point, it does not matter what brand of politics one accepts, as both Marxism and capitalism are cut from the same cloth of Enlightenment modernity. Of course, it matters practically (I have no difficulty concluding that capitalism is superior in practical terms), but neither seeks the spiritual good of society. Both systems have much in common philosophically; they both believe that human beings are basically good, and that if things go terribly wrong, it is because of the social structures that have failed to adequately "nurture" them or unleash their possibilities. Both are offspring of the secular experiment, and by confusing capitalism with Christianity, we are not only historically naive (ignoring its roots in the Renaissance and Enlightenment), but are incapable then of really assessing the spiritual damage either secular experiment has caused to the human spirit. Furthermore, both are idolatrous: Capitalism replaces God and His prominence with the "Invisible Hand of the Market," whereas Marxism makes an idol out of the state. One looks to the state as the liberator, the other to the market, but both are essentially materialistic and hostile to spiritual realities. That is why a Solzhenitsyn can come to America and find the same disillusionment, despair, and nihilism that he knew so well under a Marxist state.

For us to call into question the spiritual effects or so-called biblical origins of capitalism is not to suggest that capitalism ought to be replaced with something else; it is simply to come to terms with the fact that every human invention has its pluses and minuses. The same technology that put a man on the moon can annihilate the inhabitants of the earth, and the same systems that can deliver so much weal can also produce much woe. If we place any system or ideology in the category of divinely inspired (and therefore beyond the possibility of divine criticism), we end up turning a political or economic idea into a religion.

Not only are political solutions not, ultimately, Christian solutions because the reigning ideologies are cut from the same naturalistic cloth; it is important to realize that political solutions are not ultimate even if they are based on Christian revelation.

The whole history of Israel demonstrates that even with a king, judges, the presence of God in the temple, and the Torah, with all of the commentaries of the wisest scribes, the nation habitually failed to mirror God's heavenly peace, justice, and righteousness. Even King David was prohibited by God from having the honor of building the temple, because of his violence. Someone else will have to eventually usher in the perfect kingdom of God—some Messiah in the future, the true Son of David.

When Aleksandr Solzhenitsyn came to America for refuge, evangelicals found immense pleasure in his attacks on Marxism and his calls for moral repentance and spiritual awakening. And yet, many seemed to miss his attacks on the West—not only for its sexual immorality (which seems to be about the only form of immorality some conservatives worry about), but for its greed and exploitation. In fact, the Soviet dissident clearly disavowed any love-affair with the idea of democracy. What Solzhenitsyn favored was not an American-style democracy over a Soviet-style dictatorship, but the end of ideological regimes altogether. In other words, the "ideological war" was itself the problem, regardless of the particular side one took.[13] Both presuppose rationalism, human goodness and autonomy, and yet, at the same time, reduce man to a merely economic animal whose whole existence is nothing more than factors of production and consumption. It's just that one explicitly rejects heaven and the other simply elects to ignore it.

Instead of trying to persuade,
we want to legislate, demand our rights,
receive what's coming to us,
claim our piece of the political pie.

The problem is, evangelicals think that they are heirs to the Puritans and the founding fathers. The truth is, they are heirs of the latter more than the former. In his response to Solzhenitsyn's Harvard address, distinguished historian Arthur Schlesinger, Jr., noted,

> In its majesty and profundity, in its perception of the evil inherent in human nature, it exposes the shallow religiosity of a born-again White House that, against every Augustinian and Calvinist insight, proclaims the doctrine of the inherent goodness of man and the aspiration to produce a government as good, decent, virtuous, loving, etc., as the American people. The challenge to American smugness and hedonism, to the mediocrity of our mass culture, to the decline of self-discipline and civic spirit, is bracing and valuable. To this extent, Solzhenitsyn shares common ground with our Puritan ancestors.[14]

After all, Solzhenitsyn discovered,

This tilt of freedom toward evil has come about gradually, but it evidently stems from a humanistic and benevolent concept according to which man—the master of this world—does not bear any evil within himself and all the defects of his life are caused by misguided social systems, which must therefore be corrected.[15]

Ironically, this is the root heresy embraced by conservatives and liberals alike. Whether the main issue is seen as breakdown in traditional values on one hand or failure to unleash the power of universal compassion on the other, the problem is seen as primarily a matter of social, moral, and political reform, and the government is seen as the answer. Everyone is out to *legislate* his or her way to happiness. From the Supreme Court to the small claims court, we see our relationships in increasingly legalistic terms. Instead of trying to *persuade*, we want to legislate, demand our rights, receive what's coming to us, claim our piece of the political pie. Once more Solzhenitsyn offers his insights, from his Harvard address in 1978: "Wherever the tissue of life is woven of legalistic relationships, this creates an atmosphere of spiritual mediocrity that paralyzes man's noblest impulses."

What this also means is that Christians of both stripes find it increasingly difficult to think critically about the destructive beliefs inherent in the system each endorses. For instance, what one finds almost totally absent from the discussions of evangelical activists is a concern for the destructive effects of capitalistic materialism. Can anyone doubt that the same system that has allowed for tremendous economic prosperity and progress has itself contributed to the breakdown in the Christian view of the self as spiritual as well as material? Have any of the leading Christian activists really raised concern over the influence of the modern capitalistic society, with its consumerism and pragmatism, on the breakdown of the family? That is not to repudiate capitalism or argue for some alternative; it is simply to take all of the challenges seriously and not allow ourselves to be conformed to this world's pattern of thinking. Politics is about making concessions, and I do not find anything wrong with my belonging to a political party, even though I know that the candidates for whom I vote do not embrace what I would regard as a biblical agenda. But I know other brothers and sisters who are certain that the party *does* represent a biblical agenda. There is nothing wrong with compromising politically when one cannot be wholly satisfied, but we should at least know the difference. Neither capitalism nor socialism is "Christian." At best, they are systems created with Christian input, but regardless of how much proof-texting and Scripture-twisting each side engages in, it is the secular vision that produced both and that must never be underestimated.

Although I, for one, would hesitate to agree with all of Solzhenitsyn's commentary and would certainly regard democracy (and, for that matter, capitalism) as ethically and practically superior to any other system, it is vital for us to recognize that the issue we must face is not merely "this system" versus "that system," or "this party" versus "that party"; we need a fundamental reassessment of the legitimate role of politics in a fallen world.

Political solutions are not ultimate for the same reason that medical solutions are not ultimate. In the end, we all die from something. That does not mean that we ignore symptoms, nor that we refuse to follow the doctor's instructions and do what we can to remain alive, but it does mean that we do not treat them as the answer to life's greatest questions. While politicians manage to accomplish some things—indeed, many things which are necessary and beneficial—they cannot bring about faith, hope, and love. They may make peace with a foreign enemy, but they cannot make peace in the human heart. They may temporarily mitigate or relieve physical suffering in various parts of the world, but they do not have the power to bring happiness, joy, or lasting satisfaction. They may provide incentives to growth and industry, trade and commerce, and defend us against aggression, but they cannot give us inner security. They may be able to defend the civil liberties of their citizens (including the unborn), but they cannot provide liberty to the soul. And even though they may institute measures that *affect* the family, moral values, and public beliefs, they cannot create a good family or a good society. To believe that they can is to agree with that other myth of modernity, that evil is the product of social structures rather than the incurable depravity of human nature.

In short, government cannot make people good. It cannot make them tolerant and charitable, as the left would have it; nor can it make them sexually responsible or God-honoring. With the most Christian of governments, our secularized society (including its churches on both sides of the political aisle) would be no more benevolent and would be no closer to loving God and neighbor.

What is required in our day, as even many non-Christian thinkers are saying, is nothing less than a spiritual quest. Will we be there, ready for the ultimate questions with answers from the personal God of biblical revelation, who is the source of all truth, or will we still be entangled in the ideological movements and draw our water from streams which have run their course, progressing from a mighty ocean to a stagnant pond?

In the next chapter, we will move beyond the myths and ask some searching questions about the identity of the "enemy" in the culture wars.

NOTES

1. Randall Terry, *Why Does a Nice Guy Like Me Keep Getting Thrown in Jail?* (Lafayette, La.: Huntington House, 1993), 165–66.
2. Edwin S. Gaustad, *Faith of Our Fathers* (New York: Harper & Row, 1987), 88.
3. Gaustad, *Faith*, 101.
4. Ibid., 40–48.
5. Ibid., 297.
6. Gaustad, ed., *A Documentary History of Religion in America to the Civil War* (Grand Rapids: Eerdmans, 1982), 295.
7. According to Richard Hofstadter, during the mid-eighteenth century, "church members never amounted to more than a third of the population of New England adults and may never have been as high as five percent of adults in the southern colonies." *Anti-Intellectualism in American Life* (New York: Vintage, 1963), 89.
8. Thomas Askew and Peter Spellman, *The Churches and the American Experience* (Grand Rapids: Baker, 1984), 77; see also relevant sections of Sydney Ahlstrom's *A Religious History of the American People* (New Haven: Yale, 1972).
9. Clark Pinnock, *Grace Unlimited* (Minneapolis: Bethany, 1975), 104.
10. Charles Finney, *Revival Lectures*, (Old Tappan, N.J.: Fleming Revell, n.d.), 4.
11. Stephen Carter, *The Culture of Disbelief: How American Law & Politics Trivialize Religious Devotion* (New York/San Francisco: HarperCollins, 1993), 52.
12. Robert Dugan, Jr., *Winning the New Civil War: Recapturing America's Values* (Portland: Multnomah, 1991), 88.
13. Aleksandr Solzhenitsyn, *From Under the Rubble*, trans. A. M. Brock (Chicago: Regnery, 1981), 24.
14. The *Washington Post*, June 25, 1978.
15. *Solzhenitsyn at Harvard*, (Washington, D.C.: Ethics and Public Policy Center, 1989), 9.

3

WE HAVE
MET THE ENEMY

Many evangelicals attack "secular humanism" while the movement swallows nearly hook, line, and sinker the dogmas of modern, secular culture.

NOT LONG AGO, I had a famous house guest for dinner. Known around the world as an evangelist of self-esteem, this guest told me that doctrine got in the way of unity and insisted that Christians should stop fighting each other so that they could unite against the real enemy: *secular humanism*. Amazing, I thought to myself—just one more irony in the unraveling of classical Christianity. Here was a man who said that "the Reformation erred in that it was God-centered rather than man-centered,"[1] an evangelist who argued that salvation is the quenching of the self's thirst for glory and refused to say that people were sinners who needed to be justified before a holy God. After all, he said, "Just because it's in the Bible doesn't mean you need to preach it."[2] And yet, the *enemy*, he insisted, is "secular humanism."

In this chapter, we will examine a very disturbing irony: the evangelical attack on "secular humanism" while the movement swallows nearly hook, line, and sinker the dogmas of modern, secular culture.

"MAN IS THE MEASURE": HOW DID
A "SECULAR HUMANIST" DOGMA MAKE IT
TO THE TOP OF THE EVANGELICAL CHARTS?

Again and again, spokesmen of the Christian Right define secular humanism as a system in which "man is the measure," their oft-repeated reference to Protagoras. "Humanism is a man-centered philosophy," Tim LaHaye explains, "that attempts to solve the problems of man and the world independently of God."[3]

There is no question that the essence of modernity, rooted in the Enlightenment and a general rejection of supernatural religion, including revelation and redemption, is a human-centered rather than God-centered orientation. The substance of *secularity* is its tendency to push God to the outer fringes so that He can be called on for state functions, but not get involved in the day-to-day thinking or operation of normal life. But there are two things we must come to terms with as conservative Christians today: First, that the founding fathers were explicit champions of this philosophy, and, second, that modern evangelicals are among its leading proponents.

In the previous chapter, we saw how explicitly people like Jefferson, Paine, and Adams attacked the supernaturalism of biblical Christianity, Jefferson himself creating a bible that had such references entirely removed. This is the very essence of secularization—the process of eliminating the acknowledgment of the supernatural. Reason refuses any place to revelation; nature cancels grace; morality replaces salvation. This was the deistic religion of many, though not all, of our founding fathers.

It is one thing to say that about the founding fathers, but quite another to assert that contemporary evangelicals fit this pattern of thinking. And yet, there is a great deal of evidence to suggest that one of the reasons leaders of the Christian Right have not found too many problems with returning to the faith of the founding fathers is that deistic moralism is increasingly becoming the diet in Christian preaching, publishing, broadcasting, and discourse.

Changing Views of God and Self: "Man Is the Measure"

One proponent of Christian political activism, in fact, attacks secular humanism for making man the measure, and then writes that, "God would save all men if he could. . . . He will save the greatest number possible without violating their free will."[4] After arguing that the voluntary application of the Golden Rule ("Do unto others as you would have them do unto you") would eliminate all pollution, crime, divorce and child abuse, drugs, and war, Pat Robertson writes, "That's not utopianism, I might add, but reciprocal self-interest."[5] But again, by arguing for moral absolutes on the basis of "reciprocal self-interest," man is still the measure, still the center of the universe. One cannot attack secular humanism (with man at the center) by reinforcing its central dogma. Our Lord was not *suggesting* a "look out for number one by looking out for others" ethic, but *condemning* such self-centered motivations. In fact, according to University of California-Santa Barbara sociologist Wade Clark Roof, the self-centered, self-deifying impulse in American history is now a part of evangelical as well as New Age spirituality. God has become another source of self-fulfillment. In fact, among "born again" Christians, "This God is thought of in very human terms: God, as it were, is created in one's own image."[6]

Like the deists in 1776, evangelicals today are suspicious of creeds, confessions, and doctrinal systems. This is not a part of our "Judeo-Christian" heritage, but a departure from biblical authority and commitment to clear cognitive beliefs. "Evangelical and especially fundamentalist worldviews are anything but tightly integrated dogmatic systems; in fact, as one writer recently put it, they are a 'hodge-podge of rather loosely coupled, and even discrete, statements or tenets.'"[7] To that, Jefferson might even say, "Amen!"

Even the formulas evangelicals create for serving the Lord, Roof points out, are "geared toward self-fulfillment: By keeping one's priorities properly ordered, one will have a better life. Materialism, competition, achievement, and success—to cite the dominant secular, individualistic values of America—create the context in which evangelicals, like all others, form their beliefs, attitudes, and definitions of reality." Even though one of the evangelicals Roof interviewed said we need to realize *America* has a covenant with God to which it must return, "she does not use this biblical language in talking about *church.*" Instead, she says, "You don't have to go to church. I think the reason I do is because it helps me to grow. It's especially good for my family, to teach them the good and moral things." Another nod from Jefferson.

As Roof points out so well, this is the very epitome of self-centered individualism and secular autonomy evangelicals decry in the wider culture. Eight in ten conservative evangelicals "accept a version of 'possibility thinking,' or the belief that one can do just about anything if one believes in oneself." "Obviously," Roof notes, "many of the older, more rigid religious notions about the self have been set aside to make room for more adaptable psychological conceptions."[8]

It is impossible to build a foundation for "Judeo-Christian" ethics in culture on the basis of self-fulfillment.

Of course, the biblical interpretation of human nature must go, but that does not seem to bother most Christians these days. University of Virginia sociologist James Davison Hunter notes, "There are, in fact, strong indications that a total reversal has taken place in the Evangelical conception of the nature and value of the self. . . . For example, nearly nine out of every ten Evangelical students (roughly paralleling the number of public university students) agreed that 'self-improvement is important to me and I work hard at it.'" When asked how many agreed with the statement, "For the Christian, realizing your full potential as a human being is just as important as putting others before you," 62 percent of the evangelical college students agreed, while 44 percent of the public university students took this new psychological approach of self-fulfillment. In a Barna poll, more than half of the evangelicals surveyed agreed with the statement, "The purpose of life is enjoyment and personal fulfillment."[10]

Is it possible: Are we *more* secularized in our view of the self than the world?

The Law and "Self-Fulfillment"

This even affects our view of the Law. Not only is this recognition of God's Law essential for us to understand the reason for the Gospel; it is important for our understanding of the Law's relationship to civil society. It is impossible to build a foundation for "Judeo-Christian" ethics in culture on the basis of self-fulfillment. Often, we pitch our moral campaigns in the rhetoric of secularism, whether with new Christians or with the mass public: It will produce happiness and self-fulfillment. After all, "God only wants what's best for us." But not only is this flawed theologically, since God's laws do not exist for our happiness, but His; it is also insufficient in terms of moral persuasion.

David Walsh, a political philosopher, argues, "Morality that is statically based on social instinct, the internalization of behavior necessary for social cohesion and the common good, does not really take hold until it is united with a morality that utterly transcends any principle of self-interest."[11] It is ironic, to say the least, for one to employ self-interest as a means of challenging self-interest, but we do that whenever we appeal to the "it works better" philosophy. So, ultimately, we must argue on the basis of a transcendent revelation. The problem is, our neighbors no longer believe that God has spoken in a reliable revelation; indeed, most have never heard an intelligent defense. Therefore, all attempts to coerce or push our underlying beliefs without defending them will end in frustration for both parties.

Just when it is needed most, the church seems in no position to confront the world with its unbelief, since there is so little interest in the substance of the apostolic faith within its own ranks. Donald Bloesch speaks of an "anti-theological bias" in an evangelicalism that prefers the insights of secular disciplines. "In conservative circles," Bloesch writes, "one can detect a notable dependence on the findings of psychology and secular philosophy, while in secular, liberal theology an appeal is made to sociology and political science." Of course, this observation was made in 1973, and since then conservative Christians have also leaned heavily on sociology (trends, surveys, polls) and political science (gurus of conservative politics) as well as psychology and secular philosophy for setting the course of the church. "Yet theology, the doctrinal exposition of Holy Scripture, is often regarded with mistrust." However, because we are so often a part of popular, mass culture, our dependence is indirect. We are not aware of just how dependent we are on secular beliefs precisely because we do not reflect very deeply either on Scripture or those very beliefs. That is why Bloesch concludes that "this betrays a markedly cultural orientation in which the authority of reason is substituted for that of revelation."[12] In other words, can we really be pro-Scripture while we are anti-theology? Surely, no more than a physician can be pro-health while being anti-medicine.

Conservative evangelicals are about
as likely to defend their faith
on the basis that "it works" or
"it feels right," or on some personal
experience that validates the truth.

Sin, Grace, and Felt Needs

Sermons used to focus on sin and grace, but now they are often more concerned with addictions, recovery, felt needs, and other psychological categories. Yale professor George Lindbeck says, "Playing fast and loose with the Bible needed a liberal audience in the days of Norman Vincent Peale, but now, as the case of Robert Schuller indicates, professed conservatives eat it up."[13] In fact, Schuller argues that the traditional understanding of sin is "insulting to the human being,"[14] and must therefore be scrapped. "Reformation theology failed to make clear that the core of sin is a lack of self-esteem."[15] Thus, the problem was no longer "sinners in the hands of an angry God," but, "How can I be happy?" The great issue of religion was no longer, "How can I be accepted by a holy God?" but "How can I accept myself?" Hell, for Schuller, does not even have a vertical (i.e., Godward) dimension, but is the "loss of pride," although God does serve some sort of purpose, since He is "the ultimate and unfailing source of our soul's sense of self-respect."[16] Hunter concludes that evangelicalism has taken on board secular notions of the self "to a historically unprecedented level . . ." and "To the degree that the meaning of human nature is revised in this way, the infrastructure of traditional Protestantism is undermined."[17]

Another example of the similarities between modern evangelicals and secularists is the matter of authority. "Man is the measure" even here, in that evangelicals share with the modern secular culture an implicit faith in experience. Now here, at least, one might suspect that the widest cleavage would exist. After all, don't evangelicals stand for moral absolutes over the relativism that pervades our culture? Take a second look. Hunter, like a growing number of sociologists, historians, theologians, and church leaders, points out that evangelicals today are not only ignorant of their theology, but suspicious of theology altogether. While touting a high view of Scripture on paper, conservative Christians are as likely as the unchurched to say that church is not vital so long as one has an active, if private, "personal relationship with Jesus."

Conservative evangelicals are about as likely to defend their faith on the basis that "it works" or "it feels right," or on some personal experience that validates the truth. As Roof notes, modern people, including Christians, are united in the presupposition that "Direct experience is always more trustworthy, if for no other reason than because of its 'inwardness' and 'within-ness'—two qualities that have come to be much appreciated in a highly expressive, narcissistic culture."[18] The "testimony" ("what Jesus did for me") and personal experiences are often the most authoritative tests of truth in evangelical circles today. If one experienced something, it must be true. This too is a capitulation to the secular spirit, locating the seat of authority somewhere in oneself.

THE BASIS OF AUTHORITY

Whereas traditional evangelicals have stood by the Reformation slogan, *sola Scriptura* (only Scripture), the pressures of narcissism and subjectivism (often cloaked in pious phrases, such as "personal relationship" over "dead doctrine") have not only replaced God with self as the *object*, but have replaced God with self as the *authority* for interpreting reality. A rejection of theology is a rejection of Scripture, inasmuch as the Bible is filled with propositional statements about the character of God (theology proper) and humanity (anthropology) and God's saving action in Christ (christology, soteriology, ecclesiology, eschatology). The Bible makes definitive pronouncements on the key questions of God, the self, the meaning of life and history. It demands the priority in defining for us the ultimate problem and its solution, and this process of defining things *is* theology. If we do not care about theology, we do not care about God or revelation, and we are left to the newspapers and television to define our reality.

> *Long gone is the focus on Christ*
> *crucified for us outside the city*
> *center of Jerusalem nearly 2,000*
> *years ago for our objective sin*
> *and guilt against a holy God.*

The very popular New Age mystic Matthew Fox declares that "heart-knowledge" is the basis for all true knowledge, and that is not far off from the disdain I heard for "head-knowledge" over "heart-knowledge" growing up as an evangelical. Fox also repeated the warning of Carl Jung, a mystic who passed himself off as a scientist (successfully, one might add): The greatest threat to the soul is to "worship a God outside you."[19]

Although Jung and Maslow are criticized by evangelicals as fathers of "humanistic psychology," the entire Christian publishing, preaching, and broadcasting industry seems to be bent on "the god within" and personal, subjective, inward experience. Long gone is the focus on Christ crucified for us outside the city center of Jerusalem nearly 2,000 years ago for our objective sin and guilt against a holy God. Now, if religion is to have any "practical" meaning, it must focus on making me happier, taking me inside myself, and providing spiritual experiences. Think of all those "testimonies" in many evangelical churches. Personal experiences and "sharing" replace common study, prayer, worship, and witness. The individual's spiritual autobiography replaces the life and times of the Nazarene. Too often, we learn more about the pastor and his life growing up in wherever, and his spiritual crisis at Camp Waloopa, than about Christ and His doing and dying. It reflects a generation in which talk shows have replaced reading and in which the only thing we really know is our own experiences.

This is where another irony comes in, when the question of truth and authority is raised. Christian leaders criticize "secular humanism" for its relativism and its belief that contradictory assertions are equally true. And yet, how many times, in a doctrinal dispute (especially between Calvinists and Arminians), does one hear statements like, "There are good people on both sides" (as if one's character had anything to do with determining truth), or "We can't know," or, better yet, "They're both true." In fact, evangelical Christians, according to Barna, are almost equally divided between those who strongly agree and strongly disagree with the statement, "There is no such thing as absolute truth." Remarkably, "adults associated with mainline Protestant churches are more likely than all other adults to agree that there is no such thing as absolute truth (73% compared to 65%)."[20]

Even among conservative evangelicals, the accommodation to contemporary culture's retreat from objective truth is obvious. Hunter argues that we have moved from things "known" to "belief," further degenerating into "religious opinion," until it finally reaches its ultimate destination: "feeling." If the early church defended its convictions with, "It is written . . ." and the medieval church with, "The Church says . . .", today's evangelicals often throw out rehearsed slogans and the appeal, "I feel that. . . ." The demand today is that preaching must be "practical" and have "application" to daily living. The goal must be to show people how to live happier and more fulfilling lives. So, as Hunter notes, "The emphasis shifts from a concern with the proclamation of an objective and universal truth to a concern with the subjective applicability of truth."[21] So instead of asking, "What does this passage *mean?*", we ask, "What does this passage mean *for me?*" The self has not only become center of all things, but the "measure of all things." And if this is the definition of "secular humanism," evangelicals have swallowed the bait—hook, line, and sinker, even while they castigate others.

The reason we see this so much more clearly in the world than in our own assembly is because the worldly version is more intentional, radical, and extreme in its overt commitment to these dogmas of secularism. Furthermore, their rejection of a God-centered frame of reference is not really taken seriously until it touches on the favorite subject of contemporary evangelicals: private and public morality. But what we must realize is that when the war centers around issues of morality, the debate is already lost. We are fighting a generation that is merely acting out its beliefs. As the evangelicals in many of the mainline churches only awakened to the apostasy within their churches when they saw shifts in moral policies and were often apathetic about the much earlier doctrinal shifts, any "culture war" that chooses morality for its battle-ground is too late.

This brings us to the changing definitions of redemption itself. To the degree that sin is redefined as a negative attitude one has toward oneself rather than an offense against God, to that degree salvation is going to be recast in psychological categories, according to the dogmas of secularism. A whole new set of problems replaces the old ones, and a whole new set of solutions to match them. If sin and standing under God's judgment is the problem, atonement and justification is the solution. But if dysfunction, low self-esteem, and unmet needs are the ultimate problem, the solutions will be prescribed in therapeutic rather than theological language. This is not merely "contextualizing" the Christian message for a contemporary audience; it is conforming the message to that comtemporary audience.

This is precisely what we see today. More than four in five (83 percent) of the American adult population believe that people are basically good. But those are just those "secular humanists" out there, right? No, 77 percent of the "born again," evangelical constituency buy into this secular view of human nature.[22] In fact, when it comes to salvation, "God helps those who help themselves," according to four out of five "born again," evangelical Christians. Evangelicals are actually more likely than non-Christians to agree with this "pull yourself up by the bootstraps," self-help program.[23] One-third of the evangelicals agree that "all good people will go to heaven, whether they have embraced Jesus Christ or not,"[24] so redemption seems to depend on one's own goodness rather than on faith in Christ. Indeed, in this scheme, Jesus is not even necessary, except as a moral guide. But, of course, we recognize this as theological liberalism and as secularism when it is in the world, but I think Barna is quite entitled to demand of us as evangelicals, "What is being taught in our churches about the nature of salvation?"[25]

In his penetrating treatment, *No Place for Truth*, evangelical theologian David Wells noted with great sorrow, "In the intervening years I have watched with growing disbelief as the evangelical Church has cheerfully plunged into astounding theological illiteracy."[26] Mark Noll, Nathan Hatch, and George Marsden observe,

> Humanism, or faith in humanity, has been mixed with virtually every American religious heritage, including evangelicalism and fundamentalism. Most commonly, since the nineteenth century, many Americans, including many evangelical Christian Americans, have tended to believe in the essential goodness of humanity, in the importance of believing in oneself, in self-help, and the ability of a free people to solve their own problems. . . . Recent politically oriented critics of "humanism" seldom have attacked modern faith in humanity in any consistent or general way, since their own views have contained humanistic elements, such as faith in American "rugged individualism."[27]

That is why A. W. Tozer noted,

> The flaw in current evangelicalism lies in its humanistic approach. It struggles to be supernaturalistic but never quite makes it. It is frankly fascinated by the great, noisy, aggressive world with its big name, its hero worship, its wealth, and its garish pageantry. . . . Peace of mind, happiness, prosperity, social acceptance, publicity, success in sports, business, the entertainment field, and perchance to sit occasionally at the same banquet table with a celebrity—all this on earth and heaven at last. Certainly no insurance company can offer half as much.[28]

A FORM OF GODLINESS, DENYING ITS POWER

It is important to note that the Enlightenment succeeded not only in altering the intellectual life of New England's "culture elites"; it also succeeded on the frontier. Whenever Christians ignore the pursuit of orthodox theology, they do not end up with a simpler gospel and a closer walk with Jesus. Enlightenment always ends in Pelagianism, the age-old belief in man. Nineteenth-century revivalists may have ranted against the liberals of Boston, but they held the same basic beliefs about human nature and authority. Charles Finney, for instance, believed that humans were not born in original sin and insisted that regeneration is the work of the evangelist and the convert, not God. "Sinners Bound to Change Their Own Hearts" was one of his popular sermon titles, in sharp contrast to the preaching of the Great Awakening in the mid-1700s. Later, revivalist Sam Jones declared, "You convert yourself, and when you convert yourself, God regenerates you." This is the belief of most modern evangelicals: When I make a decision for Christ, I'm born again. Free will, cooperating with grace, is the recipe for new birth. This, however, is the sort of rank Pelagianism which was condemned by the whole Western church, Roman and Protestant, ever since it was championed in the fourth century. The Enlightenment overturned the Reformation insistence on human helplessness and divine grace, and neither liberals nor conservatives have recovered.

Not only have evangelicals been shaped by secularism in their theology; they have adopted the patterns of thinking that have opened them up to participate in the idolatry of their contemporaries.

But belief in man is only possible when the mirror (God's Law) is removed. Most evangelicals cannot even name the Ten Commandments they are so passionate about getting back into the public classrooms.[29] In fact, in a series of interviews conducted by our own organization, some respondents at an evangelical convention, when asked to name the Ten Commandments, after realizing they could not, simply replied, "I can't name them off the top of my head, but I sure do live by them." We do not know the Law, the Gospel, the attributes of God, the way of salvation, the person and work of Christ and of the Holy Spirit, the nature of the church, and there is widespread confusion over, and obsession with, the way history is going to wind up. And yet, Operation Rescue founder Randall Terry expresses the bewilderment:

We have more "gospel preaching" in America than any other nation on earth. Yet America is growing more corrupt by the week; injustice in the courts is growing; oppression against Christians is on the rise; mockery of the holy has become common; homosexuals are demanding the right to be married and have children. . . . All of our gospel preaching hasn't stopped . . . a tidal wave that threatens our very survival. . . . We have more churches, more gospel radio, gospel television, gospel literature, gospel tracts, street meetings, evangelistic crusades, gospel music, "win the world, win your town, and win your neighborhood to the Lord" training seminars than any nation on earth. . . . And yet, America is fast becoming the moral cesspool of the earth.[30]

This leads Terry, and many Christian activists, to conclude that the Gospel somehow is not enough. While convinced that the Gospel is necessary, Terry wonders why so many Christians say, "Just preach the Gospel." "Why do they cling to an obviously inadequate solution?"[31] An "obviously inadequate solution"? The Gospel is the only thing God ever calls "the power of God unto salvation." While Terry and so many evangelicals today look at the inconsistency between the *amount* of "gospel" activity and the *effect* of that activity in the culture and conclude that the Gospel somehow is not enough, perhaps, in the light of the preceding arguments, they should conclude instead that the weakness of the Christian witness today is rooted in weaknesses in the *message* evangelicals communicate. Is the Gospel clearly known in so-called "gospel-preaching" churches? Is the average Christian excited about purchasing books about God's attributes, sin and grace, the meaning of the Cross, and so on? These are the themes of the Gospel, not "How to Have a Happy Home," "How to Experience Victory," and "How I Discovered Myself by Being Born Again."

Not only have evangelicals been shaped by secularism in their theology; they have adopted the patterns of thinking that have opened them up to participate in the idolatry of their contemporaries. Believing in the essential goodness of humanity and its moral perfectability through ethical education, legislation, self-help, and political pressure, evangelicals have also accepted the idea of secular progress: Things are getting better and America is a special agent in this global improvement. Remarkably, this is going on at a time when most evangelicals still officially hold to the dispensational premillennial scheme that has dominated the movement for most of this century, a scheme that argues for a pessimistic view of history, worsening until Jesus returns. While attacking Marxism as godless statism, evangelicals have failed to realize that Marxism and free market capitalism are twin sisters of modernity, and while one may be more just and sensible, godless capitalism is just as great a threat to the soul, if not to the pocketbook. By reducing human beings to consumers, making nearly all social relationships depend on competition, and shrinking human life down to purely economic determinism, modern capitalism is just as dangerous to the soul—in part because of its marriage to religion, where apathy reigns in the face of every enemy except the threat to the "American Way of Life."

One of the nation's leading cultural analysts, Harvard sociologist Daniel Bell, wrote,

> American capitalism . . . has lost its traditional legitimacy, which was based on a moral system of reward rooted in the Protestant sanctification of work. It has substituted a hedonism which promises material ease and luxury. . . . The culture has been dominated (in the serious realm) by a principle of modernism that has been subversive of bourgeois life, and the middle-class life-styles by a hedonism that has undercut the Protestant ethic which provided the moral foundation for the society. . . . What then can hold the society together?[32]

Bell added, "To say, then, that 'God is dead' is, in effect, to say that the social bonds have snapped and that society is dead." In other words, Bell is saying that, at its root, the problem is not social, but theological. But what about the spiritual revival people were talking about in the last two decades? Stanford sociologist David Gress observes, "What has revived is a social and culturally bound form of religiosity, in which the main purpose of the churches has been to become socially relevant. . . . This phenomenon has nothing to do with genuine religion and is but another outgrowth of the modernist spirit which Bell so accurately diagnosed."[33] In other words, the more popular evangelicalism becomes (or tries to become), the more it takes on the appearances of the contemporary world and becomes a prisoner of the very culture it is seeking to convert. Evangelicals can see secularism when their neighbor wants to open an adult bookstore on the corner, but not when their own beliefs, assumptions, and tactics are dripping with secular attitudes and convictions. Jude Dougherty, dean of the Catholic University's School of Philosophy, writes, "Many outside [the] church look to it to fill the intellectual and moral void that is increasingly apparent. Yet that church as a visible organization in North America appears as muddled and as confused as the larger society that it seems more to reflect than challenge."[34]

Think about how much of our society is ruled by commercialism, consumerism, marketing, creating "felt needs" so that some company can make a fortune on the latest thing that suddenly everyone thinks he absolutely has to have. And then think about how much the evangelical church is ruled by the marketplace. Are our "testimonies" much different from the testimonials for shampoo we see on TV? Both are usually based on pragmatism ("it worked for me—you try it") and narcissism (self-fulfillment).

By contrast, the biblical testimony for Christianity was not that it "worked" for Peter: after he had tried everything else, he finally "gave Jesus a chance"; nor that Paul's quest for self-esteem was finally satisfied, nor that James was able to use Christian principles to build a happy, healthy family. Rather, their testimony was, "That which was from the beginning, which we have *heard*, which we have *seen with our eyes*, which we have *looked at* and our *hands have touched*—this we proclaim concerning the Word of life. The life appeared; we have seen it and testify to it, and we proclaim to you the eternal life, which was with the Father and has appeared to us."[35] Their testimony was not a "burning in the bosom" or a crisis experience, but the sort of testimony that could hold up in a court of law. It was the case of normal people from various walks of life being witnesses to the miracles, teachings, death, burial, resurrection, and ascension of a man who claimed to be God incarnate, and proved His claims. It is the testimony of these eyewitnesses that must have the priority in our churches and evangelism, not our own subjective testimony.

Furthermore, the triumph of secularism (whether modern or postmodern) has not only redefined the Gospel and the wider Christian message; it has redefined the nature of the Christian mission and the identity of the Church. John Leith, though himself very active in speaking out on political and social issues, addresses his concerns:

> Many sermons are moral exhortations, which can be heard delivered with greater skill at the Rotary or Kiwanis Club. Many sermons are political and economic judgments on society, which have been presented with greater wisdom and passion at political conventions. Many sermons offer personal therapies, which can be better provided by well-trained psychiatrists. The only skill the preacher has—or the church, for that matter—which is not found with greater excellence somewhere else, is theology, in particular the skill to interpret and apply the Word of God in sermon, teaching, and pastoral care. This is the great service which the minister and the church can render the world. Why should anyone come to church for what can be better found somewhere else?[36]

Ironically, Professor Leith was aiming his criticisms at the mainline churches, although today it could just as appropriately describe evangelicalism. And the critique is to the point: Instead of confronting secularism with transcendence and the merely horizontal (myself and others) with the vertical dimension (God), we are actually trying to play the game. But we are not as good or clever at it, so in our rush toward "relevance" we have actually become irrelevant. That is why, according to poll after poll, so many of the "boomers" have decided to stay away. "Religion seemed so captive to the status quo," Roof explains, ". . . more comforting than challenging," simply baptizing "a set of commonly held cultural values such as progress, security, conformity, and confident living—all wrapped up and called 'the American Way of Life.'"[37]

Many left because they thought the churches were "spiritually and theologically impoverished" and they left, ". . . not out of any strong doctrinal or moral objection, but because church or synagogue seemed irrelevant to them."[38] The church is only relevant if it stops chasing after the competing voices of this passing age and hears the golden strains from another place more real than our own. That does not mean the church resists changes in style in principle or that it never updates the language of its liturgy, but that its message is relevant precisely because it takes people who are inundated with a this-worldly and self-ward, consumeristic, therapeutic, and ideological orientation and raises their eyes toward heaven, as Nebuchadnezzar had experienced. "Then my sanity was restored," the king confessed (Daniel 4:36). The church's first task is not to support the insanity of secularism; it is to unmask it. But before we can do that, we need to know two things: the errors of this movement and the truth of divine revelation. But at this moment, at least, we are absorbing by osmosis the very insanity that we eschew in its more blatant moral forms. To reverse this trend, we must take both the truths and the heresies more seriously.

Why does a modern university professor tell his or her students on Monday morning that we cannot really know religious facts (i.e., God's existence, ultimate purpose, values, revelation, etc.) the way we know scientific facts? Because prayer was removed from the schools in 1963? Of course not, but because Immanuel Kant, an eighteenth century Enlightenment philosopher (who, by the way was not a godless secular humanist, but was reared in evangelical pietism) declared that the scientific realm (natural things) and the sacred realm were separate, the latter unknowable except through a leap of faith. Why did Kant do this? Was it a sinister plot to remove God from public life? Not at all. In fact, it was just the opposite intention: Kant wanted to remove religion from rational investigation and rest it safely on the shores of faith, where it could not be battered by the waves of doubt. After all, science *must* doubt: that is how it accumulates knowledge of the natural world, but the faithful must never doubt God. Granted, this is a simplification of a very sophisticated series of arguments, but suffice it to say that this fundamental tenet was widely accepted by pietistic evangelicals ever since: "You just have to believe, regardless of what science comes up with." So, both conservative Christians and liberal secularists happily accepted this solution: One accepted the leap of faith; the other, implicit faith in observation, science, and reason. Both assume a discontinuity and, indeed, antagonism between faith and the intellect.

So when that professor gets up to teach our children Monday morning, and says that there can be no true, objective knowledge of religious truth, he or she is merely passing on this fundamental modern tenet which was embraced by fundamentalist and atheist alike. But how much easier it is to blame secularism on a sinister plot to take America away from God by eliminating a sixty-second tip of the civil hat to the unknown god.

In the Reformation tradition, however, both nature and grace are realms of divine activity. That is why modern science was launched by the heirs of that movement: They were motivated to study what they called "the second book of God" (nature) in an attempt to understand more about nature's author and His creation. As science helped provide the answers to the "hows," the first book of God—Scripture, provided the answers to the "whys." When people like Bacon, Newton, and Leibnitz were reading Scripture or conducting experiments, they discerned a symmetry, a unified story. There was harmony. Similarly, they saw all of life—music, religion, science, industry, art, education, labor, leisure, the family—as distinct spheres of activity which were nonetheless all under the sovereignty of God and lordship of Christ. No pursuit was ultimately merely "secular"; even the shoemaker served God, said Luther, by making a good shoe and selling it at a fair price. All of life was meant to raise one's eyes to God as the source and preserver of physical as well as spiritual felicity. A day sailing with friends could do as much to raise one's eyes to God in gratitude as a "quiet time." Glorifying and enjoying God was a telos woven into the fabric of the most common, everyday experiences and activities. There was no division between "spiritual" knowledge, which required a leap in the dark, and "scientific" knowledge, which was simply given.

> *The church cannot "save America"*
> *from its moral confusion while it*
> *is itself operating, at its very*
> *core, with secular presuppositions.*

If the church does not think of all of life in a God-centered (i.e., theological) manner, surely it is not the world that should bear the blame. "Oh, that's just theology. I just want to love Jesus," is the familiar refrain in the churches these days. Giving up creeds, confessions, and doctrine in general as a fairly impractical category, the Christian is as lost as the non-Christian in trying to relate the pieces of the puzzle to the "big picture." In other words, human thought in all areas is no longer framed in terms of the character of God, the person and work of Christ, providence, miracle, sin and redemption, the meaning of history, and the church. But then, what replaced this theological casing in society? As many sociologists and historians have noted, it is the forces of modernity and now postmodernity which have been given the privilege of naming things. Sin is dysfunction or a lack of self-esteem, because the therapeutic revolution now commands authority in such definitions. The church is a "user-friendly" corporation designed to target a specific market with its product because the managerial revolution won its right to determine such things.[39] You see, the cultural war has already been fought . . . and won. Secularism not only won the world, but the church—even the evangelicals.

> We are ourselves the very "secular humanists" we discover in a more developed form through the barrel of our guns in the ongoing culture wars.

Not only did secularism win by dismantling Christian theology and by turning a faith that is passed down through generations into an individual's experience, it also won by turning biblical supernaturalism into a moral system much like a modern machine: Push the right buttons and even God is obliged to obey. Evangelists in our day have actually written of "the law of reciprocity"[40]: If you follow God's laws, you will get x,y,z. And whenever God's law or commands in Scripture are given from the pulpit, or in evangelical books, tapes, and broadcasts, it is most often in the form of, "God just wants what's best for you. He wants you to be happy." Meanwhile, in Scripture, the Law is given because it is God's moral character. In other words, because it makes *Him* happy. We cannot even discuss morality these days without adopting a human-centered, secularized frame of reference. The church cannot "save America" from its moral confusion while it is itself operating, at its very core, with secular presuppositions. Employing relativism and utilitarian pragmatism as the basis for arguing moral absolutes is about as silly and self-contradictory as a relativist making absolute statements about the truth of relativism.

As it is possible to be "so heavenly minded that we're no earthly good," it is also possible to be so earthly minded that we are no earthly good. Jesus scolded the Pharisees for attributing sin to the world instead of to their own hearts, and understanding it chiefly as *actions* instead of as a *condition*. If evangelicals are going to have anything to say to the world, they are first going to have to realize that the enemy is not left-wing politics, but *secularism* (read "sin") as a condition, and a condition which plagues conservative Christians these days just as surely as non-Christians. Inasmuch as secularism is the fastening of our eyes on ourselves, our nation, our world, our time and place, our moment, instead of fixing our eyes on Christ and His kingdom, reformation and revival, proclamation and repentance, it is evident as much in the local Christian bookstores, pulpits, Sunday school curricula, broadcasts, and religious discourse as anywhere else.

My purpose here is not to present an exhaustive case for evangelical accommodation to modernity or postmodernity. That has been done better by others.[41] But what I have attempted here and in a full-length treatment elsewhere[42] is a brief survey sufficient, hopefully, to illustrate the tragic likelihood that we as evangelicals have become our own worst enemy, that we are ourselves the very "secular humanists" we discover in a more developed form through the barrel of our guns in the ongoing culture wars.

NOTES

1. Robert Schuller, *Self-Esteem: The New Reformation* (Waco: Word, 1982), 64.
2. Robert Schuller, in an interview in *Modern Reformation* magazine, May-June issue, 1993.
3. Tim LaHaye, *The Battle for the Mind*, (Old Tappan, N.J.: Fleming Revell, 1980), 27.
4. Norman Geisler, in his essay in *A Tribute to John Walvoord* (Chicago: Moody, 1982).
5. Pat Robertson, *The New World Order* (Dallas: Word, 1991), 231.
6. Wade Clark Roof, *A Generation of Seekers* (New York/San Francisco: HarperCollins, 1993), 75.
7. Ibid., 101.
8. Ibid., 109.

9. Hunter, *Evangelicalism: The Coming Generation* (Chicago: Univ. of Chicago, 1987), 53.

10. George Barna, *What Americans Believe* (Ventura, Calif.: Regal, 1991), 92.

11. Walsh, *After Ideology: Recovering the Spiritual Foundations of Freedom* (New York/San Francisco: HarperCollins, 1990), 200.

12. Donald Bloesch, *The Evangelical Renaissance* (Grand Rapids: Eerdmans, 1973), 21.

13. George Lindbeck, "The Church's Mission to a Postmodern Culture," in *Postmodern Theology*, Frederic B. Burnham, ed. (San Francisco: Harper & Row, 1989), 45.

14. Schuller, *Self-Esteem*, 65. On the same page, Schuller explains how a new Reformation will happen: "It will happen, I am convinced, when we redefine our doctrine of sin." Psychologists like Erik Erickson are given the place traditionally given by Scripture in this redefinition. Therefore, "what is guilt but an ugly loss of self-esteem?" Original sin is nothing more than saying that ". . . we are all born with a negative self-image, an inferiority complex, if you please." This is why "The Cross sanctifies the ego trip" (75). Schuller is very deliberate about all of this, describing the Reformation as the origin of "The Reactionary Age" and concludes that "The sixteenth-century Reformation will be seen as a reactionary movement" after the new self-esteem reformation "refines all of its theological expressions around every person's daily need for self-affirmation . . ." (175).

15. Ibid., 98.

16. Ibid., 13. Schuller represents the tendency among many church leaders today to rule theological orthodoxy out of the discussion at the outset because of its irrelevance. Theology and a God-centered orientation with a commitment to Scripture may have been acceptable for the Protestant Reformers, but "time and history have changed all that." But leaders like Schuller, although their rhetoric makes it sound as if they are leaving theology behind for the more "practical" issues, are actually doing theology every bit as much as Luther, Calvin, or Edwards. In fact, Schuller is not opposed to referring to "any creed, any biblical interpretation, and any systematic theology that assaults and offends the self-esteem of persons" as "heretically failing to be truly Christian . . ." (135, italics added). So Schuller does believe in orthodoxy and heresy after all; he just wants to reverse the two as they have been historically defined. The biblical doctrines of original sin, total depravity, unmerited favor, the substitutionary atonement, justification, and so on, must be redefined beyond recognition, as the new hermeneutic is self-esteem, and the new sacred text is popular psychology. It is essential for both sides, however, to recognize that they are doing theology. It is not theology vs. more allegedly relevant operations, as Schuller indicates. Rather, it is classical, orthodox theology vs. a new theology based on the dogmas of popular psychology. Both sides have their dogmas, their sacred authorities, and their official pronouncements; it is quite unfair for revisionists to attempt to make their case, not by arguing it, but by appealing for sympathy, as if they were victims of an inquisition by those who care about theology rather than mission.

17. James D. Hunter, *Evangelicalism: The Coming Generation* (Chicago: Univ. of Chicago, 1987), 73.

18. Roof, *A Generation*, 67.

19. Ibid., 75.

20. George Barna, *What Americans Believe* (Ventura: Regal, 1991), 83–84.

21. Hunter, *Evangelicalism*, 47.

22. Barna, *What Americans Believe*, 89.

23. Ibid., 80.

24. Ibid., 51.

25. Ibid., 80.

26. David Wells, *No Place for Truth* (Grand Rapids: Eerdmans, 1993), 4.

27. Mark Noll, Nathan Hatch, George Marsden, *The Search for Christian America* (Westchester, Ill.: Crossway, 1983), 127. I would respectfully dissent from the authors' definition of humanism, however, as "faith in humanity." The term refers to the Renaissance passion for recovering the interests, sources, and pursuits of classical Greco-Roman culture and thus to the recovery of the "humanities" (history, philosophy, the arts, and related subjects). The Protestant Reformers were also humanists in this sense even though their faith was hardly in humanity. The Renaissance was a diverse movement, including those such as Giovanni Pico della Mirandola, whose faith in humanity almost matches the highest platitudes of modern self-esteem preachers, as well as the Reformers, for whom a renaissance of classical learning meant a recovery of biblical texts and doctrines.

28. A. W. Tozer, *Born After Midnight* (Harrisburg, Pa.: Christian Publications, 1959), 22.

29. George Gallup and Jim Castelli, *The People's Religion*, (New York: Macmillan, 1989), 60.

30. Randall Terry, *Why Does a Nice Guy Like Me Keep Getting Thrown in Jail?* (Lafayette, La.: Huntington House, 1993), 63–64.

31. Ibid., 61.

32. Quoted by David Gress in *The World & I*, May 1990, 485.

33. David Gress, ibid., 486.

34. Ibid., 509.

35. 1 John 1:1–4.

36. John Leith, *The Reformed Imperative* (Philadelphia: Westminster Press, 1988), 22.

37. Roof, *A Generation*, 65.

38. Ibid., 55.

39. Noll, Hatch, Marsden, *Christian America*, 203.

40. Pat Robertson, *Answers to 200 of Life's Most Probing Questions* (Nashville: Nelson, 1984) on "laws of reciprocity," 231, 264–68.

41. Os Guinness has been particularly interested in this effect of modernity. For instance, see his very helpful and concise treatment, *Dining with the Devil: The Megachurch Movement Flirts with Modernity* (Grand Rapids: Baker, 1993), especially 47 ff. See also *No God But God*, Guinness, ed. (Chicago: Moody, 1992), and John Seel's *The Evangelical Forfeit* (Grand Rapids: Baker, 1993).

42. See Michael Horton, *Made in America: The Shaping of Modern American Evangelicalism* (Grand Rapids: Baker, 1991).

4

THE
CHRISTIAN EMPIRE

The early Christians had been instructed by the apostles to pray for their rulers at a time when these very rulers were dipping believers in wax up to their necks, in order to be living candles in Nero's garden.

WHEN PRESIDENT REAGAN announced before the National Association of Evangelicals that the Soviet Union was the "Evil Empire," the assumption was, of course, that America was the Christian Empire or, in John Winthrop's words, "the shining city upon a hill."[1] Is there a possibility of a "Christian nation"? What is the relationship of the kingdom of God to the kingdoms of this world? Is there a difference between the activity of the *Christian* and the activity of the *church* in the world? These, and many like them, are questions which perplex us, and until we answer them, there will be tremendous confusion in our public witness.

The Protestant Reformers were convinced that the confusion of the Law and the Gospel, which is the topic of the next chapter, led to a confusion of things earthly and things heavenly, a confusion between the kingdoms of this world and the kingdom of God. In this chapter, we shall see just how relevant, as well as biblical, this wisdom is and how essential it is that we recover this distinction.

THE TWO KINGDOMS IN HISTORY

There are many déjà vu-like events in church history. The persecutions of the early church are well-known, but it is worth remembering that this was not because they were trying to impose Christianity by legislation or economic pressure, nor indeed because they maintained some quaint religious philosophy that differed from the majority. Rome was full of diverse superstitions and was only too happy to have more, providing they served the glory of the empire and sought the well-being of the nation. (Sound familiar?)

But Christianity was not ultimately concerned with Rome's well-being; nor indeed was it unconcerned. The early Christians had been instructed by the apostles to pray for their rulers at a time when these very rulers were dipping believers in wax up to their necks, in order to be living candles in Nero's garden. Jesus had taught them to "render unto Caesar that which is Caesar's and unto God that which is his" (see Matthew 22:21). Furthermore, Paul had counseled them to be obedient to their rulers (Romans 13), warned against counterfeit miracles (2 Thessalonians 2:9), and instructed them, "Make it your ambition to lead a quiet life, to mind your own business and to work with your hands, just as we told you, so that your daily life may win the respect of outsiders and so that you will not be dependent on anybody" (1 Thessalonians 4:11–12). They were not to respond to the persecutions either by running from the world or by trying to take over the world, but by trying to be the best citizens, employees, artisans, parents, and friends they could possibly be under the circumstances.

In spite of generations of persecutions, by the third century the church father Tertullian could announce with some pleasure that while Rome was not looking, the Christians had, by this policy of industry, wisdom, regular instruction in the Scriptures, and commitment to the good of their neighbors (Christian or not) won some of the most important places in society. "We are but of yesterday," Tertullian told a still intolerant, but largely apathetic emperor, "and we have filled everything you have—cities, islands, forts, towns, exchanges, yes! and camps, tribes, decuries, palace, senate, forum. All we have left you is the temples!" How did they do this? By launching public campaigns? Boycotts? Calling for a crusade to take over the Roman Empire? No, but simply by being Christians where they were, enduring persecution as their Savior had, because of the prize which lay before them, an imperishable crown.

This eternal perspective allowed successive generations to take a long view of history. Hardly separatistic or hostile to the world, even to a culture that had persecuted them, these believers threw themselves into proclaiming the Gospel and being "salt" and "light" in their own calling. Instead of whining and protesting their treatment, they drew from their instruction in Scripture a rich deposit of truth and employed argumentation and persuasion effectively. Rather than merely opposing the Roman games with threats of force, Tertullian, for instance, asked, "Have you a mind for blood? Let me tell you about the blood of Christ."

The success of the Gospel, according to Oxford historian Henry Chadwick, was due in part to the fact that it spoke to the deepest questions: "Divine grace in Christ, the remission of sins and the conquest of evil powers for the sick soul, tired of living and scared of dying, seeking for an assurance of immortality and for security and freedom in a world where the individual could rarely do other than submit to his fate." Further,

> The terms were those of the baptismal vows: a renunciation of sin and everything associated with demonic powers, idols, astrology and magic; and a declaration of belief in God the Father, in the redemptive acts of Christ's life, death, and resurrection, and in the Holy Spirit active in the Church.[2]

Even the moral strength of the early Christians was due to motives the average pagan could not understand: "The divergence lay in the Christian stress on the grace of God . . . (rather than the individual's self-respect) . . . and on the outgoing activity of 'charity' toward one's fellow men."[3] Instead of building homogeneous churches, where the wealthy and the poor worshiped in their own churches, they all worshiped together. The poor needed the wealthy to help them get on their feet, and the wealthy needed the poor in order to demonstrate their gratitude to God through charity. This interdependence helped knit the diverse groups within the church together and became a marvel to the cynical but watching world. The church treasuries were even used to buy slaves and release them, and Christian slave-owners willingly released their slaves, as Paul had asked concerning Onesimus "for the sake of the gospel."

What separates evangelicals from the culture today very often is not doctrine, but style, extrabiblical codes of behavior, lingo, and in-house spirituality.

Furthermore, the early Christians, in spite of persecutions, were not hermits waiting in the corner to be caught away. In his *Dialogue with Trypho the Jew*, Justin carefully explained Christianity, trying to clear it of false impressions and charges. Instead of listing the Jewish persecutions of Christians (i.e., getting locked into a "culture war"), Justin has an eye to winning Trypho. To this effort at persuasion, Trypho replied,

> This is what amazes me. . . . Moreover, I know that your teachings, written down in the so-called Gospel, are so wonderful and so great that in my opinion no man can keep them; for I have read them with interest. But this is what we cannot grasp at all: That you want to fear God and that you believe yourselves favored above the people around you, yet you do not withdraw from them in any way or separate yourselves from the pagans; that you observe neither festivals [pagan] or sabbaths [Jewish]; that you do not circumcise; and further, that you set your hopes on a man who was crucified, and believe you will receive good things from God in spite of the fact that you do not obey his commandments (10.1.2).

If the average person on the street today were asked, "What do you think Christianity is all about?", would he or she be as clear and, might I add, doctrinal, as Trypho the Jew? Have we made a compelling case? Are the pagans even aware of what it is they are rejecting? What separates evangelicals from the culture today very often is not doctrine (since, as we have already seen, many evangelicals adhere to the same basic notions as the unchurched), but style, extrabiblical codes of behavior, lingo, and in-house spirituality. Yet, Tertullian backed up Trypho's impressions of the early church's non-separatist attitude:

> Christians cannot be distinguished from the rest of mankind by country, speech, or customs. They do not live in cities of their own; they do not speak a special language; they do not follow a peculiar manner of life. . . . They take part in everything as citizens and endure everything as aliens. . . . They have a common table, but not a common bed. . . . They obey the established laws, but through their way of life they surpass these laws. . . . We are a united body. We are bound together by a common religious conviction, by one and the same divine discipline and by the bond of common hope. . . . We pray for the postponement of the end. We gather to bring to mind the contents of Holy Scripture as often as the world situation gives us a warning or reminder. . . ." (Second Apology, 10).

Justin told the Gentiles, "We, more than all other men, are your helpers and allies for peace" (First Apology 12). Christianity quickly spread through Palestine, Syria, Asia Minor, Greece, and even reached as far as India and distant reaches of Europe within its first few centuries.

In spite of such advances, the Roman Empire lashed out with one more dying gasp of persecution. In the year 303 Emperor Diocletian and his assistant Galerius presided over a public sacrifice and when the high priests could not divine the future from the entrails of the sacrificed animals' livers, the usual scapegoat was, of course, the Christians. Those believers present had crossed themselves (as if to say, "We are Christians and are not participating in this civil worship"), and the pagans superstitiously believed this had prevented the priests from success in their fortune-telling. A massive imperial campaign was launched to dismantle the cathedral and confiscate the Bibles and prayer books. All Christian gatherings were outlawed. The following year, the whole empire was commanded to sacrifice to the Caesar and the gods on pain of death.

Paradise Restored?

It was the victory of Constantine at the Milvian Bridge in 312 that secured a respite from persecution, as the new emperor converted to Christianity and brought the empire with him. In spite of the cynicism which is often directed toward this conversion, Constantine had an enormous effect on transforming the identity of the empire, which included vast social legislation (outlawing abortion, financing new copies of the Bible, building churches, abolishing slavery, enacting legislation protecting prisoners and the poor, and even forbidding the branding of criminals "because man is made in God's image"). Although he did not make the empire "Christian" in any established sense, he surely did more than tolerate it. Many Christians saw this as a vindication that Daniel's interpretation of Nebuchadnezzar's dream had come true at last. In Daniel 2, the vision of the large statue with a head of gold, chest and arms of silver, belly and thighs of bronze, and legs of iron, corresponded to the empires of Babylon, Medo-Persia, Greece, and Rome, respectively. Referring to the Roman rulers, who would come more than five centuries after the vision, Daniel said, "In the time of those kings, the God of heaven will set up a kingdom that will never be destroyed, nor will it be left to another people. It will crush all those kingdoms and bring them to an end, but it will itself endure forever" (Daniel 2:44–45).

Was this paradise restored? Did this mean that the kingdoms of this world, through the good fortune of the *Pax Romana* (Roman Peace), which united so many kingdoms under one leader, had become the kingdom of God and of His Christ? Or did it mean, perhaps, that the kingdom of Christ conquers not by swallowing up the kingdoms of this world, but rather by outlasting them and outshining them in their glory, even as the eternal outlasts the temporal and the sun outshines its rays? It was the triumph of the so-called Barbarian hordes in 410, with the sacking of Rome itself, that forced the triumphalistic, and now-prosperous—indeed, now worldly—Christians to reassess the true nature of the kingdom of God.

The City of God

No more sharply does this question come into focus than in the different responses of the two most prominent thinkers of the day, those of Jerome and Augustine. Probably as in every powerful empire with an illustrious history of conquest, the illusion of national immortality held the most committed Christians under its spell. In fact, many probably assumed that word would come any day that the valiant Roman armies had finally put an end to the intentions of the invaders, but the sacking of Rome settled the question and left everyone stunned. This is very much where I think we are in our own experience as Christians in the West in general and in America in particular, and that is what makes this story the more relevant.

Plato had made the idea of the "Republic" almost mythical—indeed, almost religious, and Rome saw itself as the incarnation of that Greek idea. As the Roman Empire took on a more Christian character, the temptation was to see Rome and Christ as each other's protector, and for a vast number of the populace, if Christianity had replaced the old gods, the new religion merely served the old uses: providing social glue and lending divine approval to the Roman state and its cultural values.

> *Inasmuch as the City of God transcends earthly splendor, it marches triumphantly (even when persecuted) through the rubble of crumbling empires to reach the ends of the earth with the knowledge of the Gospel.*

When Rome was sacked, Jerome (the great Latin father), lamented, "What is to become of the church now that Rome has fallen?" Many of the Romans blamed Christianity itself. After all, when the old gods were appeased, generals came home conquerors, but the new God failed to deliver Rome's enemies into her hand. Others of a more practical bent recalled, for instance, how Honorius, the emperor, had driven all non-Christians out of the army—including the brightest and best, just at the time when they were most needed for national safety.[4] By this time, however, the church had been so favored and had so enjoyed the patronage and wealth of the royal court that Christians themselves had become lazy, worldly, and ignorant. Indeed, one could well have wondered at the time of Rome's invasion who were the real "barbarians."[5] Although many Christian leaders enjoyed buying into the myth that Rome was Christian in some genuine sense, in reality "she had remained largely pagan, above all in the highest social levels."[6]

As the tension mounted between the old Roman families and the church officials, Augustine of Hippo, an African bishop, wrote his masterpiece, *The City of God,* in an attempt to vindicate "the glorious City of God against those who prefer their own gods to the founder of that City."[7] Now, at first glance, one might think that Augustine was setting out to defend the notion that Rome was "the glorious city of God" that had been founded by Christ Himself, and that the "Christian nation" would rise again, but the irony is that Augustine intended no such thing. Instead, he wanted to argue that the true City of God was heavenly—the kingdom of God and Christ—and Rome was a city of this world—a great city, a marvelous civilization, but temporal and earthly rather than eternal and heavenly. The believers form "the City of God on pilgrimage in this world," and even though the City of Rome may have been kind for a while to the City of God, the two were never allies; they could never be allies, for they represent two different sources, goals, allegiances, and kings. Augustine offered this definition of his classic thesis:

> I classify the human race into two branches: the one consists of those who live by human standards, the other of those who live according to God's will. . . . By two cities I mean two societies of human beings, one of which is predestined to reign with God from all eternity, the other doomed to undergo eternal punishment with the devil. (Bk. xv, chap. 1)

This does not mean, of course, that the City of Man is destitute of civil righteousness or justice. After all, even pagans can build remarkably sound societies, full of the virtues which they inherited as those who are created in God's image. Nevertheless, it is not only the image of God that we have inherited from our ancestors, but the original sin as well, and so, while civil virtues may account for the grandeur of Greek and Roman civilization, these honorable qualities elicit no divine approval, since the unbelieving heart, mind, and will—all in bondage to sin—render true obedience to God impossible.

Civilisation not a curse of the fall [handwritten annotation]

This explains why we can find so much to praise in the City of Man in spite of its sin and so much to blame in the church in spite of God's grace. Christians ought to be actively involved in the City of Man, assisting it, building it, maintaining it, and enjoying its fruit—for civilization is not a curse of the Fall, but a gift of Creation—even though the Fall ended all earthly utopias and rendered government necessary. But inasmuch as the City of God transcends earthly splendor, it marches triumphantly (even when persecuted) through the rubble of crumbling empires to reach the ends of the earth with the knowledge of the Gospel. Many, like Jerome, saw the "barbarian" invaders as the enemies of Rome and, therefore, of Christ. But Augustine viewed them as "citizens to be" in the City of God.[8] This made Augustine and those who followed his Pauline account remarkably optimistic about the future, in spite of the realism with which they accepted the fall of a civilization they too had prized.

In short, Augustine saw the invasions as a missionary opportunity, while Jerome and others fled to the monasteries and still others fought for Rome as though she were the City of God. How much more quickly would Christianity reach the ends of the earth, Augustine thought, if the ends of the earth somehow came to us! The invasion was an opportunity for the church, because the church is on a mission to bring the saving Gospel to the ends of the earth, not on a mission to defend a particular culture or empire.

In *The City of God,* Augustine not only lays out his distinction between the kingdom of God and the kingdoms of this world; he offers a magesterial apologetic for Christianity, answering the philosophical, ethical, and cultural objections. Putting forward a distinctively Christian understanding of war, good and evil, divisions in society, natural law, predestination and free will, Augustine insisted that both kingdoms were dependent on God and that their disposal is in His hands. The chief issues in life, he insisted, were not related to the City of Man (political, moral, civil, social), but to the City of God. As Henry Chadwick observes, "Augustine never supposed that the interests of the Roman empire and the kingdom of God were more or less identical" and "the barbarians who attacked the empire were not necessarily enemies to the city of God. It would be the western church's task to convert its new barbarian masters." After all, "Man's true end, Augustine argued, lies beyond this life. . . . The Church exists for the kingdom of heaven, and <u>God alone knows the elect.</u> So the meaning of history lies not in the flux of outward events, but in the hidden drama of sin and redemption."[9]

Although space does not allow us to comment further on this phenomenal treatise, suffice it to say that the evangelical world today could read no wiser, more timely, and more richly scriptural Christian classic than *The City of God.*

As the early Christians eschewed either Gnostic, "otherworldly" monasticism on the one hand or a Christian takeover of the state on the other, Augustine sought to lead the Western church toward a sanely biblical view of the two kingdoms in an effort to preserve the integrity of the Gospel and take advantage of the moment by attempting to view it through God's lens rather than from a merely human, temporally conditioned perspective.

The Medieval Synthesis

Much as Augustine's theory may have emphasized the differences between the City of God and the City of Man, the middle ages represent a synthesis or merging of the two. As with any brief sketch, this one is surely simplistic and leaves out important nuances. Nevertheless, as papal power grew in the West and the barbarians were, in fact, converted (at least to the new imperial state religion, if not always to Christ), the Roman Church increasingly identified herself as the "Mother of Christendom," and "Christendom" referred to a culture, a civilization—indeed, the City of Man. Rather than seeing the kingdom of Christ triumph *in spite of* the condition of the kingdoms of this world, the church and state bound up their interests together: cardinals were "princes of the church" and adopted the familiar dress of secular rulers. In fact, a war between the Holy Roman Emperor Henry IV and Pope Gregory VII was only concluded when the former traversed the Alps in January, 1077, crawled to the pope's residence in Canossa and knelt in the snow, begging forgiveness.

In fact, the Gregorian revolution of the eleventh century was a massive attempt, at the turn of the millennium, to perfect the kingdom of God, almost entirely identified with "Christendom," meaning both civil and ecclesiastical spheres. A remarkably imaginative mystic, Joachim of Fiore, devised an eschatology (view of last things) which divided history into three dispensations: the Age of the Father (Law, corresponding to the Old Testament), the Age of the Son (Grace, corresponding to the New Testament), and the Age of the Spirit. At any moment, just as Joachim believed grace had surpassed and obliterated the law, Christendom would move even beyond the Gospel into a state of perfection in the Spirit. "The anticipation of a terrestrial paradise," writes David Walsh, "tended to eclipse the importance of the eternal one; the message of the Spirit implied that the message of Christ had been superseded, and the Church, with its sacraments, as well as the institutions of the state, were to be rendered obsolete." As Walsh points out, this rather eccentric system was taken seriously by many intellectuals of the Renaissance and laid the foundations for the Enlightenment view of progress, which is so much a part of our modern mind-set that we often do not realize the extent of its influence in our own thinking. Petrarch was the first Renaissance figure to articulate this vision, as he believed mysticism would finally lead to an Age of Light after the "dark ages," and this age of the Spirit would at last unite the world's religions.[10] Again, we see history repeating itself in our own day.

The Reformation

Just as Augustine's mind was preoccupied with combating heresy, clarifying the cardinal Gospel doctrines of sin and grace, and establishing a Christian philosophical framework, so too the recovery of the Gospel in the sixteenth century ended up reassessing the identity of the kingdom of God and its role in the world.

Martin Luther was the first to recover the Augustinian notion of "two kingdoms," so explicit in the New Testament. As the German Reformer attacked the clergy, proclaimed a Gospel that lifted up the poor and championed the equality of all Christians in their baptism, many of the peasants began to hear in the Gospel a revolutionary message that would now liberate them politically as well, much as the Zealots of Jesus' day expected a political revolution with the coming of the Messiah. Counting on the German Reformer's support, the tragic Peasant's War led to enormous bloodshed, and, just as it was being crushed, Luther wrote a tract making it clear that the liberation of the Gospel is not a call to social revolution in the kingdom of man. The radical German knight, Ulrich von Hutten, pledged the support of his soldiers: "The liberation of the Germans is in Luther's hands!" But Luther himself wanted no part in confusing the secular sword of the state with the spiritual sword of God's Word. The Reformation would proceed *non vi, sed verbo*—not by force, but by the Word.

And yet, the Reformers were children of their age too. When Luther needed the support of the state to enforce the reforms, he fell back on the Elector John. "The result," writes political historian G. E. Elton, "was a disciplinary organisation called the Visitation, a committee of two electoral councillors and two theologians, who took over the government of the Church from the bishops. They enforced devotional uniformity, reformed the morals and manners of the clergy, and supervised the moral and spiritual welfare of the laity," with the authority emanating from the secular arm. "Luther ascribed to the Christian magistrate a duty and a right to see to the well-ordering of God's Church, and the Visitation, embodying his political doctrine, in effect turned the Lutheran Church of Saxony into a state-Church."[11]

In Zurich, Ulrich Zwingli followed the same course—in theory, embracing the two kingdoms, while in practice coming to terms with the realities of medieval structures and institutions by calling upon the authority of the state to use the secular sword where necessary. Thus, as Luther rested the temporal welfare of the church on the secular prince, Zwingli placed it in the hands of the city council.

With the next generation, there was some new thinking about this relationship. John Calvin was among those interested in aiding in a more radical transition from the medieval synthesis to a clearer distinction between the secular and the sacred, the kingdom of man, which God has given the authority of physical force, and the kingdom of God, which is given by God's spiritual authority alone.

Calvin had a city council too, but unlike Zwingli, he had less say-so in its affairs until they convinced him to return after exiling him. The reason for the exile was that Calvin insisted on the church alone having jurisdiction in the spiritual affairs of the church, including church discipline. When the pastors in Geneva barred unrepentant sinners from the Lord's table—even though these citizens were part of the aristocracy and friends of the city council members, the show-down between Calvin and the council ended in the Genevan Reformer being exiled. Nevertheless, the city fell into confusion and was under renewed threat from Rome and its allies. After repeated attempts to convince Calvin to return, he finally did so and, with a relatively free hand, was able to pursue his reforms until his death in 1564.

Despite much of the popular hagiography, Calvin was not a despot. In fact, even though he was trained in civil law and was the best trained legal scholar in the region, he had less civil power than any of the other Reformers, certainly less than Luther or Zwingli. Although he was, because of his background, employed by the city to create sanitation legislation, Calvin could never get his frequent celebration of the Lord's table through city hall during his entire ministry. Calvin's greatest concern was for the spiritual integrity of the church. With Augustine, he insisted that there were "many wolves within and many sheep without," and that the church is always a mixed company of elect and non-elect. Nevertheless, if the advance of the kingdom of God is dependent on the secular arm, Calvin believed, there would be no way for those whom God had especially called and those who had been trained to preach, teach, and defend the faith against error to preserve the church from heresy and schism. He had no respect for the "contrived empire" of the medieval world known as "Christendom," although he saw the two kingdoms as mutually supportive of each other. No, the state must support the true religion, but the two kingdoms must be kept in their proper bounds, as each serves God through its distinct goals and means: First, we must realize that we are

> under a two-fold government, . . . so that we do not (as commonly happens) unwisely mingle these two, which have a completely different nature. . . . But whoever knows how to distinguish between body and soul, between this present fleeting life and that future eternal life, will without difficulty know that Christ's spiritual kingdom and the civil jurisdiction are things completely distinct. . . . Yet this distinction does not lead us to consider the whole nature of government a thing polluted, which has nothing to do with Christian men. That is what, indeed, certain fanatics who delight in unbridled license shout and boast. . . . But as we have

just now pointed out that this kind of government is distinct from that spiritual and inward Kingdom of Christ, so we must know that they are not at variance. *(Institutes* 4.20.1–2)

In fact, like Augustine, Calvin had a very high view of the cultural capabilities of pagans. No single form of government is necessarily sanctioned by God, although Calvin himself prefers "an aristocracy bordering on democracy"—a rather liberal view to hold in his day, and probably the reason why eminent historians such as Arthur Schlesinger, Jr., note that Calvinism, with John Locke's Enlightenment twist on it, "laid the philosophical basis for the American experiment in democracy."[12] In many non-Christian societies, magistrates look out for the poor and restrain the wickedness of those who would steal, kill, or vandalize, so it is not necessary to have a "Christian" nation in order to have justice, peace, and civil morality: "I would have preferred to pass over this matter in utter silence," writes Calvin, "if I were not aware that here many dangerously go astray. For there are some who deny that a commonwealth is duly framed which neglects the political system of Moses, and is ruled by the common laws of nations. Let other men consider how perilous and seditious this notion is; it will be enough for me to have proved it false and foolish" (4.10.14). After all:

> It is a fact that the law of God which we call the moral law is nothing else than a testimony of natural law and of that conscience which God has engraved upon the minds of men. . . . Hence, this equity alone must be the goal and rule and limit of all laws. Whatever laws shall be framed to that rule, directed to that goal, bound by that limit, there is no reason why we should disapprove of them, howsoever they may differ from the Jewish law, or among ourselves. (4.20.16)

Calvin emphasizes how essential it is that Christians, whether rulers or the ruled, distinguish between the two kingdoms and the limits of each, for the safety of both.

However far Calvin may have advanced beyond the medieval synthesis, he was certainly no ardent defender of the doctrine of the "separation of church and state" in the modern democratic sense. Certainly the Puritans, following the Genevan model, were not willing to separate the civil and spiritual spheres, although they did clearly distinguish them in theory and usually in practice. And yet, just as Augustine had confused the kingdoms in his appeal to secular power against the Donatists (a schismatic Christian sect), and the Reformers had confused them by relying on the "godly prince" to enforce the true religion, so too the Puritans mixed the two kingdoms by requiring voting members of the body politic to also be members of the church (i.e., the Congregational-Puritan church of New England). (This, however, must be understood in its historical context: Most New England residents were committed to the Puritan experiment, and with certain well-publicized exceptions, dissent was rare—not because of repression, but because of consensus.) Furthermore, many Puritans in England identified the cause of Christ with the cause of England, as the Spanish Armada represented the dragon in the Book of Revelation, and the New England Puritans simply applied this to the New World, as persecuted Protestants sought to settle the kingdom of God in America. These are the roots, then, of our notion of America as having a special covenant with God, as Israel of old. (In chapter 8 we will examine this notion more fully in the light of Scripture.)

We created substitutes for everything we could find in the secular kingdom: music, books, celebrities, etc.; instead of being a spiritual beacon taking itself into the world, the Christian realm became self-absorbed and took the world into itself.

It was left to Roger Williams, a Calvinistic Baptist who was himself exiled from New England, to articulate a more well-defined notion of the separation of church and state. And yet, even that is not the separation of God and state, but of an established church from dictating statecraft and vice versa. Although the proper jurisdiction and purpose of the two kingdoms had been maintained, one could argue that the doctrines of Christian liberty and freedom of conscience, unleashed in the Reformation, were not as fully understood or experienced in political affairs until this time.

Today

In our own time, debates over the church and society are largely revivals of this age-old question of the two kingdoms or cities. Due to the pietism and escapism that dominated evangelicalism for most of this century, as well as the hostility of the increasingly secular establishment, many conservative Christians lived and thought as if they were only citizens of one kingdom, the spiritual realm, and had contempt for the world. They could not understand why a talented, young artist in their church might want to study at Julliard or a bright son or daughter would want to run off to Harvard instead of Wheaton or Biola. So we created substitutes for everything we could find in the secular kingdom: music, books, celebrities, etc.; instead of being a spiritual beacon taking itself into the world, the Christian realm became self-absorbed and took the world into itself.

Today, in spite of political activism, the evangelical world has essentially adopted the monastic worldview of the middle ages rather than the world-embracing, but two kingdoms-distinguishing outlook of the Reformers and Puritans. Instead of leaving the monastery, we simply want to turn the world into one. In our own day, the climate is very different from that of the Reformers and Puritans, where the population simply assumed that, even though the civil and ecclesiastical spheres were distinct, the citizen of one would belong to the other. Now, ours is a pluralistic nation with many false religions, and our age has more in common with the pluralistic paganism of ancient Rome. Thus, an entirely new appraisal is necessary. Old assumptions have eroded and we must not argue from "givens" which are no longer taken seriously. Instead of reviving "Christendom" (in our case, "Christian America"), we must reassess, first, whether that idea is in fact biblical and, second, whether it is naive, given the contemporary situation.

When Hegel, the German philosopher of the last century, called for a *volksreligion* ("people's religion"), he was simply reissuing that call of the mystic Joachim of Fiore and the Renaissance. It was the creation of a "civil religion" with a "benign deity," as Ben

Franklin called it, that the modern experiment needed. Sadly, evangelicals settled for that and have been settling for it ever since. One of the reasons that secularism abounds today is precisely because evangelicals have accepted peace with the culture, the comfort of a civil religion that serves the moral and political ends of the nation, rather than proclaiming the universal monopoly on truth claimed by our Sovereign King, Jesus Christ. This sovereignty must not be guaranteed by the kingdoms of this world, but proclaimed by the kingdom of Christ. In other words, in the new covenant, God is never "on our side" as a nation, but only as believers (Romans 8:30). As citizens of the kingdom of God, we announce the claims of our King through the spiritual sword, not through the physical sword (political action or coercion of any kind, including economic). This does not mean that, for instance, a Christian police officer cannot employ force in the arrest of a thief, for that is appropriate to that "kingdom." And yet, we so often confuse these swords and assume that the claims of Christ's kingdom must be legislated and enforced in order to refashion a "Christian nation."

Even the most "Christian" of nations stands under the judgment of God at the end of time. One has to ask today whether even evangelicals are caught in the trap summarized by Walsh: "The leading figures of the modern world are spoiled mystics, *mystiques manques* . . . [with] the restless, over-reaching desire to bring this whole world transformation under the control of human will. These individuals cannot endure the uncertainty of faith, and they seek perfection through the instrumentality of their own actions."[13]

WHOSE JOB IS IT?

Calvin complained that a great many of the problems in society could be settled if people would simply stop transgressing their callings. By that, he meant what Paul meant when he told the Thessalonians to work well with their hands and mind their own business (1 Thessalonians 4:11). In other words, too often politicians encroach on matters outside the boundaries of their expertise or authority (such as the family, the church, and education). This is why one should be asking, it seems to me, not only why the government funds pornographic art but, more importantly, why it funds art at all. Does this not create the impression that art is a government-sponsored activity and not independent? Further, what is the government doing determining matters of family life? Here again, conservative evangelicals and liberal mainliners alike look to the state to define such essential relationships.

Around the turn of the century, the Dutch statesman and theologian, Abraham Kuyper, argued for what he called "sphere sovereignty." As prime minister, Kuyper insisted that each realm of life—the arts, education, science, the church, and the family—retains its own unique character and mission. The purpose of government was to guarantee the freedom of each "sphere" to accomplish its God-ordained function. For instance, even the schools were run by the families, rather than by public officials, and parents were involved at every level, not just at Parent Teacher Association meetings, because they believed that the family has the authority in such matters rather than the government. It was the government's business to make certain that the nation was adequately defended against aggression and was capable of limiting the ravages of crime and enforcing civil laws guaranteeing safety and liberty. The purpose of the government was not to define the family or the role of the church, as it is now doing with the help of conservatives and liberals alike.

Our failure to give legitimate balance to the several "spheres" may be partly responsible for the power we invest in politicians in general and the presidency in particular. Even apart from any biblical justification for limitation of powers, we have modern examples. For instance, in Britain, the authority is divided into the powers of state, given to the monarch, and the powers of the government, given to the prime minister. However, in America, both powers adhere in one person: the president. So, much like the ancient Caesars or those Europeans like Louis XIV, Charles I, or Napoleon, who sought to emulate them, we love our presidents too much and also hate them too much. We create idols and then love to smash them. We must, especially as Christians, beware of overestimating the presidency even while we complain about "big government." We must remember that the president is there to outline basic domestic goals and priorities, appoint the next century's bureaucrats (the reader will permit the indulgence in hyperbole), set foreign policy objectives, and deliver speeches for four years. These are not unimportant tasks, mind you, but they are not of ultimate importance. Presidents do not shape the cultural direction any more than the media, entertainers, or others whose importance evangelicals have exaggerated.

Kuyper believed that Christianity, and particularly the Calvinistic expression of it, was capable of creating a worldview and had proved itself as a force for liberty, justice, and the civil good. Nevertheless, Kuyper himself suffered no illusion that the kingdom of man would ever become the kingdom of God either through secular "progress" or religious and moral energies, arguing that in spite of common grace, through which God restrains evil in the world, the "antithesis" between these two cities would always render a fusion impossible. Thus, while Christianity can provide a new lens through which to understand the world and restrain its downward spiral, these are not "kingdom" activities. They simply preserve the society from being as bad as it could be without divine restraint. This is important for us to realize at a time when we find it so easy to embrace the modern heresy of human goodness needing good structures. By saying that the purpose of a Christian in politics is not to create a Christian society, but merely to help restrain evil, we are not derogating the importance of such a calling. It is no small matter to restrain injustice and evil; nevertheless, no social, moral, or political activity can reshape a society spiritually.

The purpose of education, for instance, is not to form character, but to teach children how to think and help make them aware of the broad range of knowledge available to us. Recently I noticed an ad for an evangelical seminary which read, "Our programs are focused on the life of the student, not just on rigorous theological training." At this particular seminary, the "professors have the same burdens and enthusiasms you do. They're ready to get involved in your life." But is that the purpose of education—to focus on the life of the student, to share the same burdens and enthusiasms, and to get involved in the personal lives of the students? We seem to be depriving education of its mission by demanding that it form a particular religious or moral character, either the virtue of "tolerance" on the left, which inhibits academic questioning and debate (and ends up creating a hostile intolerance of anyone who is not a liberal) or the virtue of "piety" on the right, which ends up

101

Just Because the Law of Moses cannot Redeem does not mean it cannot enlighten

Same Right

creating the impression that Christian education can rehabilitate bad kids and create superior moral character in the rest. But education and morality are not necessarily related. After all, the Nazis were very well-educated, cultured preservers of "Western culture" too. Education—even *Christian* education—cannot make people good any more than the government can.

Nevertheless, Christians ought to pursue education and their children's education with vigor—not because it will make bad children good, but because it will at least help make the ignorant better informed. Just because it cannot redeem does not mean it cannot enlighten. But Christians often urge the schools to teach biblical morality and then are angered when condoms are distributed. "What's good for the goose is good for the gander." If we want the government and the schools to intrude on the realms reserved for the church and the family when the *right* folks seem to be in power, other groups have the right in a free and democratic society to attempt the same.

We are called to be "salt,"
a preservative, and "light,"
to bring to open view the
drama of sin and redemption.

Likewise, art is an indispensable gift of God for the building of culture and, as such, is a product of creation, not the Fall. Nevertheless, we cannot be saved by good art any more than by good government, good morality, or good education. In his objection to the state funding of pornographic art, George Will wrote that the purpose of art is "to elevate the public mind by bringing it into contact with beauty *and even ameliorate social pathologies*" (italics added).[14] Whereas one might surely agree with the first part of his definition, the second part is more questionable. Is the purpose of art really to "ameliorate social pathologies"? Has psychology so drowned our culture that even art has to serve some therapeutic moralism by improving society? Not at all. The purpose of art is not to improve society, nor indeed even to improve the individual. If that were the case, the Nazis should have created the most

How old earth?

pathologically-free society. Art does not exist for its pragmatic use-fulness, moral effects, or for political purposes. It is not there to indoctrinate, but to enjoy. We cannot place our faith in art to build a better society any more than we can place it in any one of these other spheres.

Science, in its proper sphere (the natural world), serves a re-markably useful purpose in culture, but when it transgresses its boundaries by trying to explain the spiritual realities and the meaning of life, it becomes, as the pioneer in brain research, Sir John Eccles, observed, "a superstition."[15] At the same time, when ministers seek to tell the geologist the age of the earth, although the Scriptures are entirely silent on the point, they too transgress the limits of their sphere.

Helping the homeless or talking a woman out of an abortion is certainly an activity in which Christians ought to be engaged especially because they are Christians; nevertheless, they are not kingdom-extending activities. While they may prepare the society to hear the Gospel, it is the Gospel alone that creates the people of God and extends the kingdom of God, through the Word and Spirit. Christians have a duty to be positively engaged in the building of both kingdoms while clearly distinguishing them.

CONCLUSION

What we must recover in this regard, therefore, is a distinc-tion between the spheres even within the kingdom of man. But we must go beyond this, to recover the distinction between the two kingdoms themselves: their distinct nature, goals, objectives, and mandate. America is no more a part of the kingdom of God in our day than Rome was in Augustine's. As Donald Bloesch puts it, "The church as a church must speak to the critical moral issues in society through its preaching of the law. It must point directions, but as a general rule it should not issue political directives nor try to determine policy."[16] As citizens in the kingdom of man (cul-ture), we are called upon to execute our calling with excellence, driven by a biblically-informed outlook ourselves, without expect-ing non-Christians to embrace it without persuasion. We are called to be "salt," a preservative, and "light," to bring to open view the drama of sin and redemption.

Martin Niemoller was a Reformed pastor, whose leadership in the Confessing Church, which opposed Hitler, rendered him the führer's own personal prisoner. Nevertheless, Niemoller always used the pulpit as the opportunity to preach eternal truths that shook people up to the immediate crisis more than he would if he had railed against the regime directly. It was his actions as a private citizen that made Niemoller a hero in the City of Man, and his preaching that made him a faithful minister in the City of God, but the pastor knew the difference. In a sermon on being "salt and light" in spite of the fact that the Confessing Christians could not sponsor rallies, protests, or the like, Niemoller reminded them, "But, brothers and sisters, that is not our concern, it is the Lord Jesus'. We have only to see that the salt does not lose its savour, that it does not lose its power. What does that mean? The problem with which we have to deal is how to save the *Christian* community at this moment from being thrown into the same pot as the world." After all, the world comes to the church and says, "You really must suit your message to the world; you really must bring your creed into harmony with the present. Then you will again become influential and powerful." Sound familiar? Then Niemoller responds, "Dear brethren, that means: The salt loses its savour. It is not for us to worry about how the salt is employed, but to see that it does not lose its savour; to apply an old slogan of four years ago: 'The Gospel must remain *the Gospel*; the Church must remain *the Church*; the Creed must remain *the Creed*; Evangelical Christians must remain *Evangelical* Christians.' And we must not—for Heaven's sake—make a German Gospel out of the Gospel; we must not—for Heaven's sake—make a *German* Church out of Christ's Church; we must not—for God's sake—make *German* Christians out of the Evangelical Christians" (italics original).[17] If we substituted "American" for "German," Niemoller's message for the nationalistic German evangelicals of his day would perhaps be as appropriate for us.

Although the kingdoms of this world are always subject to God's sovereign rule in providence now, as He preserves them, and in miracle at the end of the age, when He judges them, the kingdom of God's grace is not in the least dependent on the passing ideologies or frenetic movement of self-important lobbyists and politicians who have deceived themselves and the rest of us into

believing that politics is really the most significant concern in society. Philip Yancey wisely reminds us,

> *Although we are certainly called to pray*
> *for our nation and its leaders, is there*
> *not a danger of confusing our allegiance*
> *to the "Christian nation" (America)*
> *and to the "holy nation" (the kingdom*
> *of God) to which we belong in Christ?*

Some historians argue that the church loses sight of its mission as it
moves closer to the seat of power. Witness the era of Constantine
or Europe just before the Reformation. We may be seeing history
repeat itself. In 1991, as communism fell in Poland, 70 percent of
Poles approved of the Catholic church as a moral and spiritual
force. Now only 40 percent approve, mainly because of the
church's "interference" in politics. Modern Poland does not practice church/state separation: a new law says radio and TV broadcasts must "respect the Christian system of values," and the state
funds the teaching of Catholicism in public schools. Yet the cozi-
ness between church and government has led to a loss of respect for
the church.[18]

We have cause for concern about the confusion of kingdoms
when Christian periodicals post ads with high school students hud-
dled around the American flag pole for prayer. Although we are
certainly called to pray for our nation and its leaders, is there not a
danger of confusing our allegiance to the "Christian nation"
(America) and to the "holy nation" (the kingdom of God) to
which we belong in Christ? Perhaps it is no more than a symbolic
meeting point, but my experience with such activities makes me
wonder whether it is more akin to a shrine, particularly in light of
the statements of some evangelical leaders who spoke of the
American flag as "sacred" during the trial over its burning. Does it
offend us to hear that America has no special relationship to God
and that God has absolutely no obligation to preserve or save this
nation? Does it bother us to hear that God no more favors America than Iraq? I have no doubt as to my allegiances as a citizen, but

God is obliged by no treaties or debts. We must always beware of turning God into a mascot of civil religion.

When a leader of the National Association of Evangelicals asked, "What will happen to the kingdom of God if Clinton is elected?" I couldn't help but think of Jerome's lamentation, "What will become of the church now that Rome has fallen?" Not only did the remark demonstrate an unbelievable degree of confidence in the power of politicians; it confused the success of an earthly kingdom and a particular agenda within that kingdom with the kingdom of Christ. Those who are overwhelmed with disillusionment can, like Jerome, return to the monastery—the evangelical subculture is still warm and waiting for us—or we can wage a culture war with the "barbarian invaders," vowing to take our empire back, or we can return to the more biblically prudent, time-proven policy of creative engagement and well-informed persuasion, relying on God and His Spirit alone for the success of the City of God.

NOTES

1. Henry Chadwick, *The Early Church* (London/New York: Penguin, 1967), 216–36.
2. Ibid.
3. Edward Gibbon, *The Decline and Fall of the Roman Empire*, an abridged version edited and with an introduction by Dero A. Saunders (London/New York: Penguin, 1980), 586.
4. Ibid., 591 ff.
5. Introduction, St. Augustine, *The City of God*, David Knowles, ed. (New York: Pelican, 1972), xv.
6. Ibid., xvi.
7. Ibid., Book 18, 47–50.
8. Chadwick, *Early Church*, 226–27.
9. David Walsh, *After Ideology: Recovering the Spiritual Foundations of Freedom* (New York/San Francisco: HarperCollins, 1990), 108–9.
10. G. E. Elton, *Reformation Europe: 1517–59* (London: Fontana, 1963), 56.
11. *Solzhenitsyn at Harvard* (Washington, D.C.: Ethics and Public Policy Center, 1989), 69.
12. Walsh, *After Ideology*, 137.
13. James D. Hunter, *Culture Wars* (New York/San Francisco: HarperCollins, 1991), 239.
14. Sir John Eccles, in "Science Can't Explain," *US News and World Report* (February 1985).
15. Donald Bloesch, *The Evangelical Renaissance*, (Grand Rapids: Eerdmans, 1973), 74.
16. Selected from *Religion from Tolstoy to Camus* (New York: Harper, 1961), 325–26.
17. Ibid.
18. *Christianity Today*, August 16, 1993, 72.

5

WHATEVER HAPPENED
TO THE GOSPEL?

*In the "culture wars," the Gospel has been a casualty—
not from the shells of the secularists, but from the
"friendly fire" of its own soldiers.*

LET'S SAY YOUR CHURCH HAS BECOME a scandal to the
neighborhood for its immorality. One member is living with his
mother-in-law; late-night orgies are so common that even when
the people come together for Holy Communion, they get drunk on
the wine. The church is divided into a dozen loyalties and hobby-
horses around charismatic personalities. Believers are suing each
other. Homosexuality is tolerated. The people will listen to just
about any traveling salesman of religious wares. What would be the
first words out of your mouth? How would you clean up this mess?

This was precisely the church the apostle Paul faced in Corinth, a great commercial city of the Roman Empire. No doubt,
Paul was infuriated with the Corinthians for their immorality, and
he is very clear later in his first letter that those who refuse to
repent will never enter God's kingdom. He insists that the immoral brother must be disciplined by the church. And yet, this is
not where Paul begins. First Corinthians begins by launching a

defense of the Gospel, a message that is "foolishness to those who are perishing" (1:18). God has chosen the weak, the foolish, and the common, in order to frustrate the powerful, the wise, and the noble "so that no one may boast before him" (v. 29). "It is because of him that you are in Christ Jesus, who has become for us wisdom from God—that is, our righteousness, holiness, and redemption. Therefore, as it is written: 'Let him who boasts boast in the Lord'" (vv. 30–31). Paul reminds the Corinthians that while he was with them, he did not come with a brilliant scheme of philosophy or morality. He did not try to out-dazzle the itinerant spiritual salesmen who tried to blend Christianity and fashionable paganism. "For I resolved to know nothing while I was with you except Jesus Christ and him crucified" (2:2).

> *When we see the staggering moral crisis of our society, the first thing we turn to is an earthly kind of wisdom when the Gospel, "the power of God unto salvation" is staring us in the face.*

Paul went on to say that though the Gospel indeed does possess wisdom, it is not "the wisdom of this age or of the rulers of this age, who are coming to nothing" (v. 6). In other words, it is not the sort of "wisdom" you get from passing fads or that you are likely to see on daytime talk shows. It is a wisdom which completely misses the most sophisticated moralists and philosophers because the religion of the natural man is this: "I'm basically a good person. Give me a plan, a strategy, a program for spiritual growth." The Gospel, on the other hand, says, "You are not a good person. You need someone else's righteousness to cover your unrighteousness, someone else's holiness to cover your shame, someone else's sacrifice to satisfy the demands of a just God." Thus, the true wisdom is that Christ "has become for us wisdom from God—that is, our righteousness, holiness and redemption," which excludes all reason for boasting.

In the "culture wars," the Gospel has been a casualty—not from the shells of the secularists, but from the "friendly fire" of its own soldiers. Instead of seeing the Gospel as the source of all healing in the church, we turn to other means. Like the world, we assume that massive campaigns, crusades, marches, and protests will force change where all the king's horses and all the king's men have failed. When we see the staggering moral crisis of our society, the first thing we turn to is an earthly kind of wisdom (political and civil righteousness), when the Gospel, "the power of God unto salvation" (Romans 1:16) is staring us in the face. In this chapter, we shall take a closer look at the ways in which the "culture wars" have redefined or removed the Gospel from the witness of the church.

THE LAW & GOSPEL: GETTING IT RIGHT

"The difference between the Law and the Gospel is the height of knowledge in Christendom. Every person and all persons who assume or glory in the name of Christian should know and be able to state this difference. If this ability is lacking, one cannot tell a Christian from a heathen or a Jew; of such supreme importance is this differentiation." So urged Martin Luther, in his New Year's sermon in 1532. Similarly, Theodore Beza, successor to John Calvin as Geneva's chief pastor, wrote,

> We divide this Word into two principal parts or kinds: the one is called the "Law," the other the "Gospel." All the rest can be gathered under the one or the other of these two headings. What we call "Law" (when it is distinguished from Gospel and is taken for one of the two parts of the Word) is a doctrine whose seed is written by nature in our hearts. . . . What we call the "Gospel" (Good News) is a doctrine which is not at all in us by nature, but which is revealed from Heaven (Matthew 16:17; John 1:13), and totally surpasses natural knowledge. By it God testifies to us that it is His purpose to save us freely by His only Son (Romans 3:20–22), provided that, by faith, we embrace Him as our only wisdom, righteousness, sanctification and redemption (1 Corinthians 1:30).

Furthermore, if we do not know the difference between these two categories, we will forever be confusing them when we run across particular passages in Scripture:

We must pay great attention to these things. For, with good reason, we can say that ignorance of this distinction between Law and Gospel is one of the principle sources of the abuses which corrupted and still corrupts Christianity. The majority of men, blinded by the just judgment of God, have indeed never seriously considered what curse the Law subjects us to, nor why it has been ordained by God. And, as for the Gospel, they have nearly always thought that it was nothing other than a second Law, more perfect than the first.[1]

In Paul's letter to the Galatians, he is appalled that the Christians there had been so easily swept away from the true Gospel of grace, seduced into mixing that Gospel with Law. Nowhere else is Paul so angry in his communication with the churches. In fact, as frustrated as he was with the Corinthians, in all of their spiritual immaturity and immorality, his outrage there comes nowhere near his criticisms of the Galatian church: "I am astonished that you are so quickly deserting the one who called you by the grace of Christ and are turning to a different gospel—which is really no gospel at all" (1:6). "If anybody is preaching to you a gospel other than what you accepted, let him be eternally condemned!" (v.9). "You foolish Galatians! Who has bewitched you? Before your very eyes Jesus Christ was clearly portrayed as crucified" (3:1). "I fear for you, that somehow I have wasted my efforts on you" (4:11). This is the same apostle who urges the Galatians in the same letter to produce the fruit of the Spirit: gentleness, peace, self-control, etc.; yet when it comes to the Gospel, he will give no quarter.

But today, Paul would be likely to hear the church reply, "But that's doctrine!" "You're being divisive." "Just when we need to form a united coalition against secular humanism in this country, you're bringing up theological debates that will be sure to distract us from the real war!" If you think I'm exaggerating, what are we to make of Randall Terry's remark that the Gospel is "an obviously inadequate solution" to the moral crisis in our nation?[2] In his book Terry presents the Gospel clearly and emphasizes its importance, but then he insists that "We must expend energy in both 'preaching the gospel' in the narrow sense, as well as 'living the gospel'—the good news that the Lord is come—and extending the rule of His authority into all arenas."[3] This new "gospel" is about our extending the rule of Christ (i.e., the rule of evangelicals and a particular agenda) over Washington, D.C.

Second, if the Reformers were correct in their insistence on the distinction between the Law, which commands, judges, condemns, threatens, and guides, and the Gospel, which gives, saves, redeems, and justifies, then "living the gospel" (so often heard these days) is a contradiction in terms. We do not live the Gospel. Rather, we *believe* the Gospel. It was because someone else lived, died, and rose again that we are saved. This is not to deny discipleship. Far from it; rather, it is to place it in its proper category. Whenever the Bible gives us commands, these are to be followed, but they are not the Gospel or even part of the Gospel. Rather, they are part of the Law. That Law consists of the moral commands, from Genesis to Revelation, which make demands on our lives. And yet, we cannot obtain life or God's favor by trying to live up to God's commands, so the Law curses us, condemns us, and drives us to Christ, despairing of our own righteousness. Regardless of whether or not we give lip service to that distinction, it clearly does not occupy a formal place in defining our vocabulary and everyday discourse, especially in the "culture wars."

The Law

The rich young ruler came to Jesus looking for the "one thing" he could do to be saved (Luke 19:18). What new program was Jesus pushing? Our Lord replied by first informing him that no one is good but God alone (v. 19). Next, Jesus tells the man, well-versed in the Law, "You know the commandments: 'Do not commit adultery, do not murder, do not steal, do not give false testimony, honor your father and mother.'" And the ruler confidently replies, "All these I have kept since I was a boy." "When Jesus heard this, he said to him, 'You still lack one thing. Sell everything you have and give to the poor, and you will have treasure in heaven. Then come, follow me'" (vv. 20–22). Astonishing, isn't it, that this young man actually thought he had kept the Law since he was a boy? And yet, George Barna's surveys tell us that 76 percent of the American public thought they were satisfying God's command to have no other gods before Him; 71 percent said they didn't have any idols; 44 percent said they never swear or misuse God's name. And here are some even more surprising figures: 93 percent said they never commit murder; 82 percent insisted they are not adulterers and 86 percent do not steal. Nearly half said they never lie and just over half said they are not jealous of the things other people have.[4] Amazingly, the highest percentage of people saying they were free of transgressions of these laws were "born again" evangelicals!

Why is this surprising? Shouldn't we rejoice that, at least according to their own accounts, most Christians are keeping their noses clean? No, the reason this is surprising to us is the same reason Christ's words were shocking to the rich young ruler. He sought to justify himself, like the Pharisee in the parable Jesus told before this incident. He had misunderstood what the Law really required. He thought that because he had never thrust a sword through another man, he had never murdered; because he had never broken into a house or bank and stolen valuable possessions, he was not a thief. But Jesus tells the people in the Sermon on the Mount what the true righteousness of the Law requires: "You have heard it said to the people long ago, 'Do not murder, and anyone who murders will be subject to judgment.' But I tell you that everyone who is angry with his brother is subject to judgment." In fact, "anyone who says, 'You fool!' will be in danger of the fire of hell" (Matthew 5:21–22). Furthermore, "You have heard that it was said, 'Do not commit adultery.' But I tell you that anyone who looks at a woman lustfully has already committed adultery with her in his heart" (vv. 27–28). It is not enough to resist the temptation to steal; when we fail to do everything in our power to protect our neighbor's person and possessions, even if that means giving him or her the shirt off our back (v. 40), even if he or she is an enemy (v. 38), we are convicted thieves.

This is why Jesus tells the ruler to go sell everything he has and to give it to the poor—to show the man that he *hadn't* actually kept the Law, that he was a law-breaker like the common criminal. He had not loved his neighbor as himself. Suddenly, he was stripped of the righteousness he thought he possessed. It is indeed amazing that so many evangelical Christians are so sure they, like the Pharisees, are pulling it off, when at least the Pharisees, unlike today's Christians, could *name* the Ten Commandments.

In this light, the words of the apostle Paul strike home: "Brothers, my heart's desire and prayer for the Israelites is that they may be saved. For I can testify about them that they are zealous for God, but their zeal is not based on knowledge. Since they did not know the righteousness that comes from God and sought to establish their own, they did not submit to God's righteousness. Christ is the end of the law so that there may be righteousness for everyone who believes" (Romans 10:1-4). First, he notes that there is a zeal for God, but it is not based on knowledge. But then, many Christians today might say, that is actually a good thing: Better to have "heart knowledge" than "head knowledge"—in other words, better to have an experience than to have a concept. But Paul says the Israelites are not saved, in spite of their zeal, precisely because what they do not know keeps them from it. They do not know either the righteousness God requires (perfect conformity to the Law in the strictest sense we have just been discussing: loving God and our neighbor perfectly without a single thought of ourselves, for our entire lives) or the righteousness which God gives (in the Gospel, the robe of Christ's perfect righteousness which is placed over our nakedness). In other words, because they did not really understand the Law, they could not comprehend the Gospel.

Similarly today, few seem to understand the Law of God: the righteousness God really demands, the wrath and judgment which are associated with our failure to keep that Law perfectly. To the question, "Does God expect human beings to be absolutely perfect?" nearly every believer, in our own informal surveys, has responded, "Of course not!" And yet, in that same Sermon on the Mount, our Lord declared, "Be perfect, therefore, as your heavenly Father is perfect" (Matthew 5:48). Many people think that they are saved by trying their best to follow Jesus' example, live for the Lord, and so on, not realizing that God doesn't grade on a curve. He requires the original righteousness with which we were created. His character has not changed, and He will not accommodate His holiness to ours, His character to our own.

The Gospel

This, indeed, is the pinch: God demands absolute perfection; I don't have it. Therefore, must I be condemned? Not at all. If by trusting exclusively in the perfect obedience and satisfaction of Christ's life, death, and resurrection, I am clothed in the very righteousness of Christ Himself, even God cannot find a spot or blemish in me. Thus, we are justified not by the Spirit working within us, in our heart, but by Christ working for us nearly 2,000 years ago in the Middle East, a gift given through faith alone on account of Christ alone. It is a perfect righteousness imputed or credited to our account as though we ourselves had earned it, not an imperfect righteousness that results from our cooperation with the Holy Spirit.

This is the Gospel, with no additions and no subtractions. It was this message that Paul said was so essential that if anyone preaches contrary to it, or merely adds to it, he stands under the divine *anathema.*

Confusing Law & Gospel

But we have confused the Law and the Gospel in our day, as the Galatians had done and as the medieval church had done. We have watered down the Law, so that it's not quite so severe. God no longer requires such strict holiness and purity of heart, mind, and body. Just give Him our best, He'll do the rest: that's the message we often get these days. The Law is only there for our own good, our own happiness and fulfillment anyway, right? And, as the Law has been reduced in its terror, so the Gospel has been reduced in its liberating word of pardon and justification. Instead of the cross satisfying God's just sentence of wrath for our sins, it is now a demonstration of how much God thinks we are worth. The Law removed, the Gospel becomes a new law that is easier and user-friendly.

Of course, we do not use the term "law," but choose rather words like "principles," "steps," and "formulas." We would know better than to say, "We are saved by our obedience to the Law," but we find it more difficult to detect that "We will achieve victory by following these principles or steps" is a new way of saying just that. We have softened the Law and, consequently, trivialized the Gospel to the point where the distinction is rarely made in preaching and teaching.

BUT WHAT DOES THIS HAVE TO DO WITH CULTURE WARS?

Randall Terry calls us to participate in "a cultural civil war, a war of allegiances." He writes,

> If righteousness is going to prevail, if paganism is going to be turned back, then we must move to restore this nation to being a Christian nation. Otherwise we will lose the war for America's soul, and the United States as we know it will perish.
>
> And if we are going to reform and rebuild our country, we're going to have to deliberately infiltrate the power bases of America. We'll deliberately have to raise up men like John Adams and Teddy Roosevelt to be "morally correct," not "politically correct" statesmen. May God grant it.[5]

Terry very clearly defends himself against the charge of claiming salvation by works,[6] but the war rhetoric often blurs the clear distinctions he might otherwise wish to make. For instance, he asks, "And so, is all lost? Have we sold out with no hope of redemption?" And, of course, the answer is no, but what is the form of redemption? "God can restore us and grant us the vision and the strategy to systematically take back the power bases of our culture. America can once again be what the pilgrims and the founders sought after—a city on a hill, an example to the world, a covenant, a Christian nation."[7] Salvation by vision and a strategy for systematically taking back the culture's power bases is implied in this kind of rhetoric, appeals to orthodoxy notwithstanding. In fact, the title of one of Terry's chapters is "What Must We Do to Be Saved? (Repentance, Resistance, Reformation)." If we truly repent, that means that "If we have failed to fight in our communities for what is right—whether teaching chastity in the schools or closing the porno shop—we must fight."[8] This will also involve our placing blame on our secular neighbors. "Blame is critical. We want the pagans and God-haters and egalitarian socialist planners to bear the blame for leading our country into a wasteland."[9] "Then we will be in a position of strength to lead the country out of moral and social chaos."[10] Not only does this language sound like a bit of demagoguery; it confuses the Law with the Gospel, civil restraint with the means of salvation.

We must realize that moralism has had a rather supportive haven in evangelicalism for the last two centuries. The great moral crusades in the nineteenth century demonstrate how easy it is to get so caught up in the cause of civil righteousness that the spiritual mission of the church (reaching the lost and bringing them to worship God, announcing God's curses and blessings through Word and sacraments, maintaining sound discipline) is lost. But since we will deal more fully with this a bit later, suffice it to say here that evangelicals do have roots in this sort of idea, inspired by Charles Finney and others, that salvation is a matter of moral improvement, individually and socially. Of course, to affirm that, Finney had to jettison such classical and biblical doctrines as original sin and total inability (that is, the bondage of human nature to sin). After all, how could you get a moral campaign off the ground with an essentially negative evaluation of human nature?

With the biblical doctrine of the self and its sinfulness gone, Finney had to rid the movement of the doctrines of God's sovereignty (man and his free will had to be central), which he did in explicit language; of the doctrines of penal substitution (i.e., that Christ bore the penalty for each one of our sins), and justification by grace alone through faith alone (he called it a different gospel and insisted that it would inhibit moral reformation).[11]

> *We have turned the one true God of history and Father of our Lord Jesus Christ into a tribal deity of the American experience—we who are supposed to be the guardians of absolute truth.*

Charles Finney totally redefined the Christian message along the lines of the arch-heretic Pelagius, the latter condemned by more church councils than anyone else in history, and no one seemed to blink. The "theological casing" about which David Martin speaks was already gone. Nobody cared about theology, as long as the show was going on (evangelism) and moral victories were being won (politics). The modern church growth movement and the Christian Right are merely perpetuating this moralistic stream in American revivalism. Impressively sprawling buildings may have replaced giant tents, and moral crusades might be conducted through high-tech direct-mail marketing, but the capitulation to secular sentiment and ideology runs throughout its two-century history.

That moral sentiment is more important than theology is illustrated in the push for prayer in the public schools. According to one Christian leader, speaking in the hyperbole that has characterized the movement, the 1963 Supreme Court decision to forbid school-sponsored public prayers was the darkest hour in the history of the nation. Darker than slavery, the Civil War, or two world wars, the decision to remove public prayers in public schools had the effect of evicting God, as if He were the school mascot who had just been voted out in favor of another. And yet, what this points up is the faulty theology in the evangelical movement itself concerning the exclusivity of Christ.

Fundamentalists and evangelicals have usually been the most vocal defenders of the exclusive claims of Christ as the only mediator, the only Way, Truth, and Life, apart from whom no one can come to the Father (John 15). And yet, ironically, this is the same group that is pressing most vocally for public tributes to the "Unknown God," giving the impression that one need not have any particular god (i.e., Muslims, Jews, Hindus, Buddhists, New Agers, Fern Worshipers, et al., will be expected to pray to this amorphous American deity) or any mediator in order to approach him/her/it. Ours is the group Republicans and Democrats are both trying to please (and win) when their speech-writers throw "god" into the convention speeches. We have turned the one true God of history and Father of our Lord Jesus Christ into a tribal deity of the American experience—we who are supposed to be the guardians of absolute truth.

Again and again, the impression is given that evangelicals are more concerned about things which concern civil righteousness than about how we can stand righteous before God's face—the Gospel. The former has occupied a central place in our discourse; its agenda has so many specifics that if it were a confession of faith many would say it was far too detailed. But because it isn't a confession of faith, but an agenda for morality, it can demand our time, talents, and energies and outline the most rigorous, particular positions on nearly every conceivable political, economic, and social policy under consideration. Confessions of faith and doctrinal discussions cannot be allowed to take away our energies from spreading the Gospel, but moral agendas have *carte blanche*. This is the sort of thing for which we used to criticize the liberals, labeling it the "Social Gospel," but now it is acceptable because it's the right politics.

Peter Berger, a Boston University sociologist, where he is also the director of the Institute for the Study of Economic Culture, also happens to be a Christian, and in the 1987 Erasmus Lecture, published in *This World*, Berger was daring and bold enough to take on the project of challenging the church to return to the true Gospel. "Different Gospels: The Social Sources of Apostasy," was his title; his arguments are to the point in defining the importance of the Gospel and its Babylonian captivity to the modern political culture.

"The essence of apostasy is always the same: seeking salvation, not in the grace of Christ 'heard with faith,' but rather in what Paul calls 'the works of the law.' The specific contents of apostasy, the details of 'works-righteousness,' vary from age to age."[12] So Berger begins what amounts to a contemporary application of Paul's letter to the Galatians. But what does this have to do with "culture wars"? It sounds more like a Bible study, I hear someone saying. Observe Berger's application that "many of the harder theological contexts of the various traditions had been softened and relativized," he says, to accommodate the new American faith.[13] But this American faith is in jeopardy, so "Increasingly, major religious organizations are serving the function of chaplaincies in these armies, doing what chaplains have always done on battlefields: solemnly blessing the banners of their side and assuring the troops that their cause is God's."[14] Does the church derive its whole identity from the Gospel? Berger offers the following answer:

> It seems to me that we face precisely this question in American Christianity today—nothing less—and it is an awesome question. Compared to this question, the different moral and political options available to us pale, not into insignificance (because Christians are in the world and responsible for the world), but into what Dietrich Bonhoeffer called "penultimacy." The ultimate question is the question of salvation. Thus the issue I want to address now is not, emphatically not, the substitution of one cultural or political agenda for another. Rather, it is the issue of placing any such agenda into the place that is reserved to the Gospel in the faith and life

of the Church. . . . Any cultural or political agenda embellished with such authority is a manifestation of "works-righteousness" and *ipso facto* an act of apostasy.[15]

We must remember that the Galatians were not abandoning the Gospel overtly and intentionally. They were simply adding their own customs and traditions to the Gospel and requiring the Gentiles to adopt them as essential to fellowship and even salvation. But is that really what we are doing these days? I do not think Berger is exaggerating to suggest that we have, both mainline liberals and conservative evangelicals:

> Democracy or capitalism or the particular family arrangement of middle-class culture are not to be identified with the Christian life, and neither is any alternative Gospel, not to defend the American way of life, not to "build socialism," not even to "build a just society," because, quite apart from the fact that we don't really know what this is, all our notions of justice are fallible and finally marred by sin. The "works-righteousness" in all these "different gospels" lies precisely in the insinuation that, if we only do this or refrain from doing that, we will be saved, "justified." But, as Paul tells us, "by the works of the law shall no one be justified."[16]

The danger in hitching the Gospel wagon to the shooting stars of economic, political, social, religious, or national custom lies not in choosing the *correct* secular path to take for the Gospel's success, but in choosing to take any of the alternate paths at the fork in the road. In the sixties the chant from the mainline denominations was, "The world sets the church's agenda." Conservative preachers berated them for it as they pounded their Bibles, but in the eighties and nineties, many of them have become themselves soldiers in the army of the new Social Gospel, "the Liberation Theology of the Right," as one Christian Reconstructionist has been so bold as to call it.[17]

The only difference now is that the part of the world that sets the church's agenda is the white, upper middle-class, Republican establishment rather than the minorities, the poor, and the Democrats. "I don't know how a true Christian could be a Democrat," many evangelicals say these days. One can hardly question the spiritual state of a popular evangelist or author who fundamentally alters the basic Christian message, but one's political affiliation is decisive these days. "Political correctness" is not only a problem on the left; one finds similar tactics, attitudes, and intolerance among politically conservative Christians too, many of whom have proclaimed Rush Limbaugh the new evangelical pope, even though he does not claim to be representing any particularly biblical agenda.

This is the vision God has of building His kingdom—through the proclamation of the Gospel, not through the rhetoric and actions of war.

The tongue-lashing Paul gave to the Galatians should stand out against us in bold relief. By adding things to the Gospel, such as Jewish customs and ceremonies, and making Christian identity turn on whether one adhered to them, the Galatians had in fact embraced another gospel, which is no gospel. This is why Paul turns from announcing the Gospel all over again (justification by grace alone through faith alone, apart from all works of any kind, including the old ceremonies) to its application to the Galatian community:

> You are all sons of God through faith in Christ Jesus, for all of you who were baptized into Christ have clothed yourselves with Christ. There is neither Jew nor Greek, slave nor free, male nor female, for you are all one in Christ Jesus. If you belong to Christ, then you are Abraham's seed, and heirs according to the promise (3:26–29).

We have not only followed Galatia in so identifying the Gospel with a particular political affiliation as conservative evangelicals; it has manifested itself in blatant racism, just as it did in the Galatian church. I am not talking here about what the "politically correct" gestapo regards as racism, but what anyone should regard as such: "Would you be willing to live next door to a black or Hispanic neighbor?" According to Gallup, the Southern Baptists and white evangelicals were the first to say no.[18] Perhaps this is why there is still a National Association of Evangelicals and a National Association of Black Evangelicals and why when one thinks "evangelical," cultural and racial variety does not leap to mind.

But the answer even to this is the Gospel, not social legislation or the "P.C." (politically correct) thought-police. Paul tells the Galatians that by wrapping the Gospel up in things that are not part of the Gospel (he specifically mentions race, socio-economic status, and gender), they have in fact abandoned the Gospel, and their additions are "works-righteousness." They are seeking to be justified or saved by a prescribed program of cultural indoctrination rather than by grace alone through faith alone. "Faith alone" destroys the other gospels of works-righteousness and self-righteousness, and in the process it creates a Gospel community based on the answer to our Lord's query, "Who do men say that I am?" rather than on cultural, political, or socio-economic factors. It even buries the guilt and condemnation of the vilest offenders of God's law in the sea of atonement. The Gospel says that the pornographer, the child molester, the homosexual, drug dealer, and, yes, even the abortionist, are being invited to become co-heirs with Christ. When, by God's grace, we turn from our wickedness, acknowledge even our righteousness (the very best we have) to be "filthy rags," and throw ourselves entirely on God's mercy, we meet at the cross together, beside those who were our enemies. The cross, not cultural victory, has at last brought us together, we who were so hostile to one another. This is the vision God has of building His kingdom—through the proclamation of the Gospel, not through the rhetoric and actions of war.

The Jews believed that Gentiles were "dogs," much as some Christian activists might think of "secular humanists." Influenced by their being raised in the Roman Empire, where there were sharp divisions in society based on social and economic standing, these divisions ran just as deep in the church as in society, which James points out in his letter (2:1–7). And concerning women, the Jewish liturgy had a line in one of the prayers, "Thank you, Lord, that I am not a Gentile, a slave or a woman." Not only is this not found in the Old Testament, its very sentiment is alien to Scripture. Nevertheless, it had become part of the liturgy, and the Galatians may well have been using it. Joel prophesied that the Spirit would be poured out on women as well as men in the last days (i.e., Christ's first advent), and here Paul says that even though differences do exist—healthy, positive differences—the Gospel makes us all equal before God. This is not a modern egalitarian notion. Paul does not advocate here the redistribution of wealth, to eliminate the differences between slave and free, nor the removal of any distinctions between race, as if we could or even should deny the richness of our cultural and racial identity and diversity. Nor does he argue from this that there are no differences between men and women, as his remarks about proper roles make clear. Rather, he is insisting that before God we are equally sinners and equally justified, and that any message that requires a particular agenda, party-line, set of cultural values, or that targets or favors a particular group for its race, income, or gender is seeking to establish its own righteousness by creating its own gospel, "which is no gospel."

We would all do well to reread John Bunyan's *Pilgrim's Progress*. Many will remember such exchanges as the following, in which Evangelist describes Worldly Wiseman to the pilgrim named Christian: "The man that met thee is one *Worldly Wiseman*, and rightly is he so called: partly because he savoureth only the doctrine of this world, (therefore he always goes to the Town of *Morality* to church); and partly because he loveth that doctrine best, for it saveth him from the Cross." The evangelicals used to chastise the liberals for ignoring the Cross in favor of politics, but one wonders if the Town of Morality has been selected by evangelicals as the spot for the lifting of the burden. With hope in politics rather than in God, in works rather than in faith, many modern evangelicals are just building one more Tower of Babel alongside the many others.

Peter Berger tells of common experiences people have these days, whether in mainline liberal churches or conservative evangelical churches, both boasting in their "prophetic" ministry, while doing little more than parroting the most extreme versions of either left- or right-wing ideology. Those who lose out are the folks who come for eternal answers to eternal questions. Berger says, "These individuals come to receive the consolation and solace of the Gospel, instead of which they get a lot of politics. I can think of no clearer case of one asking for bread and being given a stone."[19] I know what Berger is talking about. Recently, I was being interviewed by a radio station, and a man called in who said he was looking for answers and had finally decided, after many years away from church, to give it a try again. He went to a conservative evangelical church and, according to his report, heard nothing but a political speech. These are the kinds of reports I used to hear conservative preachers use to show how liberals had turned the pulpit into a soap-box for radical politics. But now we are just as worldly, just as willing to embrace other gospels. Our own people cannot name the Ten Commandments, and yet we are outraged that they are removed from the public halls; vast numbers of people in our own churches cannot define the Gospel in terms of justification by grace alone through faith alone, while we treat the moral and political crises and solutions as ultimate.

MISTAKING SYMPTOMS FOR THE ILLNESS

Our greatest problem is not any particular expression of sinfulness (whether homosexuality, divorce, abortion, etc.), but our sinful condition.

> *Commonly, evangelical leaders refer to political activism as "the battle for the souls of our nation," confusing partisan politics with salvation every bit as much as a sixties liberal or liberation theologian.*

We have confused civil righteousness (righteousness before our neighbor) with spiritual righteousness (righteousness before God) by confusing moral and political crusades with the advance of Christ's Gospel and kingdom: We will do it. We will bring God back or bring America back to God. Its moral righteousness is the reason God favored it, and its lack of moral righteousness is the reason for God's abandonment. We must get Him back. We will save America. And here is how we'll do it: Vote this way, organize this group, follow this strategy, embrace this agenda. It is like following a recipe or an instruction manual: By following these laws ("principles"), God will be obligated to make America number one again.

One piece of correspondence from one leader declares, "It is time to take America back. . . . The only way to get our nation out of this crisis is to spark a national revival." Revival becomes something we control through our campaign machinery rather than a sovereign work of God's Spirit bringing people to despair of their own righteousness before the Law and driving them to Christ in the Gospel. The goal of a national revival is political, and the means of the national revival is our own works: "I am asking Christian people who care about our nation to join me in the following plan of action to save our nation: (1) Dedicate your life anew to humble yourself before God and honor Him . . . ; (2) Pray—as you never have before . . . ; (3) Join me in spreading this message to concerned Christians everywhere as we raise up a great army to overcome this evil gripping our nation." "We had the privilege of growing up in a nation where God was honored and His principles obeyed," he writes, "—we lived in a nation blessed of God—let's bring America back to these Godly principles." He closes his appeal, "And today, we are mobilizing a great army of people determined to stop the onslaught of evil in our society" as he refers to this call for revival/political campaign as "this great work of the Gospel."[20] But by calling moral and political activism "the work of the Gospel" and a "plan of action to save our nation," the author risks the same confusion as the Galatian church.

We ought to be absolutely clear that the church witnesses to the truth of the claims of Christ and His apostles, not to the truth of the Republican or Democratic party.

Commonly, evangelical leaders refer to political activism as "the battle for the souls of our nation," confusing partisan politics with salvation every bit as much as a sixties liberal or liberation theologian. In fact, "revival" is described, in part, in the following terms: "This is the time for evangelicals to grab history's helm and to determine America's course. When they do, they should not be surprised to find millions of cultural conservatives—whether they would call themselves that or not—willing to follow."[21] If one replaces "evangelicals" and "cultural conservatives" in that sentence with "mainline Protestants" and "cultural liberals," the flaw is readily apparent: What a confusion of Christianity and ideology! But here, we are told that the wedding of Christ and conservative culture is a recipe for *revival!* Of course, this is not the way revival has been understood in the past, where it was seen as a supernatural work of the Holy Spirit, working through the preaching of the Law and Gospel, bringing men and women to repentance and faith in Christ, resulting in charity, social concern, and justice. By reversing that order, we create another gospel, which is no gospel, and another revival, which is no revival. We ought not to be looking for a revival that will be so determined by its cultural, social, and political character that "cultural conservatives" will be pleased with it. If genuine revival comes, and the Word is correctly preached, cultural conservatives will have as much to lose, and cultural liberals will have as much to gain.

Evidently, it is cultural ideology that determines the contours of "revival" these days. For instance, why was Nancy Reagan asked to address an evangelical convention even though her dependence on astrologers was well-publicized, she was disinterested in church attendance, and there was an absence of any clear profession of faith? Would Hillary Rodham Clinton, an active Methodist, be invited? I doubt it, and I am not suggesting that she should be. But surely such decisions reinforce my fear that evangelicals care more about politics than about ultimate and eternal issues that transcend our earthly allegiances. The most ardent defenders of the left-wing agenda in America may be a threat to sound political wisdom, but they are not a threat to the kingdom of God. Although we certainly must not be unconcerned or apathetic about the impact of ideas in the social arena, we must not overestimate the ultimate significance of those issues for the advancement of God's kingdom. And just as we must not confuse the objectives and good of the kingdom of God with the objectives and good of America or our particular political party, so we ought to be absolutely clear that the church witnesses to the truth of the claims of Christ and His apostles, not to the truth of the Republican or Democratic party.

The National Association of Evangelicals' Robert Dugan refers to "the evangelical lobby." Imagine how uncomfortable the term, "the Mormon lobby" sounds. Or how about, "the Muslim lobby," the "Jehovah's Witnesses lobby," or the "Buddhist lobby"? What is a religion doing as a "lobby" in Washington? Does a religion exist to express a particular consensus on every public policy issue that comes down the pike? Or think of the name, "Christian Coalition." Is it possible to be an evangelical if one does not endorse that list of positions? It does not seem to be a problem if one dissents from evangelical *theology* these days, just so long as he or she stays within the limits of proper *ideology*, as prescribed by the "evangelical lobby."

This is the language of the Christian Right, and it is the language of Pelagianism, the revival of the Galatian heresy insisting that human nature is not captive to sin, but disoriented; that the greatest need is not redemption, but redirection; that Christ is chiefly a moral example who *shows* us the way rather than a sacrifice who *is* our way into the presence of the Holy One; a friend who *teaches* us righteousness more than a substitute who *is* our righteousness. It is a strategy of works-righteousness, and, as such, it is a recipe for disaster, both here and hereafter. Most of these leaders denounce "works-righteousness" gospels in theory, but the practical course suggests their influence.

Our crises, our "culture wars" and moral tragedies, horrible and significant as they may be, are not of ultimate seriousness. And yet, Berger argues,

> . . . there is a crisis of ultimate seriousness—it is the crisis brought on by the Gospel being proclaimed, or not proclaimed, in any moment of history—yet it is a crisis that has been with the Church from its beginning. We are justified by faith. This means that nothing depends on us: our personal destiny and that of the entire world rests in God's hands. It also means that everything depends on us: we are called, to the best of our ability, to serve both the Church and the world.

But to fulfill this duty, we must "recall the true meaning of Gospel, Church, and ministry, and then to put our own ecclesial houses in better order." Berger complains, however, "I see very little evidence of any of this happening in American Christianity today."[22] May it begin happening with us today.

NOTES

1. Theodore Beza, *The Christian Faith*, trans. James Clark (East Sussex, England: Focus Christian Ministries Trust, 1992).

2. Randall Terry, *Why Does a Nice Guy Like Me Keep Getting Thrown in Jail?* (Lafayette, La.: Huntington House, 1993), 61.

3. Ibid., 66.

4. *The Barna Report*, (Ventura: Regal, 1993), 113, 92–93.

5. Randall Terry, *Nice Guy*, 80–81.

6. Ibid., 106.

7. Ibid., 154.

8. Ibid., 161.

9. Ibid., 165.

10. Ibid., 166.

11. Charles Finney, *Finney's Systematic Theology* (Minneapolis: Bethany, 1976), 170 ff.

12. Peter Berger, *This World*, Spring, 1987, number 17, 7.

13. Ibid., 8.

14. Ibid., 11.

15. Ibid., 12–13.

16. Ibid., 13.

17. Not only is North apparently happy to see the movement described in this way, but the way of approaching Scripture—often ignoring doctrine in favor of *praxis* and maintaining an eschatology of redemption through dominion of the "righteous," has many parallels with liberation theology. Richard John Neuhaus observes just this point: "But the analogies are inescapable. The policy specifics may be dramatically different, but the theological rationale is strikingly similar." [*First Things*, May 1990, no. 3, 16] Neuhaus also points out the cultural imprint on the Reconstruction movement: "There is also a deeply American dimension of optimism in theonomy. The distance from Norman Vincent Peale to Rousas John Rushdoony is not so great as may at first appear. Victorious living, positive thinking, dominion theology—all are entrenched in the can-do tradition of what used to be called muscular Christianity. It is the perduring power of what Luther called 'the theology of glory,' as opposed to 'the theology of the cross'" (19).

18. George Gallup and Jim Castelli, *The People's Religion: American Faith in the 90's* (New York: Macmillan, 1989), 188.

19. Berger, *This World*, 16.

20. Jerry Falwell, fund-raising appeal in August, 1993, "Take America Back!"

21. Robert Dugan, Jr., *Winning the New Civil War: Recapturing America's Values* (Portland: Multnomah, 1991), 180.

22. Peter Berger, *This World*, 17.

PART TWO:

Defining the Solutions

6

GOD, SECULARISM, AND SANITY

The more involved individual Christians are with the evangelical subculture, including the churches themselves, the greater the likelihood that they have already succumbed to the hypnotic powers of secularism.

IN HIS CLASSIC, EPIC POEM, the *Odyssey*, Homer's hero, Odysseus, must make his journey home past the isle of the Sirens. Hypnotizing sailors with their irresistible melodies, the Sirens seduced the unsuspecting into their lair; those who thought they were up to the challenge soon learned that they did not possess sufficient powers of resistance. Knowing this, Odysseus had his crew tie him to the mast of the ship and seal their own ears with wax. In so doing, the ship passed the isle safely and resisted the Sirens' song, to advance to the next stage in the odyssey.

For us today, the song of the Sirens is secularism, a *condition* of contemporary life that has resulted from the *process* of secularization. While there is neither the space nor the scope here for a detailed definition, suffice it to say that secularism is largely the product of two movements: The first, modernity, is rooted in the Enlightenment, which repudiated the supernatural (miracles, salvation, revelation, etc.), leaving room only for naturalism (laws of nature, moral improvement, progress, reason, etc.). The second is postmodernity, which in many ways is reacting against the arid triumphalism of modernity and rationalism by emphasizing experience over reason and the inner realities of the soul over the external realities of the objective world. Both are very secular movements, and yet Christians have often surrendered, usually unwittingly, to this process. Often, it is in the name of "relevance" and what one might today call "contextualization," whereas in other cases it is simply a matter of slowly accommodating to the spirit of the age, with very little thought to making intentional concessions.

Confident in their powers of resistance to worldliness, many conservative Christians today, like the mainline denominations earlier this century, naively assume that because they are so involved in church and the evangelical subculture, with its own music, art, events, conferences, books, and broadcasting, that they are sailing safely past the isle of the Sirens. Nevertheless, the more involved individual Christians are with the evangelical subculture, including the churches themselves, the greater the likelihood that they have already succumbed to the hypnotic powers of secularism.

The remedy, as I see it, to our crisis of secularism is not a renewal of earth-bound movements (even Christian ones), but a recovery of the vision of God. It is a recovery we find in the Lord's Prayer: "Our Father which art in heaven . . . ," and in that one sentence we find the balance between the personal aspect of our relationship with God, so often played up in our day by both liberal and conservative Christians, and the transcendent and eternal perspective of God's holiness and sovereignty. With this chapter, we turn from the criticisms of the "culture wars" approach to a positive strategy for reformation and revival, based on the Lord's Prayer. The following chapters will gather our thoughts around each of the petitions, recovering a sense of biblical transcendence, reverence, the kingdom and will of God, daily concerns in this world, redemption; resisting the lure of secularism; and recovering God's glory, kingdom, and power as the axis upon which our entire thought and life turns.

"OUR FATHER WHICH ART IN HEAVEN"

Church history records the swing from an over-emphasis on transcendence to immanence and vice versa. Transcendence refers to God's being "wholly other," completely distinct from His creation, and therefore the things that are related to Him are from another place, another world. Transcendence underscores God's distance from us in the Creator-creature relationship. Immanence, however, refers to God's nearness. If we ignore God's transcendence, God becomes a buddy who is little more than a rather huge version of your best friend, girlfriend, or boyfriend. (Much of modern Christian music leans in this direction.) If we ignore God's immanence, God becomes a distant, unknown and unknowable being with whom we cannot have a personal relationship.

The Scriptures show us the balance we must have in holding to both the transcendence and immanence poles. When the people of Israel wanted to worship God in the form of a golden calf, they were simply seeking a more immanent way of worshiping the true God. They wanted a practical, personal, tangible deity; it was hard to have a personal relationship with an unseen God who would not allow Himself to be discovered or understood on man's terms. St. Augustine spoke of the essence of original sin as being "curved in" on ourselves, much as an older person might be bent over, unable to see more than a few feet ahead. Such a person's world is often tragically limited and joyless, as he or she is unable to take in the beauty of the world beyond his or her own two feet. The natural man or woman only sees a place for "god," therefore, somewhere within that limited, narrow horizon, within that "practical," earth-bound frame of reference. He or she can only think of "god" in earthly terms, as a companion who helps one achieve purely earthly, secular goals. When the church accommodates this "god" of pagan experience, it may momentarily meet a "felt need," but unless it challenges that limited, utilitarian, secular view of "god" and his place, it ends up merely buttressing secularism and human lostness.

This is the human problem, often identified as the "hedonistic paradox": By running after self-fulfillment, we only find emptiness. It is only by dying to self that we really begin to live, and it is only by having our eyes raised toward heaven, by God's grace, that we begin to know true joy. This is the theme of Ecclesiastes, where everything ends up being meaningless if one's world is merely "under the sun"—that is, focused on this world and unable to see even the simplest pleasures in the world as gifts lowered down to us from

Self centered

God's fatherly hand. Similarly, John Calvin said that the uncon-
verted person is like a man blind-folded in a glorious theater.
Apart from transcendence and revelation, even this world does
not make any sense. We can understand the pieces of the puzzle *as
pieces;* that is, we can obtain sophisticated data, but we cannot
understand the "big picture," how the pieces fit together.

AN AGE OF HUMILIATION

Of course, putting ourselves in God's place at the center of
existence did not begin in the modern age. It was Adam and Eve,
remember, who wanted to be gods long before Nietzsche declared,
"If there were gods, how could I endure not being one?" Similarly,
at his brother's graveside in 1879, humanist Robert Green Ingersoll eulogized, "Happiness is the only good. The time to be happy
is now. The place to be happy is here. The way to be happy is to
make others so," so that even the goal of morality was self-interest. After all, said Ingersoll, "Life is a narrow vale between the
cold and barren peaks of two eternities. We strive in vain to look
beyond the heights. We cry aloud, and the only answer is the echo
of our wailing cry."[1] The agnostic philosopher Bertrand Russell
declared, "Every man would like to be God, if it were possible,"
and this is true not only of individuals in isolation, but of individuals in groups. Nationalism is a form of collective narcissism, as the
psychologist Karl Menninger seems to indicate: "The sin of pride appears most conspicuously in group pride—tribalism, nationalism, jin-
goism, and racism."[2] While this tendency toward self-infatuation
has been a part of fallen human nature ever since the Fall, we see
it expressed very blatantly in our own day. In fact, Solzhenitsyn
insists that we are at a major historical turning-point, just as revolutionary as the Middle Ages. Our question to be tackled in this
new revolution will be, "Is it true that man is above everything?"[3]

"You shall be as gods" has been the lie for which we keep
falling in each generation, and I fear that, as the surveys we have
studied earlier seem to indicate, the human-centeredness and hu-
man-elevating message of so many churches today has contributed
to the very secularization those same churches denounce in its
moral manifestations.

GOD AND SANITY

Never before has there been so much information, technological sophistication, and so little sanity. In fact, entire professions and recreations depend on the insanity of modern life. Daniel 4 records the story of the Persian king Nebuchadnezzar, proudly pacing the roof of his palace, overlooking the bright lights and big city: "Is this not the great Babylon which I have built by my power and for the glory of my majesty?" he boasted. But God put the king in his place: driving him from society into the wild to live like an animal. "At the end of that time, I, Nebuchadnezzar, raised my eyes toward heaven, and my sanity was restored." He went on to praise the one true God who "does as he pleases," without getting human permission. "Now I, Nebuchadnezzar, praise and exalt and glorify the King of heaven, because everything he does is right and all his ways are just. And those who walk in pride he is able to humble" (Daniel 4:28–37).

> *How long will we train our eyes on the altars our hands have made—the clever, sure-fire, proven techniques, the programs, the worship styles?*

While his eyes were on his own glory and splendor, Nebuchadnezzar had no sense of the transcendent. Thus, the king lived like an animal and his fingernails grew like claws. The insanity of Nebuchadnezzar reminds one immediately of Howard Hughes in his last years, with claw-like fingernails and a fearful isolation from the world. It was only when this transcendence (raising his eyes toward heaven) was realized through divine humiliation that reality finally fell into place for Nebuchadnezzar. He realized he was not God or a god, that he was neither the center of God's universe nor indeed even his own. To the extent that modern evangelicals have resisted humiliation, to that extent they are incapable of understanding Nebuchadnezzar's joy and sense of release at discovering the majesty, holiness, and sovereignty of God. They have lost

135

transcendence in their pursuit of their own power and splendor and a god within their heart who can be managed with the proper proven formulae.

Repeatedly, the children of Israel are called to raise their eyes. On their pilgrimages to Jerusalem, as they made that ascent to the City of God, the Israelites would sing the 121st Psalm: "I lift up my eyes to the hills—where does my help come from? My help comes from the Lord, the Maker of heaven and earth." In other words, the people ask, "Where is my salvation? Is it up there on those high places off on the horizon, where the nations sacrifice and worship their idols? No, our hope is not in those hills all around us, but in the Lord who sits on His holy mountain."

God promises Isaiah a restored vision: "In that day men will look to their Maker and turn their eyes to the Holy One of Israel. They will not look to the altars, the work of their hands, and they will have no regard for the Asherah poles and the incense altars their fingers have made" (Isaiah 17:7). One wonders how much we, like the children of Israel, insist on worshiping a god who meets us on our terms, the god of modern church growth, who is there to please us, to show us how to find ourselves, enjoy ourselves, and glorify ourselves. And this god is very "practical," very "relevant." He is not holy or separate from His creation, but "He walks with me and talks with me" in the garden "while the dew is still on the roses." How long will we train our eyes on the altars our hands have made—the clever, sure-fire, proven techniques, the programs, the worship styles? Do we think our salvation comes from these "high places"—modern altars of psychology, sociology, business and marketing strategies, political agendas and ideology? How many Christians today look to Capitol Hill rather than to Calvary for their hope of revival and salvation?

When will we raise our eyes to heaven, away from the hills? Are our services God-centered or man-centered? Do they train us to raise our eyes to heaven, or do they perpetuate our tendency to focus on earthly things like success, pleasure, and self-fulfillment? Do they encourage us to look to the hills and high places of self-fulfillment, or do they lead us to place our trust in God instead of in our own flesh? Is there a sense of awe, reverence, and transcendence as the holy and majestically enthroned Lord of heaven and

136

earth is celebrated? If not, why should the world not conclude, with Ingersoll, "We strive in vain to look beyond the heights"?

The apostle Paul warned a church in an upscale city that even many in the church "live as enemies of the cross of Christ. Their destiny is destruction, their god is their stomach, and their glory is in their shame. Their mind is on earthly things. But our citizenship is in heaven" (Philippians 3:18–19). Paul was calling the early believers to resist the Sirens' song of pagan society and raise their eyes toward heaven. Obsession with self-fulfillment is hardly a modern phenomenon; it is just that the strides in technology have made "you shall be as gods" sound a bit more realistic. This is why Paul warned Timothy, "In the last days men will be lovers of themselves, lovers of money, boastful, proud . . . , lovers of pleasure rather than lovers of God" (2 Timothy 3:1–5). What Paul probably did not bank on was the possibility that the evangelicals at the end of the twentieth century would actually capitalize on this sinful "self-fulfillment" orientation and turn it into a gospel. The same apostle tells the Colossians, "Since, then, you have been raised with Christ, set your hearts on things above, where Christ is seated at the right hand of God. Set your minds on things above, not on earthly things. For you died, and your life is now hidden with Christ in God" (Colossians 3:1–4).

Have we lost the radical impact of Paul's announcement here? In baptism, we were buried with Christ. While we are still citizens of this world, our ultimate citizenship is heaven. That does not mean that we have no responsibility in and to this world; just the opposite is true. It is because we are citizens of heaven that we must be involved in the world God created. And yet, we live as aliens, realizing that we are citizens of heaven not only when we die, but here and now. For, Paul says, in a very real sense we already have died, and our identity is defined by the resurrection of Christ. We are seated with Him in heavenly places, and this will radically alter the way we view life here on earth.

If there is one thing that the postmodern version of secularism preaches in the matter of religion it is divine immanence. That is, in its reaction against a deistic rationalism that removed God and the spiritual realm from the interest of everyday thoughts, many secularists today are turning to a very aggressive *where is God?*

spirituality, usually in the form of pantheism (everything is a part of god) and the god within. Superstition is most common, according to surveys, among the college-educated, so this growing paganism ought not to be considered a passing fad inspired by tabloid journalism.

But what Paul tells us here is that we must not place our faith in the idol of reason (modernity), nor in the god of experience (postmodernity); not in the god known only through reason, nor in the god within, but in the God outside of us and yet made known to us in the written and living Word.

At a time when the culture wants the church to be the church—however unpopular that course might end up being—will we continue to follow the world in its human-centeredness?

I worry about the extent to which the church has participated in the triumphalism of modernity. Until now, our eyes have been on our own kingdom, power, and glory. At our conventions during the eighties, we boasted of our majesty and splendor in Washington. In the nineties we are confident in our earth-bound programs that focus on this week's fads and "felt needs." Instead of worshipers, we are the audience. What God has done *for me* today is the topic of conversation rather than God Himself. We need desperately to raise our eyes toward heaven. It is vital for evangelicals who think they are "with it" when it comes to analyzing the "baby boomer" charts and church growth to realize that when they focus on temporal problems and turn the church into a giant twelve-step group, they are doing so just at the time when the culture is regaining an interest in the transcendent. "A widespread sense that a particular phase has reached its conclusion now prepares us to contemplate again the God who for so long has been displaced at the center of our existence," writes David Walsh, chairman of political science at the Catholic University of America.[4]

Have we actually read the surveys—I mean *really* read them? Gallup says that the negative attitude toward the church is due to disillusionment with "the shallow and superficial stance of so many church members; the inability of congregations to deal with the basics of faith." It is not because they did not find contemporary worship styles or felt bogged down with doctrine. Quite the contrary, they found too much of the world in the church. They complain in every survey of a *lack* of doctrinal substance. "There is a great hunger among the churched as well as the unchurched for a sharper focus on the primary questions of life," but half of the unchurched are convinced that "most churches and synagogues today are not effective in helping people find meaning in life." In fact, "most churches and synagogues today are too concerned with organizational as opposed to theological or spiritual issues," a statement with which even half of the *churched* agreed.[5]

The message is loud and clear: People don't *want* more programs and self-help groups catering to every felt need. They are disappointed with the lack of a theological focus. "Superficial Christianity was alarming to many young people," writes Gallup. "Their heavenly hopes are far from fulfilled in the earthbound churches."[6] In other words, they want to hear something that nobody else is saying. They want to hear about God, Christ, salvation, heaven and hell, sin and redemption. We send people to Russia to "give them the Gospel" after all these years under Communism, when it might be we who need to hear it first ourselves. As Nebuchadnezzar was "earthbound" by his obsession with self and success, so as a church and individuals, we must raise our eyes to heaven for a restoration of our sanity. At a time when the culture wants the church to be the church—however unpopular that course might end up being—will we continue to follow the world in its human-centeredness?

Walsh observes, "We live in a post-ideological age to the extent that we have lost faith in all systems and, with it, the faith that had inspired system builders from Descartes on: in the power of humanity to dominate reality as a whole."[7] Our experience leads us to conclude, "The age that began with the glory of the Renaissance, the bright expectations of the Enlightenment, and the energies of the scientific, industrial, and political revolutions has devolved to the horror, vacuity, and mediocrity of the twentieth century."[8] We placed the whole weight of our souls on man, and the experiment blew up in our face. Two world wars demonstrated that man was *not* basically good and that no nation, system, moral or political enterprise can make him so.

Weary of trying to be gods creating new worlds through political, moral, and social campaigns, today's thought-leaders will not tolerate political saviors of the left or the right any longer. "How can an age that sets itself up to surpass all predecessors in satisfying the needs of humanity surpass all others in the suffering inflicted on human beings?"[9] That is the paradoxical question of the postmodern person. Nietzsche foresaw the collapse of hope in his announcement of the so-called "death of God," assisted by the clergy. In fact, he thought that the search for a "Christian" morality without a Christian theology would destroy both in the process. Referring to modern Europe, "One still hopes to get along with a moralism without a religious background: but that necessarily leads to nihilism." Is that not exactly what we are now experiencing? Nietzsche spoke of "the end of Christianity at the hands of its own morality,"[10] although that was in part due to his misunderstandings of what that morality constituted. We have reason to suspect those who come to offer us a place in society as the providers of the moral glue to hold things together. If "Judeo-Christian" means not handing out condoms, it is reduced to the trivial, and, ironically, anything meaningful it may have to say about condom-distribution is disregarded because it is not taken seriously. Christianity is a religion, a theological confession first and a moral system only secondarily.

The existentialist philosopher Heidegger told *Der Spiegel* in 1966, "Philosophy will be unable to effect any immediate change in the current state of the world. This is true not only of philosophy but of all human endeavor. Only a god can save us." Similarly, philosopher Paul Ricoeur refers to "the new level of anguish" due to our loss of meaning beyond the here and now.[11] We have endured Nebuchadnezzar's experience, felt his trial. We have had a time of humiliation, where we became animals instead of men and women, and where sanity was attempted through drugs, sex, therapy, and causes. I think we can all agree with the concerns of New York Governor Mario Cuomo, expressed in a college commencement address, where he targeted the parents:

We've never had it so good, most of us. Nor have we ever complained so bitterly about our problems. The closed circle of pure materialism is clear to us now—aspirations become wants, wants become needs, and self-gratification becomes a bottomless pit. All around us we have seen success in this world's terms become ultimate and desperate failure. Teenagers and college students, raised in affluent surroundings and given all the material comforts our society can offer, commit suicide. Entertainers and sports figures achieve fame and wealth but find the world empty and dull without the solace or stimulation of drugs. Men and women rise to the top of their professions after years of struggling. But despite their apparent success, they are driven nearly mad by a frenetic search for diversions, new mates, games, new experiences—anything to fill the diminishing interval between their existence and eternity. . . . [Could this be Nebuchadnezzar's "insanity"?]

Do you think they would believe us if we told them today what we *know* to be true: That after the pride of obtaining a degree and maybe later another degree and after their first few love affairs and after earning their first big title, their first shiny new car and traveling around the world for the first time and having had it *all*—they will discover that none of it counts unless they have something real and permanent to believe in?" (italics original).[12]

Weary of looking to earth for salvation, our contemporaries are just in the spot for the good news about God's saving action in Christ. They are ready, in other words, to hear about the realities of another kingdom and to raise their eyes toward heaven. "But how shall they hear without a preacher?"

OUR FATHER

Even in this brief prayer our Lord gave us, we have the proper balance between transcendence and immanence. God is completely above and beyond us (transcendent), but we are instructed to call Him "our Father." Isn't this a contradiction? Not at all. For in Christ, the Father reconciles us to Himself and adopts us as His own children, co-heirs with Christ.

In the parable of the prodigal son, Jesus gives us a picture of the Father's love for us. Having deserted his family and blown his entire inheritance on wine, women, and song, the son finally is brought to his senses and returns home, prepared to be nothing more than a servant. "But while he was still a long way off, his father saw him and was filled with compassion for him; he ran to his son, threw his arms around him and kissed him" (Luke 15:20). The son knew that he merited his father's rejection, and acceptance merely as a servant would have been merciful, but the father "was filled with compassion." "'Quick! Bring the best robe and put it on him,'" the father commanded the servants. "'Put a ring on his finger and sandals on his feet. Bring the fattened calf and kill it. Let's have a feast and celebrate. For this son of mine was dead and is alive again; he was lost and is found.' So they began to celebrate" (vv. 22–24).

Similarly, we were "dead in trespasses and sins." And, "Like the rest, we were by nature objects of wrath. But because of his great love he made us alive with Christ even when we were dead in transgressions—it is by grace you have been saved. And God raised us up with Christ and seated us with him in the heavenly realms in Christ Jesus, in order that in the coming ages he might show the incomparable riches of his grace, expressed in his kindness to us in Christ Jesus" (Ephesians 2:1–8). We were not always children, but were "like the rest, children of wrath." And yet, God chose to reconcile us and become our Father. He did this even while we were sinners, by sending His Son to atone for our sins and to satisfy divine justice and holiness on our behalf. And then He even gave us the faith to believe before we ourselves chose it: "Because of his great love he made us alive with Christ even when we were dead in transgressions."

Like the father in the parable, our heavenly Father places the robe of Christ's righteousness, "the best robe," Jesus called it, on the sinner who trusts in Him and "comes home." The smell of the pigpen does not keep us from our Father's embrace, because all He smells is the sweetness of Christ; all He sees is the purity of Christ; all He touches is the holiness of Christ. In this way, the holy can adopt the unholy and enter into a personal relationship with those who are in themselves unworthy of anything but God's wrath. It is not because we were worth it, but "because of His great love."

Modernity has been a quest to build from earth to heaven and to transform earthly chaos into heavenly peace through human effort. But the Christian message, if it gets through, is the greatest challenge to that Adamic myth. It tells not of a person or a nation

142

or a race climbing up the ladder to heaven, but of a person—namely God Himself, coming *down* the ladder to save a lost world. Secularism tries to deal with the tension between transcendence and immanence either by denying the former, or by trying to force its way into God's transcendent presence, past the heavenly guards, to see Him as the mystics sought—as He is, *Deus nudus* (the nude God).

But no man can see God and live, God told Moses. He is too holy, too transcendent, too—well, too everything we're not. But in Christianity, the transcendent and immanent meet in the person of Christ, God *and* Man, two natures in one person. The triumph is not humanity becoming God, or a person, race, or nation becoming the universal ruler and savior, but of God becoming man. How contradictory of every modern dogma! In the cross of Christ, what appears to be a sign of defeat, we find the ultimate victory over the powers of death and the wrath of God. The greatest victory was achieved *for* us at the cross, not *by* us in Washington. And that Gospel is proclaimed, not by rallies and marches, but by the explanation of sin and redemption from the Scriptures.

It is that victory of Christ's cross and resurrection that gives the church its reason for existence, not its usefulness in society for propping up the crumbling American Dream, just one more Tower of Babel and one more high place of paganism to distract the children of Israel on their pilgrimage to the Holy City. It is only because of that cross that we can raise our eyes toward heaven in true hope and without fear, for apart from Christ "our God is a consuming fire" (Hebrews 12:29).

This is why, when we raise our eyes to heaven, it is not to peer into God's presence and see Him or somehow discover Him as He is in Himself; nor is it to speculate about the streets of gold and mansions, but it is to place our confidence in God as He has revealed Himself in Scripture and in the person and work of Christ. This is a vital point, because postmodernism makes a great deal out of rejecting the idols of modernity—the earthly utopias and panaceas; it speaks a lot concerning eternal, transcendent solutions and a return to "the spiritual." Nevertheless, for Christians, looking for "the spiritual" for salvation is no better than looking to this world for salvation. We are not satisfied with a revival of pagan "spirituality," and we do not proclaim salvation through a mere recovery of "the sacred." It is a particular sacred reality and a particular Person who creates that reality who becomes the hope of Christians. To raise our eyes to heaven is not merely to search for the spiritual side of life, but to ". . . fix our eyes on Jesus, the author and perfector of our faith, who for the joy set before him endured the cross, scorning its shame, and sat down at the right hand of the throne of God" (Hebrews 12:2). To look to heaven is to look not to the things which our hands have made, nor to ourselves, nor to causes and movements, ideologies or strategies, for our salvation; but neither is it to look within or above for general spiritual realities, but to look to that hill in history where God's foolishness triumphed over man's wisdom that afternoon outside the gates of Jerusalem.

> *The problem in America today, as in the West generally, is not that people, for the most part, do not know godliness, but that they do not know God.*

At least one of the answers, therefore, in our pursuit of something beyond a culture war is a conversion of both the church and the culture from self-salvation to the sovereignty of God in His grace. Just as Nebuchadnezzar was humiliated until he recognized "that God is sovereign over the kingdoms of men . . . , does according to his will among the hosts of heaven and the people of the earth, and no one can hold back his hand or say to him, 'What have you done?'", so too the contemporary church will have to swallow some difficult theological realities about the sovereignty of God. He is not the hapless deity of American sentiment who ought to be pitied rather than feared, but the Almighty God who has yet to experience failure. If, ever since the nineteenth century revivals, we have reduced salvation to moral improvement and championed a puny god who could do little without our permission and cooperation, why should we blame the world for secularism's triumph? J. B. Phillips correctly captured the world's charge against the church in the title of his book, *Your God Is Too Small.* Any true reformation or revival in the church or in society today must begin not with a campaign for traditional values, but with a campaign for the knowledge, worship, praise, fear, and service of God.

The problem in America today, as in the West generally, is not that people, for the most part, do not know godliness, but that they do not know God. Hosea was informed that the moral crisis in Israel was not due to insufficient laws, but because there was no knowledge of God in the land. "A people without understanding will come to ruin!" God declared (Hosea 4:1, 14). As Solzhenitsyn explained the modern crisis, "Men have forgotten God; *that* is why all this has happened" (italics added). It has not happened because of a lack of public rites and acknowledgment of God, but because His identity is lost to us in this generation. That is a theological and spiritual problem; the moral and political effects are merely symptoms. And the illness is as easily diagnosed in our churches as in our society.

> *What I fear is that evangelicals today*
> *do not seem to long for God and His*
> *presence so much as they long for power*
> *(spiritual or political) itself.*

How can we blame the schools and government for forgetting God until we remember Him in our own families and churches? When our sermons and our worship are about God and His saving grace again, *then* we will see the tide of secularism roll back. When was the last time you heard a series on the attributes of God? Do the sermons you hear concern God and His redemptive activity as it unfolds in biblical history? Or are they essentially pep talks seasoned with personal anecdotes and helpful illustrations? If the church does not take God seriously, will the world? As long as the churches prefer trivial pursuits to the knowledge of God, secularism will not only prevail, but it will eventually attempt to rule every sphere in the land. Secularism is nothing more than unbelief and ignorance of the Creator and Redeemer, and by that standard, the churches are as secular these days as the society. Even in the pursuit of biblical morality, we can become secular if the focus of our preaching, witness, and worship is not God as He has revealed Himself in Scripture and in Christ.

> *When we recover our sanity, raise our eyes to heaven, and fix our eyes on Christ, then the glory of the Lord shall fill the earth and the nations will be glad.*

As Israel learned during her exiles, the greatest tragedy comes not when God's people are exiled and must endure slavery in a foreign land. Rather, it comes before that, when God's glory leaves the temple, when God's own people no longer know, understand, feel, fear, or serve Him, when His presence is no longer felt "in the cool of the day," or in the wilderness by fire and cloud. The people in this condition will turn to anything: to the rituals, tools, techniques, or even gods of the nations, in order to get back this powerful presence of the Transcendent God. What I fear is that evangelicals today do not seem to long for God and His presence so much as they long for power (spiritual or political) itself. They do not need God back, except as a means to the end of getting America back. And yet, there are Christians seeking the true God as he has revealed Himself. The signs and wonders movement, inner healing, spiritual disciplines, the impressive, if shallow, immediacy of contemporary worship: these are all attempts to recover this lost sense of God's presence among us. And yet, God's presence has never been secured by the clever and holy elite who steal their way into heaven and find this or that key that will open His chamber. Seeking God directly, apart from Christ, such disciplines, principles, tactics, and experiences will always end in the Spirit descending in judgment, as at Babel, rather than in blessing, as at Pentecost. God's presence cannot be commanded, as if a servant could command the king. Rather, He maintains His presence "in Spirit and in truth." Where He is rightly known and worshiped and acknowledged in Christ's name, there He maintains His powerful presence.

Every awakening and every reformation that has brought lasting change has been the direct result of the preaching of the Law and the Gospel, sin and grace, judgment and justification. God's sovereignty and grace, when proclaimed with the accompaniment of the Holy Spirit, have been the stuff of which the greatest movements of God in church history are made. When we recover our sanity, raise our eyes to heaven, and fix our eyes on Christ, then the glory of the Lord shall fill the earth and the nations will be glad. May we pray with the Psalmist, "Be exalted, O God, above the heavens, and let your glory be over all the earth. Save us and help us with your right hand, that those you love may be delivered. . . . Give us aid against the enemy, for the help of man is worthless" (Psalm 108:6, 12).

NOTES

1. William Safire, ed., *Lend Me Your Ears: Great Speeches in History* (New York: Norton and Norton, 1992), 174.

2. Karl Menninger, *Whatever Became of Sin?* (New York: Hawthorne, 1973), 135.

3. Cited by David Walsh, *After Ideology: Recovering the Spiritual Foundations of Freedom* (New York/San Francisco: HarperCollins, 1990), 19.

4. Ibid., 2.

5. George Gallup and David Poling, *The Search for America's Faith* (Nashville: Abingdon, 1980), 16–18.

6. Ibid.

7. Walsh, *After Ideology*, 10.

8. Ibid., 9.

9. Ibid., 12.

10. Friederich Nietzsche, *Will to Power*, trans. Walter Kaufmann (New York: Vintage, 1974), 7.

11. Quoted by Walsh, *After Ideology*, 41–42.

12. Safire, *Lend Me Your Ears*, 934.

7

IN GOD'S NAME

Theology, not morality, is the first business on the church's agenda of reform, and the church, not society, is the first target of divine criticism.

"Hallowed be thy name."

How do we get people to take the name of God seriously at the end of the twentieth century? Although nearly everyone in America says he or she believes in "god," "This is not the 'jealous God' of the Old Testament . . . ," according to a best-selling survey of American attitudes and trends. "For most Americans, God is not to be feared or, for that matter, loved." He is irrelevant.[1] Another survey tells us that most Americans view "God" as a friend, rather than a king. They see themselves as basically good—especially the religious people think this way, including the evangelicals. Furthermore, they define for themselves what is right "for them." (No wonder they think they're pulling it off!) "Most Americans (82 percent) profess to believe in an afterlife that includes both heaven and hell (55 percent of us believe in the existence of Satan). We are confident, however, that our future prospects are bright. Almost half of us (46 percent) expect to spend eternity in heaven versus only 4 percent who see their future in hell."[2]

Without any knowledge of God, there can be no fear of God, and without any fear of God, there can be no hallowing of God's name. So we are back to the original thesis: *Theology*, not *morality*, is the first business on the church's agenda of reform, and the *church*, not *society*, is the first target of divine criticism.

After all, why should society take God's name seriously today? "God loves you and has a wonderful plan for your life." The bumper sticker god of contemporary evangelicalism commands little respect: "God Is My Co-Pilot," "Give Jesus a Chance," "Try God," "Jesus Is the Real Thing," "This Blood's for You," "God Is Rad, He's My Dad."

Meanwhile, preachers try to usher in the kingdom of God through moral crusades in which the politicians and often the preachers themselves are caught in the strangest moral scandals themselves. Nobody talks about God—His attributes, self-revelation, saving action in election, redemption, justification, sanctification, and so on, but we're certain we want the pagans to pray to him/her/it in public anyway. Successful evangelists use God's name for prosperity and healing, leaving disillusionment with God's name in their wake when "god" doesn't come through for them.

Why is God's name so abused in our day? Is it because of the "secular humanists"? Or does it start with us, the people of God who bear that name and have used that name falsely?

One is reminded of God's lamentation, through Jeremiah, against those "false prophets who prophesy their lies in my name . . ." (Jeremiah 23). False prophets would never dream of telling the truth, warts and all—that would risk their popularity, so, "They dress the wound of my people as though it were not serious. 'Peace,' 'peace,' they say, when there is no peace" (Jeremiah 8:11). One is also reminded of our Lord's repetition of this charge, as He refers to the final judgment: "Many will say to me on that day, 'Lord, Lord, did we not prophesy in *your name*, and in *your name* drive out demons and perform many miracles?' Then I will tell them plainly, 'I never knew you. Away from me, you evil-doers!'" (Matthew 7:22).

Surely, taken as a whole, the evangelical witness in our day, in sharp contrast to the general witness of evangelicals in past eras, could stand to hear God's charge, reiterated by the apostle Paul: "You who brag about the law [traditional Judeo-Christian values], do you dishonor God by breaking the law? As it is written: 'God's name is blasphemed among the Gentiles because of you'" (Romans 2:24).

But this is where we turn from the criticisms to the hope God offers us as a church in Christ. After explaining to Israel that she is being oppressed because of her own unfaithfulness to the name of God, He declares that a day will come when they and the nations themselves will know and revere the name of God. "Therefore my people will know my name; therefore in that day they will know that it is I who foretold it. Yes, it is I." And then in that passage, God follows with His wonderful vision of the kingdom of Christ reaching the ends of the earth: "How beautiful on the mountains are the feet of those who bring good news, who proclaim peace, who bring good tidings, who proclaim salvation, who say to Zion, 'Your God reigns!'" When the Servant of God appears, salvation will come. "The Lord will lay bare his holy arm in the sight of all the nations, and all the ends of the earth will see the salvation of our God" (Isaiah 52:6–10).

This is the message entrusted to us: The Servant of God has come, the holy arm of God has brought salvation to the ends of the earth, and peace with God through the cross of Christ is now secured for all believers. At last, the name of God is revered, as even Gentiles—those who were aliens and enemies—place their hope in the name of the God-Man, Jesus Christ, and no longer in themselves or their own projects, or the nations. As Peter declared, "Salvation is found in no one else, for there is no other name under heaven given to men by which we must be saved" (Acts 4:12).

If this is the case, if by calling on the name of the Lord, we can be saved, why is God's name so abused in our day? Is it because of the "secular humanists"? Or does it start with us, the people of God who bear that name and have used that name falsely?

HALLOWING GOD'S NAME IN POLITICS

There is no need to remind the reader of all of the crusades that have been launched by self-confident humanity in an effort to champion a cause which, in retrospect, we can see to have been actually contrary to God's written, expressed will. Who among us today would argue that the Crusades in the Middle Ages, in which "Christendom" slaughtered Muslims and Jews in the name of God was not a misuse of that name? Would not even the most radically political Christian today recognize the error in confusing the Holy Roman Empire with the kingdom of God? And yet, it is more difficult for us, living in the middle of our own time and place, to see how we have confused America and the kingdom of God and have used that confusion to casually invoke God's name for everything from the Strategic Defense Initiative (S.D.I.) to specific domestic policies. One could even detect among many Christian groups a mentality in the Gulf War that had more to do with Saddam Hussein being the Antichrist, and a "holy war" against Babylon, than with strategic or human rights violations. This, however, should come as no surprise, since the pundits of end-times prophecy have been selecting nations and antichrists according to their relationship to America for some time.

But does this mean that we can never appeal to God's name for support of particular positions in the political sphere? Not at all.

In the last century, contrary to a long-standing position in the Dutch Reformed Church (the majority church in South Africa), white leaders began to argue that God was on the side of the Afrikaaner (the white South African), as the victories over the British (who had placed Afrikaaners in concentration camps) as well as over various African tribes, appeared to them to confirm. Much as the English had thought of themselves as Israel (the Protestants) at war with Babylon (the Catholics) in the defeat of the Spanish Armada, and just as the American colonists trusted in their "most favored nation" status with God against England, so white South Africans began to create their own myths, drawing upon biblical history and placing themselves in the position of Israel, the kingdom of God.

Although there are as many black or colored (mixed) Calvinists in South Africa as white, the Dutch Reformed decision-making body declared in 1857 that it was acceptable for churches to be built on racial lines. As John de Gruchy has argued, this was chiefly a pragmatic missionary strategy, much like today's church growth idea of "homogeneous" churches, since, as church growth architect Donald McGavran stated, "People like to become Christians without having to cross cultural, linguistic, or racial barriers."[3] What began as a pragmatic idea in the churches was used by the politicians to create apartheid. The oppression of the blacks by the whites received official sanction from the churches across denominational lines, much as evangelicals in America at the same time remained silent during the civil rights movement here. That is why, when the church finally condemned apartheid, it did not condemn it as "racial injustice," or "misguided public policy," nor "a violation of civil rights," although it was all of those things; the church called it what only the church could call it: heresy. Since the political system was justified by Scripture-twisting, the system could only be dismantled by naming the heresy.

Nationalism and Christianity

One wonders how many setbacks to the progress of the Gospel and the kingdom of God have been due to the church's willingness to allow the two kingdoms to become merged in the interest of power and control. Are we Christians first or Americans first? Christians first or Afrikaaners first? Of course, the same confusions with nationalism can be found in a variety of cultures. Karl Barth, Martin Niemoller, and other leaders of the Confessing Church (so-called because they believed that the church's greatest power against Hitler was not political, but a recovery of loyalty to the Gospel as expressed in the Reformation confessions) remind us again and again of the dangers of what the former cynically called the "healthy evangelical national piety" which lent its support to Hitler's nationalistic crusade.

One can see the same confusion of the name of God and the names of things ("isms") among black Christians in America, where God is identified with every policy put forward by the NAACP. Instead of being one body with one message and one voice, we have become *white* evangelicals, *black* evangelicals, *Hispanic* evangelicals, evangelical *feminists*, and *anti-feminists*. We are a collection of competing special interest groups, not a church united in its proclamation of the kingdom of God and in its witness to the possibility of hope in the name of God and the new society He is building as a contradiction to the world's societies.

It's a very serious business, this name of God. People were executed in the Old Testament, by divine command, for misusing it, and while God has not given the church in the New Testament the physical sword, He does promise that there will be many condemned by Him on Judgment Day who really thought they were doing the Lord's work in the Lord's name.

Positive Political Involvement

At this point, therefore, it is necessary to distinguish the *legitimate* use of God's name in politics.

Once we have settled that God's name cannot be attached to the names of things ("isms"), we are ready to build a positive notion of political involvement. After all, the church does have a responsibility to call the nations of the world and their leaders to account, not only as individuals before God needing redemption, but as public servants of God who are meant to carry out justice. The following are some rules one might put forward to assist in determining whether we are properly using God's name in the political sphere. Remember, we may pursue all sorts of goals in a democratic society as *individuals*, but neither individuals nor the church can speak on their own authority in the name of God.

(1) Make sure it is *theological,* not *political.*

I use those terms in their most etymological sense. In other words, what we offer is a critique of particular political situations based on biblical revelation concerning God, humanity, sin and redemption, the meaning of history, and so on. Whereas individual Christians may be called to the noble task of forming particular public policies, this is not the *church's* calling as an institution. For instance, the church must speak out in defense of the sacred character of life. Human life derives its dignity, not from the importance attached to it by law or by judges, but from the significance

God attaches to it, since human beings were created in His image. What does this mean for abortion? Surely that Christians and indeed the churches should speak out, and each believer must be convinced in his or her own mind precisely how to tackle the problem; but it does not mean that the Christian faith demands one particular public policy position or another, except in very unusual circumstances. In God's name, we may all seek to end abortion-on-demand, because we have His will concerning human life on record in Scripture, and even radical pro-choice proponents will concede that the life in the womb is indeed human. Nevertheless, we are left to our own wisdom (which, we hope, will be illumined by God through prayer) in specific strategies and policies. For the latter we must not claim God's expressed blessing or commandment, and Christian liberty must not be denied to those with widely divergent views as to how justice is to be done.

> *Although we have every right to use God's name to call the world to account, we cannot identify that name with particular agendas or policies to which He has not committed Himself in print.*

If we are thinking theologically as a church, we realize that violence against the unborn is surely no more heinous than violence against civilians in such war-ravaged areas as Bosnia. And yet, in spite of regular reports in which we see children lining the streets in pools of blood, a genocide in the name of "ethnic cleansing," the churches seem to be silent. Where are the protests? Where are the impassioned defenses of human life for these children *after* they are born? Similar questions ought to be asked about children in our own country, since more than 20 percent of the nation's children live in poverty.

Francis Schaeffer, who got the church moving on the abortion question, thought theologically. He was calling evangelicals to rediscover the doctrines of creation, the Fall, redemption,

God's concern for the environment, and a variety of other issues. The same man who spoke out against abortion in *Whatever Happened to the Human Race?* wrote *Pollution and the Death of Man.* Schaeffer also had some fairly stern things to say about the attitudes of white evangelicals to their non-white brothers and sisters.

But this is characteristic of our history as evangelicals, if not of our contemporary approach. B. B. Warfield, the staunch defender of orthodoxy at turn-of-the-century Princeton, not only defended the inerrancy of Scripture, he also wrote impassioned pleas for the civil rights of the emancipated slaves. It is impossible for historians to separate the struggle against slavery, child labor, and other injustices in the modern industrial era from the history of evangelicalism. And yet, aside from the abortion issue, if the evangelical movement were committed to defending the oppressed today, without capitulating to typical left-wing or right-wing solutions, the secular press would be at a loss for words. If we thought theologically, we would more readily see the connections between these issues, but we think politically. It is particular public policies, devised in the laboratory of the secular conservatives or secular liberals, not particular doctrinal convictions, that guide our concerns and involvement. Our involvement is, therefore, predictable and unbelievers eventually become quite cynical about our casual invocation of the name of God for policies that always happen to coincide with the particular position of our political party.

Throughout the Old Testament, the prophets invoked the name of God in judgment against bloodshed, mistreatment of the poor and the alien, sexual immorality, and the like. So while we know that we can use God's name with confidence in our outrage at the genocide in Bosnia, we must wrestle with the complicated issues involved in this age-old crisis and distinguish between the calling of the church to remind the world of the larger issues involved, and the calling of the state to make specific foreign policy decisions which are beyond the church's expertise and legitimate authority. After all, there are foreign policy experts on both sides of the debate over the use of military intervention, and both are arguing from the conviction that the savagery must end. Although we have every right to use God's name to call the world to account, we cannot identify that name with particular agendas or policies to which He has not committed Himself in print.

(2) Make sure it really is a universal absolute and not a relative application.

It is not only in the realm of politics that Christians are bound to the Protestant conviction of *sola Scriptura*—"only Scripture"; even in doctrine, we cannot speak where God has not spoken. In ethics, we have no authority to command the conscience where God has not bound it, by requiring or prohibiting that which God has not clearly addressed in Scripture. In the Reformation tradition, this is called the realm of *adiaphora,* or "things indifferent." It is, in other words, the "grey area," where Christians are not bound to take any prescribed position, but are free to exercise their own judgment and Christian liberty. This is precisely where we must see all but the most exceptional policy issues. It is not that all policies are equally good, but although all Christians, for instance, are commanded to seek racial justice and reconciliation, this Christian affirmation does not come with an attached policy commitment either for or against affirmative action, health care programs, welfare, and so on. On each of those issues, we are left to the "big picture" God gives us in Scripture, and we must carefully distinguish between that which He commands and that which we infer or pursue on our own in the light of those commands.

God's name is surely not misused when we call for the protection of human life in all of its phases, but when one claims the divine blessing of one party, or one set of policies, or even claims God's favor on behalf of the nation as a whole, he is taking liberties with God's name. "I have not sent that prophet or given him my words, and yet he speaks in my name," God says of us in such cases, as He said of the false prophets of Jeremiah's day. In the matter of what to do about the Balkans, the faithful prophet in our day talks about being created in God's image; he doesn't talk about air strikes, regardless of whether he is personally for or against such action. He is merely a messenger, and his message is written. He comes with no *carte blanche* from the Sender.

Yale professor of law, and one of the nation's leading experts on constitutional law, Stephen Carter, writes,

> As a deeply committed Christian, moreover, I have always been deeply offended by politicians, whether on the left or right, who are ready to seize on the language and symbols of religion in order to grub for votes. When members of the clergy use those symbols as divisively as they did in Houston [at the Republican Convention in 1992], presuming to cast their opponents into the outer darkness, I tremble with anger—and, since that decision is not really within the scope of their ecclesiastical authority, I tremble as well for their souls.
>
> Yet I am equally offended by suggestions that our politicians are wrong to discuss their views on the will of God, or that members of the clergy have no business backing what candidates they will, or that voters should never choose among candidates based on their religious beliefs.[4]

So often, when the liberation theologians were playing fast and loose with the biblical text in the interest of ideology, conservative evangelicals were more than willing to enlist the assistance of evangelical theologians and exegetes to expose the fallacies, but when it is the conservatives themselves doing the damage, those same individuals who would call people to appeal to the Bible with integrity are viewed as disloyal to the cause. Carter continues:

> During the anti-Vietnam War movement of the sixties and seventies, for example, many liberal activists were driven by and publicly invoked deep religious commitments. From the Berrigans to William Sloane Coffin, some of the best-known antiwar figures were members of the clergy and freely invoked God's name. They were often criticized by conservative evangelicals—but only on the ground that they were taking the wrong position on the war. (*Christianity Today*, for instance, supported the war effort to the end, often in terms more hawkish than those of the government itself.)[5]

After telling the story of a sermon in which a divinity student turned the moment into an opportunity to preach against American foreign policy in Central America, Carter observes, "And she was, it turned out, a sort of left-wing Oliver North, whose evident view was that it was our Christian duty to support the good (left-wing) terrorists in their holy struggle to massacre the bad (right-wing) terrorists." She exemplified this "problem of the political tail wagging the scriptural dog," but the same horrors can be found at many a local conservative church today, too. "Thus, there is no essential difference between the almost repressive patriotism of many of the churches in the 1940s and 1950s and the often relentless egalitarianism of many of the mainline denominations today. In both cases, the churches take the values of their members and put them in the mouth of God, thus confirming for the members their own essential righteousness."[6]

(3) Make sure you distinguish between the church's calling to proclaim the Law and the Gospel (revealed in Scripture) and the state's calling to enforce civil justice, based on natural revelation.

Even in the realm of morality, *sola Scriptura* (only Scripture) stands. Just as we cannot dictate the personal behavior of individual Christians beyond Scripture (although we do it anyway), we cannot dictate public morality *in the name of* God beyond that which is written into the human conscience by creation. We cannot even attempt to force the Ten Commandments on a godless society. This does not mean that we do not *preach* them and call all men and women to repentance by the preaching of the Law, but it does mean that we cannot really enforce the Ten Commandments.

I realize that this is a controversial position today, so let me explain it. First, remember that the "first table" of the Law concerns our relationship to God, prohibiting the worship of other gods, the false worship of the true God, reverence for the name of God, entrance into God's Sabbath rest: These are things that the courts and police cannot enforce, as the true worship of God depends on a right relationship with God, and this belongs only to those who have been reconciled to God by Christ alone through faith alone.

Unless we truly believe that it is the business of government to force people to become Christians, the first table of the Law is not to be legislated by the state, but is rather to be proclaimed by the church and is to shape the witness of the church as it is properly related to God by the Gospel. It is the duty of every person, but it cannot and ought not to be the duty of the state to enforce it.

That leaves us with the remaining commandments regarding our relationship to each other. Surely, it is not the place of the state to enforce love, and yet Jesus tells us that this is what the Law commands. The state can keep me from murdering my neighbor with my hands, but it cannot keep me from murdering my neighbor in my heart.

It seems clear from the Scriptures themselves that God gave His written Law to Israel as part of the covenant, and not to any other nation. When Moses was informed that, because of God's anger with that unbelieving generation, it would be left to Joshua to lead the next generation into the Promised Land, the patriarch reminded his holy nation, "What other nation is so great as to have their gods near them the way the Lord is near us whenever we pray to him? And what other nation is so great as to have such righteous laws I am setting before you today?" (Deuteronomy 4:7–8). Thus, a sign of Israel's elect status was the nearness of God in prayer and in the Ten Commandments. No other nation enjoyed such an intimate relationship with God that they were actually in covenant with Him: "I shall be your God and you shall be my people" was addressed to no other nation.

If, as I shall argue in the following chapter, Israel was the only nation in history to enjoy the linking of the two kingdoms, then no nation can be "in covenant" with God as was Israel. Even the most Christian nations stand under God's judgment and enjoy no special relationship with Him. Although those nations whose institutions are founded on a Judeo-Christian understanding of righteousness and justice are far more likely to execute their secular callings wisely and justly, there is no guarantee that they will, and there is no guarantee that pagan societies will not. That is because the Law of God is written on the conscience, and even the heathen have a sense of right and wrong. In fact, Paul argues in Romans that Gentiles, without the Law, do that which is contained in the Law, although very often the Jews themselves, though confident because they had the Law given to them, lived contrary to it. In summary, Paul says, both Jew and Gentile stand under the Law's condemnation, for "there is none who is righteous, no not one" (Romans 3:10).

But just because there is no one who has kept God's Law *perfectly*, either as it is written on the conscience or on tablets of stone, that does not mean that it is impossible for men and women to discern right from wrong. This is why John Calvin argues, for instance, that as you "look around and glance at the world as a whole, or at least cast your sight upon regions farther off, divine providence has wisely arranged that various countries should be ruled by various kinds of government." Although Calvin certainly did not deny that the moral Law of God is the standard of true righteousness, he strongly criticized the idea held by many Christian "revolutionaries" in his day "who deny that a commonwealth is duly framed which neglects the political system of Moses, and is ruled by the common laws of nations."[7] It is not a question of what God requires, but of what the *state* must require. God demands total obedience in heart and life, and this must be proclaimed by the church to the world, while the state is simply concerned with civil order, safety, and justice.[8]

(4) Make sure that natural law is your common ground.

This leads us inevitably to the discussion of "natural law." If we cannot enforce the Ten Commandments in American society, how on earth can Christians persuade non-Christians to obey a higher authority than the Supreme Court?

Here again, we find help in Augustine's and Calvin's interpretations of Scripture, but first in the infallible authority itself. The apostle Paul declared that even the most godless "secular humanists" have accurate knowledge about God. They cannot know everything about Him, not even some of the most important things: That He is a Trinity, that He has spoken through the prophets and brought salvation to the ends of the earth through the life, death, and resurrection of Christ, and so on. But they do know enough by nature to condemn them apart from supernatural revelation (Romans 1:18–20).

This knowledge of right and wrong and the transcendent divine authority above their judgments of right and wrong implies that even pagans can set up just societies. And what is implicit here is explicit in 2:14: "Indeed, when Gentiles, who do not have the law, do by nature things required by the law, they are a law for themselves, since they show that the requirements of the law are written on their hearts, their consciences also bearing witness, and their thoughts now accusing, now even defending them." They cannot be justified before God by their occasional obedience to the law written on the conscience any more than the Jews can be excused by their occasional obedience to the law written on tablets. Nevertheless, there is enough there for what philosophers and theologians have called "natural law."

Although the church may insist on universal equity (justice) in the name of God, it may not claim God for democracy.

The medieval theologian, Thomas Aquinas, was one of the most brilliant exponents of this notion of "natural law" since Augustine, but modern historians are agreed that John Calvin was one of the chief architects of our modern understanding of this theory, a theory which has been rejected today in favor of relativism and pragmatism. This "natural law" is not a rival to God's Law, but rather it is that same universal divine mandate imprinted on humanity's conscience as part of God's image. But since modern nations are not in a covenantal relationship with God, as Israel was, the rule ought to be "general equity," as it was established by constitutions and interpreted by courts. Mark Calvin's comments:

> Equity, because it is natural, cannot but be the same for all, and therefore, this same purpose ought to apply to all laws, whatever their object. Constitutions have certain circumstances upon which they in part depend. It therefore does not matter that they are different, provided all equally press toward the same goal of equity.

First, notice that here Calvin is employing the principle mentioned above: Distinguishing over-arching universals, clearly discovered in Scripture, from particular applications or policies, which differ from nation to nation.

> It is a fact that the law of God which we call the moral law is nothing else than a testimony of natural law and of that conscience which God has engraved upon the minds of men. . . . Hence, this equity alone must be the goal and rule and limit of all laws. What-

ever laws shall be framed to that rule, directed to that goal, bound by that limit, there is no reason why we should disapprove of them, howsoever they may differ from the Jewish law, or among themselves.

> *The church must realize that it still has an obligation to expose unbelief and immorality as a matter of ultimate consequence and therefore more serious than politics, and yet it does not have the power of the state to enforce this, but the sword of God—namely, His Word.*

Then Calvin refers to the example of stealing. God's law forbids stealing, but prohibitions of this nature are found, he observes, in "the very ancient laws of other nations" as well. However, the civil penalties imposed varied from society to society: "They do not agree on the manner of punishment. Nor is this either necessary or expedient," since each society has its own particular problems which require specific policies and punishments.

> How malicious and hateful toward public welfare would a man be who is offended by such diversity, which is perfectly adapted to maintain the observance of God's law! For the statement of some, that the law of God given through Moses is dishonored when it is abrogated and new laws preferred to it, is utterly vain. For others are not preferred to it when they are more approved, not by a simple comparison, but with regard to the condition of times, place, and nation; or when that law is abrogated which was never enacted for us. For the Lord through the hand of Moses did not give that law to be proclaimed among all nations and to be in force everywhere; but when he had taken the Jewish nation into safekeeping, defense, and protection, he also willed to be a lawgiver especially to it; and—as became a wise lawgiver—he had special concern for it in making its laws.[9]

Therefore, although the church may insist on universal *equity* (justice) in the name of God, it may not claim God for democracy, even though many of the great biblical doctrines suggest a form of government that is certainly compatible and perhaps even most consonant with democracy, as Calvin himself argues in that same chapter. Our defense of the unborn ought to be made on the same basis as our defense of civil liberties for everyone in this country: equity, which can be argued on the basis of natural law, without requiring people to first accept the Bible's authority.

But in our day, not only do we seem to have trouble distinguishing *natural revelation* from *special revelation*; we have trouble also, it seems, distinguishing *absolutes* from *non-absolutes*. Any compromise in the political arena is regarded as a fatal blow to principle. Even questioning the free enterprise system could be tantamount to heresy, since, as Falwell argues, America's free enterprise system was patterned on "the clear teachings of Scripture."[10] Justly outraged at a moral relativism that has rendered it almost impossible to say that anything is true, good, or beautiful (except, of course, for the dogma of relativism itself), many Christians refuse to acknowledge that there is any place in the political, social, or moral arena for "things indifferent" (i.e., the "relative"). It is true that we ought to be "black and white" on the sanctity of life, stewardship of the divinely-given earthly resources, the dignity of work, civil liberty, and other absolutes we not only find in Scripture, but find written on the human conscience. Nevertheless, general wisdom guides our application of these universal aims and truths, a wisdom that is always fallible and conditioned by particular factors.

CONCLUSION

Thus far, we have distinguished two kingdoms, one heavenly, the other earthly. Further, we distinguished ultimate issues (sin and redemption) from proximate issues (politics, morality, justice, etc.). Then we distinguished the expression of God's universally binding will in special revelation (the Ten Commandments) from that same universally binding will expressed in natural revelation (the conscience). Finally, we distinguished universally binding principles *for which we may claim divine sanction* from locally binding policies and applications for which we may not claim divine sanction.

It is the role of the church to make known God's revealed will in Scripture, including the Ten Commandments; it is the state's role to enforce God's will revealed in nature by pursuing justice ("equity") through wise counsel, legitimate government, and the rule of constitutional law. I am convinced that if the church were to deal seriously with these categories, we would see more fruitful dialogue and less hostile rhetoric that squelches meaningful advances. The church must realize that it still has an obligation to expose unbelief and immorality as a matter of *ultimate* consequence and therefore more serious than politics, and yet it does not have the power of the state to enforce this, but the sword of God— namely, His Word. This alone can bring conviction, as the Spirit works with the Word to bring a person to repentance. And it is also the church alone that has the ultimate remedy to this ultimate crisis: the Gospel. As it stands, the church is perceived, both left-wing and right-wing, as an instrument of ideology, along with every other special interest group, engaged in the modern quest for the "will to power."

> *Whenever a cup of water is given in Christ's name, the Bible says, God's name is hallowed. Whenever we pursue our calling with excellence, God's name is glorified. Whenever we care for our families, respect is given to the name of God, even by those who do not yet know Him.*

No one person or group of individuals may rise up and impose its will even in the name of God and Christ. For we are all sinners—still, yes, even we Christians. Self-righteousness only intensifies the damage the will to power can create. *I* must change. *I* must repent and believe the Gospel. *I* must forgive my neighbor and seek his or her forgiveness of my wrongs. Repentance is always *my* duty, always a burden and a joy which *I* must carry, not a weight of judgment which I may place on someone else.

This, I think, is Jesus' point in Luke 11:46, 52: "Jesus replied, 'And you experts in the law, woe to you, because you load people down with burdens they can hardly carry, and you yourselves will not lift one finger to help them. . . . Woe to you experts in the law, because you have taken away the key to knowledge. You yourselves have not entered, and you have hindered those who were entering.'" This is also why Paul told the immoral Corinthian church to mind its own business and get its own house in order. "What business is it of mine to judge those outside the church? Are you not to judge those inside? God will judge those outside" (1 Corinthians 5:12).

Therefore, while the church warns of a day of judgment on the horizon, it may not take it upon itself to seek to *bring* down God's wrath before that day. "Do not judge, or you too will be judged," Jesus told the religious people of His day. "Why do you look at the speck of sawdust in your brother's eye and pay no attention to the plank in your own eye?" (Matthew 7:1–6). That is not because there is no such thing as absolute truth or morality, nor because it is impolite to judge. Nor indeed ought this be interpreted to mean that Christians ought not to discern good laws from bad laws and encourage the former. What it does mean is that we must not confuse the civil role of the state in exercising its temporal judgments for the preservation of good order, peace, safety, and justice with the divine judgment at the end of history. The church proclaims the latter and calls all men and women to account, making God's absolute truth and morality clear from the text of Scripture.

> *It is an irony that at a time when evangelicals are the most worldly themselves they would be at such a judgmental and even self-righteous pitch.*

If we want to see God's name hallowed or revered in our day, judgment must begin not in the world, but in the house of God. We have severely damaged God's credibility in our age, and that is something we are all going to have to come to terms with if there is to be reformation. We are the ones who are regenerated and are being reshaped into the image of Christ. We are the ones whom

God has taken from every tribe, tongue, people, and nation to be a kingdom of priests, a city of hope in the middle of the hopeless cities of the modern kingdoms. We are, as John Stott has described the church, the true counterculture, pointing the way to real meaning and transcendence, not just by what we say but in the way we relate to each other and reach out to our neighbors. Whenever a cup of water is given in Christ's name, the Bible says, God's name is hallowed. Whenever we pursue our calling with excellence, God's name is glorified. Whenever we care for our families, respect is given to the name of God, even by those who do not yet know Him.

But the problem in our day is that we are *not* this counterculture the New Testament describes. We are extensions of the cultural, social, economic, and racial divisions already present in the City of Man. The statistics demonstrate that evangelicals are about as materialistic, self-oriented, and hedonistic as the unbelievers.[11] It is an irony that at a time when evangelicals are the most *worldly* themselves they would be at such a judgmental and even self-righteous pitch. If we are living no differently from the world, what is wrong with these very things we are complaining about? If the children of believers are watching more MTV than the children of unbelievers, as one poll attests,[12] should we not begin in our own homes before we poke our noses into the homes of those who are not even Christians? If we want to end abortion, why don't we start by explaining the doctrine of creation to our own congregations, since evangelicals account for one in six abortions in this country? If we want the state to enforce public prayers, we would do well to ask ourselves whether we prayed with our kids this morning. And if we expect the schools to teach morality and then get upset when it is not our particular moral beliefs that are taught, we should ask ourselves, Am I teaching my own children about God, sin and redemption, the person and work of Christ, and other great and indispensable truths of the Christian faith?

The evangelical world is in a state of confusion: theologically, nobody seems to know anymore what holds us together; ethically, we are scandal-ridden and worldly from head to toe; socially, we are confused as to what our relationship to the world ought to be. It seems to me, especially in the light of these New Testament warnings about judging those outside the church, that our own plate is full; that our own crisis is sufficient to warrant our full attention, and for *this* sort of reformation we can surely claim the name of God.

NOTES

1. J. Patterson and Kim, *The Day America Told the Truth* (New York: Plume/Penguin, 1992), 201.

2. Ibid., 204.

3. Donald McGavran and Win Arn, *How to Grow Your Church* (Ventura: Regal, 1973), 44–46. In an interview style, Arn asks McGavran about this business of "homogeneous" church growth. McGavran states, "University professors will tell you that they love factory workers, and I suppose they do; but as a matter of actual fact, men who work in factories don't feel comfortable when they go to a church attended largely by university professors. . . . We must make sure that we ask people to become Christians where they don't have to cross barriers of language and culture and class and wealth and style of life. Every man should be able to become a Christian with his own kind of people." When Arn asks if this is segregation, McGavran replies, "Pride, arrogance, exclusiveness and segregation—these truly are sins. But I am speaking about something different, about a normal, natural, innocent fact that people like to be with other people of their own kind." First, one wonders how such a "normal, natural, innocent fact" like that is not, at its root the very prejudice McGavran eschewed in the beginning of the sentence; second, the Gospel refuses to allow barriers of this kind. Is this not just the sort of "homogeneity" Paul saw in Galatia and James corrected in his stern epistle? McGavran gives an example of "the fantastic growth of Southern Baptist churches in California," among transplanted Southerners. "When the Southern Baptist churches came in, these Southerners said to themselves, 'Ah, here's our kind of church,'" once they spotted the Southern accent. This philosophy does not intend to give Christian sanction to worldly divisions, but it does just that, it seems to me. How can we be a "counterculture" or God's new society, contradicting the world's injustice, inhumanity, and intolerance, and how can we be a light to the nations if we cave in to the world's way of thinking?

4. Stephen Carter, *The Culture of Disbelief: How American Law and Politics Trivialize Religious Devotion* (New York/San Francisco: HarperCollins, 1993), 48.

5. Ibid., 49.

6. Ibid., 71.

7. John Calvin, *Institutes of the Christian Religion* 4.20.8, 14.

8. It is true that Calvin and the other Reformers thought that government should also defend the true religion, but this is in the context of "Christendom," where there is a particular, shared, public faith embraced by the population. Surely in our day, which resembles the early church context under the pluralistic paganism of Rome, the last thing we would want is state interference in religious affairs.

9. Calvin, *Institutes.*

10. Jerry Falwell, *Wisdom for Living* (Wheaton, Ill.: Victor, 1982), 102.

11. George Barna and William McKay, *Vital Signs: Emerging Social Trends and the Future of American Christianity* (Westchester, Ill.: Crossway, 1984), 140–41.

12. George Barna, *The Barna Report,* (Ventura, Calif.: Regal, 1993), 124.

8

THY KINGDOM COME: WHAT THE KINGDOM IS, HOW IT COMES, AND WHERE IT IS GOING

We don't want to wait for the return of Christ for the kingdoms of this world to be made the kingdom of God and Christ. But wait we must.

THY KINGDOM COME, THY WILL BE DONE, on earth as it is in heaven."

This line from our Lord's prayer urges believers to petition God to bring heaven to earth. In the Garden of Eden, the kingdom of God *was* Eden. Heaven on earth, this ancient Paradise was where God maintained His holy presence among His holy creation. Here, God and the creature He made in His own image, the human being, enjoyed concord. Work was a pleasure as Adam named the animals, cultivated the garden, and exercised his stewardship over the earth God had entrusted him to care for and, in turn, enjoy.

Therefore, the notions of culture, the world, human experience and ambitions, work and one's calling were gracious divine gifts of creation, not curses of the Fall. In Calvin's words, "It is not nature, but the *corruption* of nature" that is the problem. We are not evil because we have bodies nor because we are in the world, surrounded by the natural sphere with matter and pleasures. Rather, we are evil because ever since Adam's fateful choice, we have been born *corrupted*. It is not the sphere of nature as nature, but the whole creation (spiritual and material) as *fallen* that so disturbs the believer.

When Adam and Eve fell, God judged them—and us all with them. The joy of work would become mingled with tedium, weariness, and difficulty. Nature would now work in opposition to its human caretaker and would now experience the decay that was to parallel that of the human body itself. The joy of childbirth would be mingled with its pain. Culture would no longer be linked with the kingdom of God and would be mingled with evil and disaster. Again, it is not that these *realms* are evil, but that the curse of the Fall and the sinful condition renders every realm, secular or sacred, a battleground instead of a rest area. Eden was *Jeru' shalom*, the City of Peace, but when God judged the human race and removed His City back to heaven, Eden was no longer a sacred plot of land.

Nevertheless, this did not mean that the kingdom of God was totally absent. After judgment came promise. After the condemnation of the Law came the good news of the Gospel: the promise that the seed of the woman would eventually destroy the serpent, securing the victory over evil that Adam failed to achieve for his posterity. In anticipation of this redemption, God covered the couple's nakedness, which they had attempted to disguise with their own wardrobe, by sacrificing an animal and clothing them with its skin. This, of course, pointed to the Lamb of God who takes away the sin of the world, whose righteousness would cover the believer's sin. For like the fig leaves, "our righteousness is like filthy rags" (Isaiah 64:6) before God's holy eyes.

In fact, when Eve gave birth to Cain, she exclaimed, "With the help of the Lord I have brought forth a man" (Genesis 4:1). Many scholars point out that since the article is not present in the Hebrew, it could just as well be translated, ". . . I have brought forth *the* man," indicating that Eve believed that God's promise of salvation through her seed had been fulfilled, that she had given birth to her Savior, her Messiah, who would defeat evil and bring redemption.

170

But, of course, we know just how quickly that dream turned into a nightmare, as Cain killed his brother Abel for receiving the divine blessing, since Abel sought no other sacrifice than the one God had commanded. Believers have always had to deal with the disillusionment of unfulfilled expectations regarding the coming of the kingdom. If indeed Eve was disappointed that the one she had hoped to be the Messiah ended up being an "anti-Christ," this was to mark the history of human expectations. You will remember Sarah, doubting God's promise that through her seed the nations of the earth would be blessed.

Further, after the exodus from Egypt, a generation that had grown cynical about God's promise was barred from entering the new "Eden" or "promised land" of God's presence. As the writer to the Hebrews reminds us, God barred them from the land because although they had the Gospel preached to them, "the message they heard was of no value to them, because those who heard did not combine it with faith" (Hebrews 4:2). So God swore in His wrath that they would not enter His rest (v. 3). Land, promise, rest: These are the recurring themes throughout the Old Testament. After forty years of wandering in the desert, the Jews wondered if it was all a pipe dream, a ridiculous vision of a group of patriarchs led by Moses. When the nation was led into Babylonian captivity, and once more God removed His residence from Israel, posting cherubim at the east gate of the temple, just as he had done at the east gate of Eden, the people of God in captivity cried out, "'Is the Lord not in Zion? Is her King no longer there? . . . The harvest is past, the summer has ended, and we are not saved'" (Jeremiah 8:19–20).

And then finally, when the Messiah does arrive on the scene, He is rejected. If He had overthrown the Roman rule of Israel, as the Zealots had hoped, surely then He would have been hailed as the Messiah, but He told Pilate, "My kingdom is from another place." And yet, He said, "The kingdom is among you." What does all of this mean? It means that the kingdom of God has come, with Christ Himself being the fulfillment of these types and shadows. He Himself is the true Israel, and all who are united to Him by faith, Jew or Gentile, form that new nation. He is the true temple, greater than Solomon's in all its glory (Matthew 12:6;

26:61). And yet, all who are united to Him are also "living stones [who] are being built into a spiritual house to be a holy priesthood, offering spiritual sacrifices acceptable to God through Jesus Christ." Thus, whereas the nation of Israel was once called a holy nation and kingdom of priests (Exodus 19:6), now this is applied to the church: "But you are a chosen people, a royal priesthood, a holy nation, a people belonging to God, that you may declare the praises of him who called you out of darkness into his wonderful light." And to be certain that we knew he was talking about the church and not just referring to Jews, Peter added, "Once you were not a people, but now you are the people of God; once you had not received mercy, but now you have received mercy" (1 Peter 2:4–10).

And yet, even though Christ has come, that same apostle Peter warned, "First of all, you must understand that in the last days scoffers will come, scoffing and following their own evil desires. They will say, 'Where is this "coming" he promised? Ever since our fathers died, everything goes on as it has since the beginning of creation'" (2 Peter 3:3).

So this question of timing has always been central. In our Lord's own day, He was constantly asked, by His own disciples, if He was restoring the kingdom. They meant, "Are you going to overthrow the Romans and restore and perfect the Davidic theocracy?" To them, the kingdom of God was still a national thing, with the physical temple and sacrifices. And yet, Jesus made it clear that He was the fulfillment of these shadows. One day yet in the future, the Messiah will return to restore Eden. Only then will the City of Man become the City of Peace, as the New Jerusalem (meaning "City of Peace") comes down from heaven again.

But did this mean that the kingdom of God was not present at all, simply because the kingdoms of this world had not yet become the City of God? Not at all. Jesus told the Jews, "But if I drive out demons by the Spirit of God, then the kingdom of God has come upon you" (Matthew 12:28). At last, this is the man Eve was looking for, the seed of the woman who would drive the serpent out of Paradise, unlike Adam; Jesus was saying, "I am that one who has come to cast out the serpent, and to prove it, I will drive out these demons." In one sense, the kingdom of heaven, Jesus says, is like a mustard seed that grows until the tree extends its branches across the borders, or like a bit of yeast that works itself into the dough. It is also like a net that catches fish or a sower who plants seeds. All of these parables from Matthew 13 immediately make us think of the missionary task of the church, do they not? This is the nature of the kingdom in its present form. It is the extension of the Gospel to all nations. And yet, as our Lord makes clear in those parables, this kingdom is not yet perfect. There are false seeds among the genuine seeds (vv. 1–23), wheat and weeds growing together (vv. 24–30), and good fish and bad fish caught in the net (vv. 47–48). But in each of these cases, Jesus insists that the final separation of believer and unbeliever is left to God "at the harvest" for the wheat, when the weeds will be burned (vv. 29–30), and "at the end of the age" for the fish, when "the angels will come and separate the wicked from the righteous and throw them into the fiery furnace, where there is weeping and gnashing of teeth" (vv. 49–50).

In other words, those who are clothed in Christ's righteousness, as God clothed Adam and Eve and those in Israel who trusted in the promise, will be saved, and those who are clothed with their own fig leaves ("filthy rags," Isaiah 64:6), will be condemned.

But this separation, Jesus makes clear, comes at the end of the age. It is not like the kingdom of God in the Old Testament, where the unbelievers were driven out of the land, but for now both will live side by side, even in the church, leaving the final judgment to God alone at the end of the age. This means that our business as a church is not to judge the world, nor to save it, but to proclaim the judgment of God and the salvation of God. The kingdom is here in its spiritual reality, advancing through Word and sacrament, by the power of the Holy Spirit who makes us Christ's witnesses, but only at the end of the age will the kingdom of God and the kingdoms of this world become one, subject to one King for all eternity. At last, the cherubim posted at Eden's east gate and at the east gate of Jerusalem's temple, barring any human attempts to restore "heaven on earth," will be withdrawn from the watch and the two cities will become one. We all long for that day when the loud voices in heaven declare, "The kingdom of the world has become the kingdom of our Lord and of his Christ, and he will reign for ever and ever" (Revelation 11:15).

KEEPING THE BALANCE

Dutch theologian and prime minister, Abraham Kuyper, used to explain the relationship of the two kingdoms in terms of *antithesis* and *common grace*. On the one hand, we are told, "Do not love the world or anything in the world" (1 John 2:15). I remember growing up hearing that verse quoted for everything from attending high school dances to going into "secular" callings like filmmaking, writing, politics, and other fields considered evil at worst and a waste of a Christian's time at best. And yet, John makes it perfectly clear what he means by "the world": ". . . the cravings of sinful man, the lust of his eyes and the boasting of what he has and does . . ." (v. 16). John is not calling us to hate the people; nor does he want us to hate culture, education, science, the arts, and so on. It is not the world *per se*, but the vanity, materialism, and narcissism of the world that the apostle condemns.

Nevertheless, there is this *antithesis* between the Christian and the non-Christian and between the church and the world for that very reason. When God judged Cain for murdering his brother, He stripped him of his vocation as a farmer (Genesis 4:11) and sent him wandering, like a restless midwestern teenager looking for the bright lights of the big city. "You will be a restless wanderer on the earth," God told Cain.

> *Our whole modern era has been an experiment in this idea: restoring Eden (world peace and an end to suffering and pain, disease and poverty) ourselves, with our own bare hands, through the activities of culture.*

Worried that he would himself be murdered if God drove him from the land, Cain was assured, "Not so; if anyone kills Cain, he will suffer vengeance seven times over." Why is this? It is because God, in His common grace, was going to allow Cain to build a city, a civilization. God still considered cultural activity important and wanted to advance civilization in spite of the Fall, but no longer would this be "kingdom" activity. It would be common, not holy—divinely ordained, approved, and guided by God's providence, but no longer part of the Kingdom of God. "Then the Lord put a mark on Cain so that no one who found him would kill him. So Cain went out from the Lord's presence and lived in the land of Nod, east of Eden" (v. 16). Notice that Cain was driven from the "Promised Land" and lived "east of Eden," and there Cain began building a city—outside the kingdom of God.

But that is not the end of the story, of course. "Adam lay with his wife again, and she gave birth to a son and named him Seth. . . . At that time men began to call on the name of the Lord" (vv. 25–26). The list of Cain's descendants tells us how the key figures were the founders of the various activities in culture: Jubal "was the father of all who play the harp and flute. Zillah also had a son, Tubal-Cain, who forged all kinds of tools out of bronze and iron," and so on (vv. 21–22). But here, in this very next passage, we turn to the birth of Seth and his line. Instead of highlighting his descendants' achievements in culture, the text marks Seth's family significance by the statement, "At that time men began to call on the name of the Lord." In other words, here we have the two cities going in two distinct directions. One is horizontally-oriented; the other is vertically-oriented. Henceforth, God is not working through one family (the human family, via Adam and Eve), but through elect families. Although the children of Seth participate in culture, they are the heirs of the heavenly promise, and they must not intermarry with the Cainites, for that would pervert their faith. Thus, it is clear that salvation will not come through the building of the city, but through "calling on the name of the Lord."

Why is all this important? Because we often confuse these kingdoms and believe, if only subconsciously, that salvation does come through our efforts in the building of the city. Our whole modern era has been an experiment in this idea: restoring Eden (world peace and an end to suffering and pain, disease and poverty) ourselves, with our own bare hands, through the activities of culture (politics, morality, science, technology, the arts, education, etc.). But even conservative Christians find this vision alluring. Instead of proclaiming salvation by calling on the name of the

Lord, we see salvation in terms of accomplishing political or moral victories and making America a "Christian nation," as Israel of old. But there are no Christian nations, ultimately. There are nations that are influenced and shaped by Christian beliefs and values to varying degrees, but there are no special nations on earth anymore. The city Cain began building so long ago is still the city humanity is building through its cultural pursuits today. It is a city established by God's creation and providence, but because of the Fall, it is removed "east of Eden," beyond the realm of salvation, until the end of the age. We may, as Christians who are called to be "salt," preserve society and restrain the culture's decline, but, ultimately, no nation or empire can save itself, much less the world, from its own decadence. History proves this of all great civilizations.

At first, this sounds terribly pessimistic, but it is not, when taken as a whole. As Jesus told the disciples, "In this world you will have trouble." That is because Cain has forever been persecuting Abel. There is an antithesis between the two kingdoms. And yet, even when Israel was in captivity to Egypt and Persia, the Israelites were generally treated well, participated in the customs and civic life of the foreign culture, and even returned to the Land of Promise with new knowledge and skills which they were able to put to use. This leads us to the other side of the coin. If "antithesis" reminds us of the historical and eschatological struggle between the two kingdoms, "common grace" reminds us of what both believer and unbeliever hold in common and may, by God's gracious providence, attempt in common.

COMMON GRACE

When explaining the effects of the Fall, Calvin distinguishes between what we have *supernaturally* (faith, love of God and true love of our neighbor, zeal for righteousness, etc.) and what we possess *naturally* (talents, wisdom, knowledge, reason, morality, creativity, etc.). God is the author of both in creation, but the former, lost in the Fall, can be recovered only by God's gracious, supernatural intervention.

There is no question that all people are born into the world totally depraved, in the sense that their will is enslaved to sin, and even the good they do is perverted by self-love, so that there is no health in us before God. But just because God can see the perversity in even our best actions does not mean that we can see each other's. Although we are incapable by nature of spiritual righteousness after the Fall, we are capable of civic virtue. The rays of the divine image that shine through one's depravity "show him to be a rational being, differs from brute beasts because he is endowed with understanding," even though that understanding is clouded with ignorance. The unregenerate man or woman is capable of understanding in things earthly, but not in things heavenly (1 Corinthians 2:14).

There are two reasons unbelievers can create just laws, good music, and sound education: First, they are still created in God's image and rays of light still shine through. Second, God's common grace, exercised through His providential sovereignty, restrains wickedness, vice, and ignorance from the depths to which our depravity and ignorance could take us.

Many leaders of the Christian Right tell us that only Christians have a right to rule the nation. But this comes from a general misunderstanding in fundamentalism which assumes that non-Christians are not worth reading, worth listening to, or worth enjoying, either for their company or for their work. Once more, I think, Calvin's insights strike home here:

> Whenever we come upon these matters in secular writers, let that admirable light of truth shining in them teach us that the mind of man, though fallen and perverted from its wholeness, is nevertheless clothed and ornamented with God's excellent gifts. If we regard the Spirit of God as the sole fountain of truth, we shall neither reject the truth itself, nor despise it *wherever it shall appear*, unless we wish to dishonor the Spirit of God. . . . What then? Shall we deny that the truth shone upon the ancient jurists who established civic order and discipline with such great equity? Shall we say that the philosophers were blind in their fine observation and artful description of nature? . . . Shall we say that they are insane who developed medicine, devoting their labor to our benefit? What shall we say of all the mathematical sciences? Shall we consider them the ravings of madmen? . . . Those men whom Scripture [1 Corinthians 2:14] calls "natural men" were, indeed, sharp and penetrating in their investigation of earthly things. Let us, accordingly, learn by their example how many gifts the Lord left to human nature even after it was despoiled of its true good. (Italics added)[1]

Even at a time when the Muslim Turks had invaded "Christendom" and were threatening to conquer all of Europe, Martin Luther once said, "I would rather be governed by an honest Turk than a dishonest Christian."

Although spiritual discernment is wholly lost until one is regenerated, there is much natural wisdom, excellence, virtue, and beauty of which unbelievers are capable. These gifts come from the hand of God even though they are not received as such. Furthermore, the Christian himself is still a sinner—regenerate, to be sure, but wicked also.

> *Redemption does not change our*
> *participation in culture; rather,*
> *it changes us and, therefore,*
> *the character of that involvement.*

We live at present in this period of "common grace," when "God sends the rain on the just and the unjust alike," and commands us to treat unbelievers in the same way (Matthew 5:45). When a Samaritan village did not welcome Jesus, James and John asked, "Lord, do you want us to call fire down from heaven to destroy them?" "But Jesus turned and rebuked them and they went to another village" (Luke 9:54–55). There is a time coming when fire will come from heaven, but that is for the end of the age. For now, it is neither the right time nor are we the right judges. It will be His time and His judgment. Even if the church is being persecuted, it is commanded to pray for the rulers and those in secular authority (Romans 13), since even wicked rulers are "ministers of God."

CHRIST & CULTURE

At the time of the Reformation, there were three approaches to this question of how the church is to relate to society. First, there was the medieval Roman Church. Combining the ancient Roman idea of a divine Caesar with the Christian notion of a pastor, the church argued that with the pope as the head not only of the church, but of the culture ("Christendom") as well, the theocratic kingdom could be restored at least to some degree. So, off went the crusaders, driving the "Canaanites" out of the Holy Land, as medieval knights saw themselves as David's warriors, defending the *Holy* Roman Empire.[2]

Then the Anabaptists took a different approach. Adherents of what is called the "Radical Reformation," because they sought to go further than the Protestant Reformers, the Anabaptists insisted, as *The Schleitheim Confession* (1527) argues,

> We are agreed on separation: A separation shall be made from the evil and from the wickedness which the devil planted in the world; in this manner, simply that we shall not have fellowship with them [the wicked] and not run with them in the multitude of their abominations. This is the way it is: Since all who do not walk in the obedience of faith, and have not united themselves with God so that they wish to do his will, are a great abomination to God, it is not possible for anything to grow or issue from them except abominable things. For truly all creatures are in but two classes, good and bad, believing and unbelieving, darkness and light, the world and those who [have come] out of the world, God's temple and idols, Christ and Belial; and none can have part with the other. . . . He further admonishes us to withdraw from Babylon and the earthly Egypt that we may not be partakers of the pain and suffering which the Lord will bring upon them.

This means that Anabaptists must not only avoid Roman and Protestant churches, but must also shun "drinking houses, civic affairs," and so on. "From all these things we shall be separated and have no part with them for they are nothing but an abomination, and they are the cause of our being hated before our Christ Jesus, who has set us free from the slavery of the flesh and fitted us for the service of God through the Spirit whom he has given us."[3] Notice the Gnostic tendencies of dividing the world into "light" and "darkness," the Spirit and the "flesh" (implying here "matter," not as Paul intends it, referring to the sinful nature), and the notion that "it is not possible for anything to grow or issue from [unbelievers] except abominable things." There are no distinctions between common grace and saving grace, the image of God and the sinfulness of man. It appears that nature itself, not merely the corruption of nature, is the problem.

The Reformers avoided both tendencies: on one hand, to confuse the two kingdoms (Rome) and, on the other, to divorce the two kingdoms and reject any Christian involvement in the kingdom of culture (Anabaptists). Instead, they insisted that Christians should be involved in the world. They should neither seek to escape it, like the monks, whose lives were often more "worldly" than the world, nor seek to rule it, like the popes, whose own houses were not quite in order. Every believer is a "priest" before God, and each person (believer *and* unbeliever) has been given a vocation or calling, by virtue of creation, to participate in some way in culture. We are social beings, created to enjoy each other's company, whether Christian or non-Christian. Redemption does not change our participation in culture; rather, it changes *us* and, therefore, the character of that involvement. Separation from the world is not physical, according to the Reformers; rather, it is a matter of divorcing our dependence on the things of this world: its vanity and rejection or perversion of things heavenly. Luther and Calvin said that the calling of the magistrate or public official was "one of the noblest" (Calvin), inasmuch as it serves the society so well.

Protestants, therefore, encouraged their children to pursue secular callings in education, business, government, diplomacy, the arts, and science because they believed that these were all spheres of God's providence. If God, who is perfectly holy, can patiently endure evil (especially our own) in the world and water the crops of the just and the unjust alike, surely we who are sinful may not self-righteously "separate" from the world as if that meant separation from worldliness. For we cannot separate from ourselves. As Luther said of his own experience as a monk, "I entered the monastery to be rid of sin and free of the world, but I found that I had simply brought that rascal into the cell with me."

Therefore, the Reformation vision stands on three legs: Creation, which affirms the goodness of the world and the possibility of civic virtue, truth, and beauty being produced even by non-Christians; the Fall, which explains the depravity of our own hearts and renders any "perfect society" the impossible dream; and Redemption, which not only tells us of our own salvation from sin's penalty and power in this life and its presence in the next, but also promises a full restoration of Paradise at the end of history, but not within it. With these three biblical doctrines in view, there can be neither escape from the world (for involvement is our Christian duty as well as our creation mandate), nor domination over the world. For like Daniel in the Babylonian court, or Joseph as Egypt's prime minister, God's people are always exiles. They should, like Daniel, seek to excel in their learning and skill. They should be the best in their fields, for the glory of God and the good of both kingdoms. But they are always God's people in exile. Their activity in the world is never mistaken with a struggle for the power bases in order to take over society.

A CHOICE OF THREE

It seems to me that we have one of three choices of "eschatologies" or beliefs about the nature of the kingdom, history, and the future. Two of the options come from one ancient heresy that just won't seem to die.

Many of the New Testament epistles were written to counter the incipient heresy which would soon emerge as "Gnosticism." This heresy maintained that matter was basically evil. Therefore, at the high end of the chain of being was the spirit, and at the low end was matter. The Gnostics twisted the biblical message beyond recognition, blending Christianity with Greek philosophy. The Fall was redefined too; no longer was it a fall from a state of righteousness to a state of depravity, but a fall from spirit and light to matter and darkness. Whereas in Christianity, God made us living bodies and this was "good," as He Himself declared, in Gnosticism the body, being material, is evil, and man's physical body is a curse. Therefore, salvation in the Gnostic scheme was not the salvation *of* the body through the Resurrection, but salvation *from* the body at death.

Gnosticism—Abandoning the World

Most Gnostic sects, therefore, had little use for the world. They formed monastic communes where they tried to keep their focus on spiritual things, denying their bodies by severe self-denial or indulging it in orgies and the like, since they were not really responsible for what their bodies did. Gnostics insisted that the world of matter had to be transcended by an effort of the human will and spirit, rising above physical existence and achieving one-ness with the divine spirit.

This worldview was at once quietistic (that is, ignoring the problems of the world) and revolutionary. The Anabaptists revived this tendency in the sixteenth century, as some rejected any Christian involvement in society, separating into their own communities, while others attempted a communist, polygamous "utopia" through violent revolution. The modern era is an experiment in secular Gnosticism. In fact, this point has been argued most eloquently by philosopher-historian, Eric Voegelin, from the University of Munich: "The saint is a Gnostic who will not leave the transfiguration of the world to the grace of God beyond history but will do the work of God himself, right here and now, in history."[4]

Gnosticism—Remaking the World

The Gnostic is the one who believes Satan's ancient lie, "You shall be as gods," and utopianism is the eschatology of this heresy. Either the Gnostic will escape the trappings of material existence or convert those "external" structures into the spiritual Paradise. In other words, he will either enter a monastery or insist on turning the world into one. If the spirit is basically good and the real problem is society, institutions, structures (i.e., matter), all we have to do is either abandon or conquer the schools, the government, and the arts, and free the human spirit. Gnosticism went from the individual ("you shall be as gods") in Eden to a whole civilization ("Nothing will be impossible for us") at Babel. Progress is an eschatological idea. Babel's "Nothing will be impossible" is the collective version of "I will be as God." We will divinize ourselves through self-effort, and then we will divinize society.

Of course, evangelicals have not bought into this to the same extent as modern secularists, but it is an idea that has worn out its welcome in intellectual circles, just at a time when American Christians seem to think so highly of human nature and the possibilities of a Christian nation. Karl Barth's warnings at a time when German Christians had confused the two kingdoms strike home in our efforts at building the "Christian nation." Speaking of the "high things" or Towers of Babel we raise in order to build our kingdoms, Barth wrote:

Christianity does not set its mind on *high things*. It is uneasy when it hears men speaking loudly and with confidence about "creative evolution"; when it marks their plans for perfecting the development of pure applied science, of art, of morals and of religion, of physical and spiritual health, of welfare and well-being. Christianity is unhappy when men boast of the glories of marriage and of family life, of Church and State, and of Society. Christianity does not busy itself to support and underpin those many "ideals" by which men are deeply moved—individualism, collectivism, nationalism, internationalism, humanitarianism, ecclesiasticism. Christianity is unmoved by Nordic enthusiasm or by devotion to Western culture, by the visions of Youth or by the solid and mature wisdom of middle-age. . . . It watches with some discomfort the building of these eminent towers, and its comments always tend to slow down this busy activity, for it detects therein the menace of idolatry. . . .

Seeing men balanced midway between earth and heaven, and perceiving the insecurity of their position, it finds itself unable to place serious confidence in the permanence of any of these human *high places*, in the importance of any of these "important" things, or in the value of any of these "values." Christianity perceives men moving, it is true, but moving to deprivation. It beholds a hand shaking the foundations of all that is and will be. It hears the joists creaking mysteriously. Christianity cannot simply disregard what it has seen and heard.[5]

While Barth, in his laudable attempt to raise our gaze to heaven rather than to earth for salvation, may downplay the reality of common grace, he challenges us to take seriously the judgment of God upon all of our towers of babel, even the Christian ones. "Christianity knows itself at least more akin to ascetics and pietists, strange though their behaviour may be, than to 'healthy evangelical national piety,'" which Barth knew in the form of the Nazi regime, supported by many evangelicals.[6] In other words, although abandoning the world is clearly not the answer according to the Protestant reading of Scripture, at least that approach is better than participating in the pagan enterprise of placing our confidence in "this great Babylon which I have built for my power and majesty"—Nebuchadnezzar's boast before his humiliation. It is at least to be preferred to self-confident nationalism and the confusion of kingdoms.

The Doctrine of the Kingdom

But there is the third alternative to the Gnosticism which abandons the world as well as to the one that attempts to divinize its own culture, values, customs, and nation. The third alternative is the Christian doctrine of the kingdom. It is a kingdom that is already here (Satan has been driven from the heavenly Paradise, where he accused us day and night; the Gospel is being preached to the nations and they are streaming to Zion, the City of God), but not yet here in its fullness (final judgment of wickedness, the end of war, suffering, violence, poverty, and sin). At the Tower of Babel, the Holy Spirit fell on the people in order to confuse the languages and scatter the proud nations. At Pentecost, He fell on the people in order to bring their languages and nations together, as "each man heard the Gospel in his own language." It was a sign of what we are to aim at now, but which we will only fully arrive at later.

CONCLUSION

Only Christianity gives a person justification for seeking to *change* things rather than passively accepting fate, yet providing at the same time a sword-bearing angel at the gate of Utopia. Theologians often speak of the kingdom of God in terms of the "already" and "not-yet." It is difficult for us to wait for things, especially in our highly automated, service-oriented society. We refuse to wait for the redemption of our bodies, so we "name and claim it" here and now; we want money, success, happiness. It is like the line from the pop song, "I want it all, I want it now." We don't want to wait for the return of Christ for the kingdoms of this world to be made the kingdom of God and Christ. But wait we must.

The kingdom of God is here, as Christ said, but it is spiritual. And yet, we have the promise that one day there will be Utopia, that the kingdom of earth will become the kingdom of Christ, as Eden and Israel were designed to foreshadow. One day, those who cause war will be driven from the City of Peace; those who oppress through violence and injustice will themselves be imprisoned, and the Sun of Righteousness will be the light of the world. But until

all nations are Egypt

that day, we must be content with the spiritual presence of that glorious kingdom. We must not place our hope in projects of building "Christian nations." We are not called to take over power bases, but to be "salt" and "light" wherever we are, knowing that vengeance and final judgment belong to God.

Even in America, we are in exile. Our nation does not correspond to Israel in Scripture, but to Egypt. All nations are "Egypt" to the believer. It is a constructive exile, where we learn skills, pursue our callings, raise our families, participate in common life with unbelievers, and enjoy fellowship with our fellow-exiles. We may even have, hopefully, a Joseph or two in Washington every now and then, but it is always Egypt, always the exile. Whenever we worship as the assembly on earth, through Word and sacrament, the Holy Spirit links us to the heavenly congregation where, with them, we are feeding on Christ and seated with Him in heavenly places (Ephesians 2:5). This is what it means to pray, "Thy kingdom come, thy will be done on earth as it is in heaven." As those believers who have gone to their reward are seated around the throne, caught up in praise and worship, may we worship God in Spirit and truth here on earth until the Gospel has been preached to the ends of the earth. "Then the nations shall know that I am the Lord your God." And only then will God bring heaven to earth—this time, forever.

NOTES

1. Calvin, *Institutes* 2.2.15.
2. Of course, Hebrew ideas were mingled with more secular attitudes derived especially from Plato and his much later radical interpreter Plotinus. Platonism regards the material world as merely the ephemeral projection of heavenly "ideas," but there can be no doubt that after Gregory, popes increasingly saw themselves as seated on the throne of David as the vicar of the Son of David (Christ), in the "land of promise" (the Holy Roman Empire).
3. Mark Noll, ed., *Confessions and Catechisms of the Reformation* (Grand Rapids: Baker, 1992), 53.
4. Eric Voegelin, *The New Science of Politics* (Chicago: Univ. of Chicago, 1952), 147.
5. Karl Barth, *Commentary on Romans*, trans. Edwin C. Hoskyns (Oxford: Oxford Univ., 1968).
6. Ibid.

9

FELT NEEDS AND
DOWN-TO-EARTH PROBLEMS

It cuts across the grain of our modern sentiments to think that God exists for His own happiness, not ours, and that we, in fact, are merely part of that universal design to bring pleasure to the Holy One of Israel.

GIVE US THIS DAY OUR DAILY BREAD."

Just as our Lord gave us the biblical balance between God's nearness ("Our Father") and His distance ("who art in Heaven"), this prayer also gives us the balance between things heavenly and things earthly. It is important to notice that our Lord first draws our attention to things heavenly: God and His name, His kingdom, His will. Similar to the Ten Commandments, the Lord's Prayer begins with our prayer concerning God and His name and then descends to contemplate our own needs and the world around us. Apart from God, the most important relationships between people and ideas are without definition, meaning, and purpose. When we begin with God, even the most mundane, common, everyday activities somehow become rooted in eternity.

Furthermore, we begin with God and things heavenly (theology) because, frankly, God is more important than we are. That is an odd thing to say because, on one hand, it seems so obvious to say, and yet, on the other hand, it sounds too offensive. It cuts across the grain of our modern sentiments to think that God exists for His own happiness, not ours, and that we, in fact, are merely part of that universal design to bring pleasure to the Holy One of Israel. By putting God first in the prayer, Jesus puts theology before our needs, that which is universally true before that which is practical for one's own personal life or for society.

What we consider practical is not the study of God, but the study of how we can become happier and more fulfilled, and even our moral campaigns are pitched in the language of self-fulfillment, instead of justice and duty.

Today, we want to run immediately to the "practical" or the "relevant," as if God were irrelevant. We look suspiciously at those who want to talk about theology and eternity and we say, "You have your head in the clouds; let's talk about the *real* problems." But that assumes that the *real* problems are temporal and, if there is any time left over, we can get around to the eternal questions. That is the essence of secularism, but it is widely embraced in our own churches.

Ever since the pietists and the orthodox divided the heart from the mind, and the Enlightenment made the divorce official, we have concluded either that those who look to eternity for answers are not "hip," or that those who take their calling in this world seriously are too "worldly." Heaven and earth have never been so separated in our minds. What we consider practical is not the study of God, but the study of how we can become happier and more fulfilled, and even our moral campaigns are pitched in the language of self-fulfillment, instead of justice and duty.

But here, Jesus insists that we be chiefly concerned with the glory of God and the holiness of His name and only secondarily concerned about our own needs, whether real or felt. This is a priority we must get right and a priority which, I fear, the church growth movement has gotten wrong in its insistence that the primary purpose of the church is to meet the "felt needs" of the un-churched, rather than to teach and lead the unchurched to recognize their greatest priority to be worshiping the one true God and believing His Word. It is God's command (the Law) and God's invitation (the Gospel) that form the community of faith, not our own felt needs. It is also a priority many Christian activists have gotten wrong, as they confuse moral and political campaigns with building the kingdom of God.

Having said that, our needs are important. After all, just because they are secondary, it does not follow that they are unimportant. There are many things of secondary importance that are vital. For instance, an education for our children is very important, but it is not essential to their very existence, as the experience of countless people around the world and in our own country can attest.

> *God is the source of our whole*
> *existence, not just of redemption;*
> *and second, His providence extends*
> *over every person, not just*
> *believers; and preserves culture,*
> *not just the kingdom of God.*

Some years ago, Donald Bloesch made this crisp observation: "It is commonly said that legislation is not an answer to social ills, but conversion. Yet legislation is a proximate answer even as conversion is the ultimate answer."[1] At the time of the Reformation, as alluded to earlier, there were three dominant approaches to the "Christ and culture" relationship. Rome saw the two kingdoms as one empire, the pope at the head. The Anabaptists regarded the kingdom of man as "an abomination" out of which no good could come, and in which no good could be done. The Reformers, however, insisted that this kingdom or realm of culture was neither something to dominate, nor to escape. It was the place where man and woman belong, where God placed them in creation, and where He commanded them to "be fruitful and multiply" and cultivate the earth. We do not serve at our post in society in order to "take back" power bases, nor in order merely to evangelize, but to exercise our cultural mandate as redeemed stewards.

Therefore, once we raise our eyes toward heaven, realizing that God's name and kingdom are more important than anything going on in Washington, D.C., we are ready to ask God for "daily bread," that is, the satisfaction of practical, everyday needs. I am not criticizing Christian activists for arguing that Christians should be interested in political or social reforms, but for confusing the proximate with the ultimate. As Donald Bloesch remarks, "The hope of the church certainly does not lie in new strategies, programs and techniques. Instead it lies in a rediscovery of the catholic and evangelical roots of the faith in an attempt to apply these to the critical social issues of our time."[2]

By petitioning God for "our daily bread," we are engaging in an act of worship. God is pleased to see us acknowledging what is true whether we acknowledge it or not: that apart from His fatherly goodness and care, which He owes to no one, neither spiritual nor physical life is possible. The irony is that even the most bitter atheist depends on God for the oxygen he uses to curse Him and requires divine provisions of food and drink to sustain his rebellious existence.

There are, it seems to me, two very important things we need to learn from this petition: First, that God is the source of our whole existence, not just of redemption; and second, that His providence extends over every person, not just believers; and preserves culture, not just the kingdom of God.

First, God is the source of our whole existence. I have always liked Peter and found enormous personal comfort in knowing that the chief of the apostles was slow on the uptake. The first time he was confronted with the power of Christ to provide for earthly concerns was on a fishing trip. At this point, Peter was "Simon," and he had no idea and probably little interest in Jesus' sermon as the Master stepped into his boat and continued teaching. "Put out into deep water, and let down the nets for a catch," Jesus instructed. I have been on deep sea fishing trips with real fishermen, and one thing I've learned, especially with those who have no aversion to using very strong language, is how important it is to keep my mouth shut. However many times Jesus had gone fishing, He was not as experienced as someone who had done this for his living.

Nevertheless, with a characteristic boldness that came from his confidence that He was the God incarnate who created the fish, Jesus told Simon to put down the nets, even though it was the end of a rather unproductive fishing day. But because Jesus was a rabbi and even the most irreverent sorts tipped their hats to the men of the cloth, Peter agreed to humor the man. You know the rest of the story. The nets began to break, they were so full of fish. Then another boat arrived, and both boats began to sink with their bounty. And then Luke records a most astonishing response from Simon Peter: "When Simon Peter saw this, he fell at Jesus' knees and said, 'Go away from me, Lord; I am a sinful man!'" (Luke 5:1–11).

That is a strange response, isn't it? Imagine a healing crusade today, where the most common response was fear rather than joy. A strange power, this; being in the presence of Someone who had such control over common things surely must be divine. The presence of the divine is the presence of the holy. It is this presence that makes us uncomfortable. Notice that the most surprising miracles are not when we see God exercising power over the sun, moon, and stars, but when He intervenes in the most common, everyday affairs. In fact, it is more difficult to see God as active in the mundane than in the dramatic moments in history. We can very easily see the hand of God in an earthquake or in the collapse of Communism, but we often miss His fatherly hand in providing for us every day in kind and unusual ways.[3]

The Enlightenment had a lot to do with the way we look at God's involvement in daily affairs, Deism insisting that God is the Creator who sets things into motion, but that He leaves the real running of the universe to laws of nature. Ironically, even those today who so emphasize "signs and wonders" and think they are defending the biblical supernaturalism against deistic naturalism so easily fall into the Enlightenment way of looking at things. By ignoring the biblical doctrine of providence, which comforts us in the knowledge that God is active in and in control over the ordinary as much as the remarkable, we have unwittingly encouraged a tendency to deny the supernatural. This tendency is seen when, on the one hand, we ignore the supernatural, or, on the other, when we redefine the supernatural to fit naturalistic assumptions and laws.

"Poverty is a curse," Pat Robertson states, and one cause of poverty is "a lack of knowledge of God's principles of blessing."[4] After all, the Laws of Miracles work as predictably as the Law of Gravitation or any other natural law.[5] Although he denies a "mind over matter" philosophy, Robertson argues that positive confessions are "the master key to miracles": "Do not ask the storm to stop. Tell it to stop!! . . . There cannot be doubt in the inner man in the heart. . . . You know without question the storm is going to be stopped. You know the finances are going to be provided. . . . Begin to possess it. Taste it, touch it, feel it in your spirit. When it is already yours in the Spirit, it is also yours in the visible world."[6] In fact, Robertson offers the following advice:

> Most people ask God for a miracle but many omit a key requirement—the spoken word. God has given us authority over disease, demons, sickness, storms, and finances. We continue to ask God to act, when, in fact, He has given us the authority to act with divinely empowered speech. We are to declare that authority in Jesus' name. We are to command the money to come to us, command the storm to be stilled, command the demon to come out, command the leg to grow, command the cancer to leave.[7]

We have a growing tendency in our society to blend science with the supernatural. But I believe that this is a serious misunderstanding of the doctrine of providence, among other things. In His providence, God governs in predictable ways (so predictable that we call them "laws"), but the miraculous is not the effect of scientific laws but, rather, the superseding of those laws. Miracles cannot be "expected" or "demanded," for they are by definition divine surprises. A miracle astonishes, as Simon Peter was astonished. A miracle contradicts laws of nature as well as our expectations of the way things should happen, rather than conforming to them. Nothing makes a miracle happen but the sovereign will of a loving heavenly Father. He may use our prayers, but there is absolutely no causal necessity involved.

This is essential for two reasons: First, so we will recover a confidence in God's control over "daily bread"—including the events we often consider catastrophic to the kingdom—and, second, so we will ask more serious questions of those among us who presume to possess a power over nature and circumstances that

God reserves for Himself. God is not surprised by any world event, nor is He dependent on gifted human beings to save His plans from disaster. Imagine an elected official announcing that God had entrusted him or her with power over storms, planets, wealth, and disease. This not only contributes to culture wars, it also contributes to false impressions of Christianity in an already confused and secular nation.

These more obvious forms of the so-called "prosperity evangelists" point up a larger problem even in more evangelical circles, and that is a general failure to appreciate or incorporate the doctrine of providence. This makes it very difficult for us to appreciate the "daily bread," which measures the gulf between our secular view of history and the providential view of history embraced by Augustine and the Reformers. They did not require the miraculous in order to see God at work. Brother Lawrence, a monk, wrote his little classic, *The Practice of the Presence of God*, more than three hundred years ago, and it still speaks to this problem. Whether he was bustling around the kitchen preparing meals or on his knees, he was equally in God's presence. "I am doing now what I will do for all eternity. I am blessing God, praising Him, adoring him, and loving Him with all my heart,"[8] so that this life is already the beginning of eternity.

We do not have to have interruptions of natural laws or a confusion of natural law with promises God never made, in order to enjoy the presence, love, provision, and pleasure of God. Have we become so influenced by the noisy, spectacular displays of human excitement that we demand that God entertain us or meet our temporal needs in certain predictable ways that defy natural explanation, if we are to take Him seriously or commend Him to the world? Must we approach religion in the same way we approach a shopping mall?

The irony, then, is that even as many seek to make God's presence "real" in their services and lives, the end result props up the Enlightenment myth that God is not involved in the mundane, but only in the spectacular. The only difference is that "the spectacular" is pursued with vigor. We actually end up removing the sense of God's presence from the common, so that when God's presence is not felt in the spectacular (i.e., the miracle didn't happen even though one followed the Law of Miracles), the net response is often the secularization of the disillusioned soul, individual and collective. What we need is a recovery of that transcendent vision that fills even the most common moments of our lives with meaning, an opportunity to "glorify God and enjoy him forever," beginning now. The great seventeenth-century poet, George Herbert, described the image of a person looking *at* a window versus looking *through* it:

> A man that looks on glasse,
> On it may stay his eye;
> Or if he pleaseth, through it passe,
> And then the heav'n espie.

Putting his Reformation theology to poetry, Herbert grasped the practical implications of seeing everything—even the most common, mundane activities—as gifts of God meant to raise our eyes to heaven in gratitude. Our work is not merely something we do so that we can have time and money to spend in "spiritual activities," nor are our experience and worship of God limited to the miraculous or astounding "victories." Rather, spirituality extends to the simple joys of family and friends, food and drink, love and study, work and leisure. When all of life is viewed from this theological, God-centered perspective, Herbert adds, as he addresses God,

> All may of thee partake:
> Nothing can be so mean,
> Which with this tincture (for thy sake)
> Will not grow bright and clean.
>
> A servant with this clause
> Makes drudgerie divine:
> Who sweeps a room, as for thy laws,
> Makes that and th'action fine.
>
> This is the famous stone
> That turneth all to gold:
> For that which God doth touch and own
> Cannot for lesse be told.[9]

It is important for us to recover the doctrine of providence. When legs are lengthened and the blind can see, we say, "Ah!

Now there's God at work!" But when we go to work or enjoy a good meal with friends or rear a family, these are mundane, common, everyday things that don't really demand God's involvement. But this is far from the biblical view, which presents God as active in the most minute details of our lives, even the most trivial. For instance, "The lot [die] is cast into the lap, but its every decision is from the Lord" (Proverbs 16:33). "Are not two sparrows sold for a penny?" Jesus asked. "Yet not one of them will fall to the ground apart from the will of your Father. And even the very hairs of your head are all numbered" (Matthew 10:29–30). Paul told the Athenians the identity of the "unknown God": "He is not served by human hands, as if he needed anything, because He Himself gives all men life and breath and everything else. From one man He made every nation of men, that they should inhabit the whole earth; and He determined the times set for them and the exact places where they should live" (Acts 17:25–26).

Apart from Christ, all of us as individuals deserve God's wrath, and that is just as true of the nation as it is of its people.

God is as much at work in the days we forget as in those we remember; He is always there, providing, caring, ruling, and protecting. He has been there all along, even in our suffering and lack.

HE CARES FOR SECULAR HUMANISTS TOO

So much is said today as if God only took care of the believer, and as if one reason for becoming a Christian is that God brings blessing and prosperity believers' way in material terms. In fact, much is made in the Christian Right about God's supposed covenant with America. If we follow divine principles (i.e., elect the right people), God is forced by His own laws of reciprocity to open up heaven to shower blessings upon the nation.

Nevertheless, providence is not, like redemption, something that is limited to the realm of believers. Although God's saving grace extends only to those who have accepted it, His common grace or providence does not ask whether one is a believer. Nor is God obliged to shed His common grace on America any more than on Iraq. Apart from Christ, all of us as individuals deserve God's wrath, and that is just as true of the nation as it is of its people. Not only in its worst days, but in its finest hours and most God-honoring speeches, there has been reason enough for a holy God to extinguish the life of our nation at any given moment. It is nothing but the sheer mercy of God that accounts for the blessings God sends our way.

In fact, our Lord uses this kind of "common" love or favor as an example of how we are to love our enemies: "He causes his sun to rise on the evil and the good, and sends rain on the righteous and the unrighteous" (Matthew 5:45). You love your friends? Big deal, Jesus says. "Love your enemies" (v. 46).

This helps us when we realize that there are many who never pray for God's name to be hallowed, but instead profane it; who couldn't care less about God's kingdom and will, as they are too preoccupied with their own. And yet, these same people have the provision of their daily bread, just as the Christians. That almost doesn't seem fair, does it? And yet, we must remember that creation and providence embrace all of humanity. Every person is created in the image of God, and every person is cared for by that Creator because of divine goodness. Redemption and providence are two distinct categories. This is why some pagans enjoy prosperity, while some believers have to serve them in poverty and disgrace. If this still doesn't seem fair to us, we ought to remember that God is giving us all more than we deserve, even if all we have is breath.

GOD TAKES BREAD SERIOUSLY

"Our daily bread" may not be the first thing our Lord mentions, but He does get around to it. It may not be ultimate, but it is proximate in its importance.

But this petition is no more individualistic than the others. We not only pray for our own personal needs to be met; we look beyond ourselves to a world in great need. There is pain and suffering, injustice, violence, immorality. And are we to do nothing about it? Are we to stand on the sidelines and wait for the Great Escape? Not if we take the Scriptures seriously. In the context of discussing the return of Christ, does Paul say, "It is all going to burn anyway, so just witness and occupy yourselves with spiritual things?" No, his commands for the end of the age are very different: "Make it your ambition to lead a quiet life, to mind your own business and to work with your hands, just as we told you, so that your daily life may win the respect of outsiders and so that you will not be dependent on anybody" (1 Thessalonians 4:11). "Whatever you do, work at it with all your heart, as working for the Lord, not for men . . ." (Colossians 3:23). It is an agenda, not of dominion (taking over power bases), nor of withdrawal into the new monastery of the evangelical subculture, but of diligence in our calling, care for our families, and concern for our neighbors. This is how we are "salt" and "light," not by saving the world or becoming heroes, but by preserving society from the extremes into which it could plunge, through positive involvement on a daily basis, right where we are. As Os Guinness puts it, "The problem today is not that Christians are not where they should be; it is that they are not what they should be right where they are."[10]

"Give us this day our daily bread," therefore, is a category that covers a good deal more than our own three square meals each day. It links the ultimate (things heavenly) with the proximate (things earthly). It neither confuses them, nor divorces them, but it links them together in proper order.

Falling under this category, of course, are our concerns about morality, politics, social justice, the environment, hunger, and so forth. In this petition, heaven embraces the earth. Concern for God and His kingdom, though not identified with these daily concerns, is nevertheless expected of the Christian. Once the priorities are established and we have put theology before ideology, eternal needs before earthly needs, God before ourselves and society, then we are invited to petition God's assistance for daily concerns.

To that end, let us take a brief look at how we can engage in civic life without confusing kingdoms, gospels, and spheres.

OUR DAILY POLITICS

An elected official, after hearing me explain the importance of putting eternity before the here-and-now, asked me, "Are you saying that my job isn't important?" He was put off particularly because he was a victim of that epidemic disease we seem to have today in regarding politicians as more important than they really are. But his concern went beyond that. He misunderstood me to be re-echoing the pietistic call to withdraw from society and concluded that I was simply one of those separatists who was "so heavenly minded that he's no earthly good." Some readers will also misunderstand the comments of the preceding chapters in this direction, but here is my opportunity to clear it up.

The discipline of politics, as a distinct sphere of study, is the product of the Renaissance and Reformation. In fact, many historians regard Calvin, Beza, and the theologians of "federal" or "covenant" theology as the architects of political federalism and constitutional democracy.[11] Although Calvin never sought to dictate public policy in Geneva, he did insist on the freedom in his pulpit and study to paint the big picture. Thus, the doctrines of God's sovereignty, creation, the Fall, redemption, the nature of the kingdom and the church's relationship to the world, vocation, civil and spiritual liberties, representative government, resistance to tyrants—all become major features of reformed political and social theory. Far from "pie in the sky bye and bye," Reformed theology was down-to-earth, but it did not start with this world; it started with God (theology) and applied that knowledge to worldly problems.

In the 1950s, during the civil rights movement, most evangelical leaders remained silent, insisting that the purpose of the church is not to interfere in politics. They lashed out at the mainline liberals for confusing social action with the Gospel. Certainly, in the latter criticism, they were justified, but to remain silent in the face of obvious injustice—injustices which find clear parallels in Scripture—is a guilty silence. We never have repented of that silence as a body. I have never heard remorse from evangelical leaders at political rallies and conventions. During the sixties and seventies, as Francis Schaeffer reminded us, the children of Christian parents rebelled along with everyone else, because they saw the church as little more than a place where white, middle-class American self-interest was baptized and the ethic of "personal peace and affluence" received its justification from the pulpit.

In the eighties, we went a step further, and, realizing that those values of the fifties were no longer the "status quo" that we could simply baptize each Sunday, we entered the political arena to fight for them. It stood to reason, then, that since we were silent when blacks were being denied voting privileges, it would take something more near and dear to our own hearts to get us to our feet: free enterprise capitalism. While the Scriptures were said to be unclear about racial injustices, suddenly the Bible became a textbook for the right to excess and greed. No liberation theologians in Central America could have so carelessly torn passages from their context in the interest of ideology, as leaders of the Christian Right exploited verses like "If the Son shall make you free, you shall be free indeed" and "Where the Spirit of the Lord is, there is liberty" as a defense of whatever particular propositions and policies its leaders deemed necessary. And then there were the endless references to 2 Chronicles 7:14: "If my people, who are called by my name, will humble themselves and pray and seek my face and turn from their wicked ways, then I will hear from heaven and will forgive their sin and heal their land." Never did it seem important to check the context of this verse, placed as it is in the middle of the dedication ceremony of Solomon's temple. America was selected as the "holy nation" whenever we came across such passages, despite the casual abuse of Scripture our interests rendered necessary.

Instead of "our daily bread," we want the whole bakery, and we want it not necessarily for the good of our neighbors.

Indeed, one Christian leader in Washington tells us, "As Israel came out of Egypt, our forefathers came out of Europe. Their 'wilderness' was the Atlantic Ocean."[12] These kinds of myths of America's "manifest destiny" pervade evangelical nationalism.

This same leader praises Jefferson for proposing "a national seal portraying Moses leading the chosen people into the promised land . . . ," even though he acknowledges that Jefferson was a deist.[13] My question is this: When we praise our founding fathers for their faith in God, are we talking about the same deity? Is the god to whom deists refer as the Governor, or the Benign Providence, or equal impersonal and relativized terms the triune God of Scripture who became man in the womb of a Jewish virgin, bore our sins, rose from the dead, and is destined to come again to judge the world? If not, they did not worship God any more than a Hindu worships God. Israel learned the hard way, again and again, that simply "any god" will not do; this is a lesson we desperately must be taught in our day. "Infidel" was the name ascribed to Jefferson, Adams, Franklin, and the like by their evangelical contemporaries, who nevertheless worked with them in the great democratic experiment. But today, these men are not only national heroes (as they should be), but saints in the American pantheon.

> *When the* church *becomes that political action committee and is perceived as a special interest group for a particular segment of society, it loses its integrity and public witness.*

In the nineties, divisions abound, and rather than being agents of reconciliation, evangelicals are perceived as radicals who want power. This is partly the result of media "smear tactics," based on the very public announcements, rhetoric, slogans, and actions of many Christian activists. They not only speak of fighting to have a voice (surely a legitimate request in a democracy), but of "taking America back" and ruling, with only Christians qualified to rule. Instead of "our daily bread," we want the whole bakery, and we want it not necessarily for the good of our neighbors, but, if the rhetoric is any indication, as our own part in the "will to power." We do not seem to be very interested in those things which concern those outside our particular socio-economic or racial interests.

For instance, National Association of Evangelicals executive, Robert Dugan, makes it clear what the organization's Office of Public Affairs is fighting for in Washington: It is against Aid to Families with Dependent Children and the Family Home Leave Act. One might argue that these programs actually end up undermining the family, but who can say that they are directly calculated to be "anti-family"? Many, especially evangelicals who are single working mothers (yes, there are millions of them!), might consider such programs pro-family. The NAE is also for higher "sin taxes" on alcohol and tobacco, and the organization, in the name of evangelicals generally, lobbies for support of public prayer and the teaching of morality in the public schools.[14] That needs some explanation, of course, since it is the evangelicals who have been doing the most complaining about the "secular humanism" of these public schools. We would like for the "secular humanists" to lead our children in prayer and teach them morality? Although the average evangelical Christian may identify with some or even all of the above positions, is there not a tremendous danger in an official ecclesiastical organization speaking so definitively for God and His church where God has not spoken? Surely there is a place for political action groups and lobbies, but when evangelicals participate in these in such a way as to be presuming to represent God and His church (with names such as "Christian Coalition" and the "National Association of Evangelicals"), we give the secularists some cause for cynicism concerning our allegedly "spiritual" causes.

Can anyone deny that the Christian Right is predominantly white and middle-class? There is nothing wrong with being white and middle-class. In fact, there is nothing wrong with special interest groups and lobbies existing in Washington to speak for the interests of white, middle-class people. But when the *church* becomes that political action committee and is perceived as a special interest group for a particular segment of society, it loses its integrity and public witness. Then it no longer exists to represent the whole truth for the whole world, but it becomes a tool of partial truth for a part of the world, masquerading as the church.

This is just as true, of course, for the Left. *Boston Herald* columnist Don Feder writes, "Mainliners aren't merely tolerant of idolatry; the churches themselves are steeped in paganism. . . .

Joan Brown Campbell, head of the National Council of Churches (Heresy Central), compares family-values advocates to pre-Civil War apologists for slavery. Paul Sherry, president of the United Church of Christ, called the gay rights march on Washington, where topless lesbians and male transvestites cavorted on the Mall, a 'marvelous moment.'" Feder asks, "With such shepherds, is it any wonder the flock is deserting in droves?" and concludes with the observation of one concerned mainline pastor, "They're committed to an ideology rather than a theology."[15] But this is true also today of conservatives. Instead of fighting ideology with ideology, the evangelicals must return to theology. Ideological radicals will die. Give them time.

This petition, "Give us this day our daily bread," brings us back down to earth. Those other crusaders may claim to be more "down-to-earth" than our discussions about raising our eyes to heaven, and so on, but they are just as heavenly-minded. The difference is, they believe they are building their towers *to* heaven. But in this petition, we are reminded that all of our activity in this world, though important, is not to be taken with inordinate seriousness. We are not building any towers to heaven by our activity; we are simply working for daily solutions to daily problems. The state exists to restrain evil and defend justice, not to make people less evil or more just. Nevertheless, restraining the damage that our evil hearts can accomplish is no small or insignificant task.

That is itself an important distinction, because we often confuse eternal and temporal solutions. For instance, when someone says, "Christians shouldn't care about politics; just preach the gospel," he or she is confusing salvation (eternal solution) with social concern (temporal problem). The Gospel is not the answer to everything. It is not the solution to the welfare crisis, to environmental decay, to health care. These are temporal problems demanding temporal solutions. Some solutions may work better than others, but no single solution to these particular problems comes with God's express support, and none, no matter how good, will ever be anything more than a temporal solution. If everyone became a Christian, the world would still require government, courts, police, and prisons, because Christians are still sinful. To think that conversion is the only answer to temporal problems is to assume that unbelievers are worse than they are (denying natural capabilities for justice, truth, and beauty) and that believers are better than they are (denying ongoing sinfulness in the Christian).

But this works the other way too. Just as conversion (eternal solution) is not the only answer for temporal problems, so political and moral solutions can never achieve ultimate victories. Think about it. Christians have, after all, been in charge of societies where great immorality, injustice, and horror prevailed. They have not only been inspired by Scripture to set slaves free; they have twisted Scripture to enslave masses. Genocides have been justified on the basis of building Christian civilization, so there is no guarantee that things will be rosy if Christians get into power. We are sinners too. Just as Paul criticized the Jews for thinking that the mere possession of the law meant that they were somehow better than the Gentiles, I think he would criticize us as well for assuming that adopting "Judeo-Christian principles" guarantees a good society. Must we be reminded of the pious evangelical Otto von Bismarck, who was nevertheless a nationalistic dictator, architect of "Germany Over All," and precursor to Hitler? Indeed, when piety serves a particular ideological agenda, even a relatively harmless injustice and tyranny can become infinitely more dangerous.

> *The objectives of the kingdom*
> *of God are not to make this world*
> *a better place, but to bring the*
> *lost to a saving knowledge of*
> *Christ and worship of God.*

Many leaders of the Religious Right employ language that causes the hearts of leaders on the Left to leap in delight that their caricatures have taken on flesh and bones. Many readers will be familiar with certain leaders' suggestions that only Christians and Jews are fit to govern the nation and prophecies concerning the day when Supreme Court justices will be speaking in tongues from the bench. Recently, the founder of Christian Coalition promised that "when the people say, 'we've had enough,' we are going to take over," the moment of desperation every dictator has exploited.[16]

I am not for one moment suggesting that Robertson wants to become America's first dictator. However, he could help avoid that impression if he would stop framing his speech in such demagogic terms. Reed's references to "stealth tactics" were widely publicized in recent months as well. "You don't know it's over until you're in a body bag," he warned the political enemy. [17]

CAN WE LEGISLATE MORALITY?

As long as we realize that our activity in the moral and political sphere is of temporal rather than eternal consequence, is it appropriate for Christians to attempt to influence legislation? Without question, it is our right and our responsibility. No one can seriously question the fact that every time a law is passed, morality has been legislated. Even our debates over health care are ultimately moral issues. Obviously, the only question is, *Whose* morality will be legislated? But before we act too hastily, let us assess our responsibilities to the two kingdoms.

> *Too often, I think, we do not realize*
> *that by trying to gain the world, we have*
> *lost our soul—and not only our own,*
> *but that of countless men and women*
> *who are hostile to Christians for reasons*
> *other than the scandal of the cross.*

First, in the kingdom of man, we can participate in the political process by voting, supporting candidates, running for office ourselves, protesting, and through other constitutionally protected means. But we are not only obligated to this kingdom; we are also members of another kingdom. The objectives of the kingdom of God are not to make this world a better place, but to bring the lost to a saving knowledge of Christ and worship of God. We must ask ourselves whether any given approach, agenda, or activity in the one kingdom will adversely affect the advancement of the other kingdom. If we put the interests of God's kingdom first, that activity cannot undermine the other kingdom, but a reversal of that order surely will adversely affect both. The priorities of the kingdom of God are no less essential for the church as a whole than for individuals: "But seek first his kingdom and his righteousness, and all these things will be given to you as well" (Matthew 6:33).

Surely individual Christians may participate in rallies and protests (although we must question the real long-term value of such tactics). Furthermore, we should encourage young people to enter a career in public service, as well as in other centers of leadership—not to "take over," but to work side-by-side with our non-Christian neighbors in that wide space called "common grace" and common ground. But the church itself must be aloof—not from real problems, but from particular political solutions and policies. Too often, I think, we do not realize that by trying to gain the world, we have lost our soul—and not only our own, but that of countless men and women who are hostile to Christians for reasons other than the scandal of the cross. They do not see us genuinely interested in helping them, but as one more minority demanding its rights. On the contrary, a politician who is a Democrat and one who is a Republican should be able to worship in the same congregation and hear God's Word preached in such a way that both can agree that it was God who was speaking through His servant.

Many engaged in these discussions refer to the "politicization of evangelicals," but we must be careful to distinguish two possible meanings. In one sense, it refers to the realization in the 1980s that Christians could make a difference in the political process and were poor stewards of their citizenship by not participating. Christian leaders called the faithful to exercise not only their rights, but their responsibilities, and many did so in a non-partisan manner. This "politicization" was quite proper. But there is "politicization" in another sense, all too common today. This refers to the confusion of heavenly and earthly things, that which is ultimate and that which is proximate in importance. Evangelicals may no longer be certain where that line is, frankly, because they are sophisticated neither in things heavenly (theology) anymore, nor really in things earthly (politics, cultural issues, literature, the arts, humanities and the sciences, philosophy, etc.). We are too ignorant to act in either sphere with integrity, beyond memorized rhetoric, simple slogans, and well-organized campaigns. In things heavenly, it's "try God" or the Four Spiritual Laws; in things earthly, it's "Aren't You Glad You Weren't Aborted?" If such approaches are not working (and they are not in either sphere), the proper response is not simply to turn the volume up, but to rethink the entire enterprise.

Therefore, we must begin not only to distinguish between heaven and earth; we must begin to question our public witness as Christians in terms of its likely impact on the progress of the Gospel. For instance, I do not oppose crusading against gay rights because I think homosexuality is acceptable; God calls it an abomination, and so must we. Furthermore, I would not have any moral problems with keeping the laws on the books making such an unnatural act criminal. But we have to come to terms with the facts: The crisis in America is not political or even moral at its root. The problem is that people have so suppressed their natural knowledge of God that such things have become "natural" (see Romans 1 and 2). Therefore, we must go deeper to the problem, deeper than politics or morality, deeper than protests and crusades. It must be a spiritual battle for hearts and minds—nothing less than a revival and a Reformation in our time.

> *Let us take this world seriously, with no illusions of a "Christian society" and at the same time, no embarrassment in seeking to influence our sphere of activity, to the glory of God and the good of our neighbor.*

Christianity, then, is the answer—the only answer—to the greatest problems humanity faces. But it is not necessarily the answer for everything humanity faces. While we look to God not only for salvation (the eternal), but daily bread (the temporal), we realize that He gives us the one through miracle (the new birth) and the other through providence (common grace, culture, politics, etc.). Simply because we will never have in this present age a holy nation, as Israel was and the church is in a spiritual sense, does not mean that we cannot have a better nation and that we cannot, as Christians, seek to make it a better place for our children and our neighbors. For God is not only concerned about our life in the next world, but about our life here and now, and it is not only souls, but bodies also, that fall under His jurisdiction. He is not only the Savior of the church, but the Sovereign of the state, even if that is not acknowledged by the Nebuchadnezzars of this world. One day they will be humbled. We must announce that and warn about that day. But we cannot bring that day to pass. It has already been appointed by the Father.

BEYOND POLITICS & MORALITY

When we think of Christians being "salt" and "light," we almost always reduce this public witness to evangelism, morality, and politics. But, as argued throughout this book, politics is not as all-encompassing and culture-shaping as other spheres. We have also seen the indictments from secular art critics for Christians attacking art, while producing little positive in that arena themselves, in contrast to their heritage. The following challenge from Thomas Fleming, in the journal *Chronicles*, ought to be taken seriously:

> Will this nation be a Christian America, whose reading is limited to *Heidi*, *Pollyanna*, and the confessions of Pat Boone, or will it be an open society that reads *Justine*, *Tropic of Cancer*, and *Last Exit to Brooklyn?* . . . I had several discussions with Christians who did not want *Sex* in the library. . . . When I asked each of them about their other attempts to influence library policy, they told me of previous controversies over questionable books. Had any of them actually asked the library to buy a book? Did their churches request books? Rockford is a heavily Lutheran and Catholic town. Were the works of Luther and Melanchthon available in German (and Latin) or even in translation? What about standard editions of the Church Fathers? St. Thomas? . . .
>
> The answer to all of the above is no. American Christians in this age of the world do not care for such things, neither the laity nor the preachers. They are too busy with stewardship, financial planning, and bingo. So long as the library does not positively offend them, they are content to let their taxes be squandered on best-selling novels and books, on rose gardening or travel. . . . Instead of working to improve the common culture, they are content to rail against the immorality of the "secular humanists." After de-

cades of efforts to ban nasty books, rate movies, and put warning labels on records, the Tipper Gores of America have contributed nothing, literally nothing positive to our culture. If only we could take all the money wasted on "decency" (including the money sent to TV evangelists) and spend it on good books by living authors. We could dominate the best-seller lists and enable decent writers to earn an honest living outside universities. We would have the beginnings of a cultural counterrevolution that could bypass the corrupt political process and go straight to the hearts and minds of the American natives.[18]

As long as fundamentalists and evangelicals have a *theology* that places them constantly in an adversarial relationship to this world and its culture, they will continue to involve themselves with art only when trying to censor it; with politics, only when it is a quest for control; with science, only when they want to oppose evolution; with victims of AIDS, only when they remind them that they deserve it; and with education, only when school prayer, sex education, and condoms are discussed. Where are we when the S.A.T. scores are falling? Telling the world that it is because public prayer was banned in schools in 1963!

Thus, our involvement in this world, inasmuch as it falls under "our daily bread" (i.e., the issues of this world), must not only be negative; it must be positive. It must not only be political and moral; it must be cultural, and it must not depend on mass organization, but on the responsibility each one of us has to fulfill his or her calling. Each one of us, whether a factory worker or an Ivy League professor, is responsible to contribute positively to his or her own sphere of influence which includes one's calling, family, relationships, neighborhood, and nation. Let us take this world seriously, with no illusions of a "Christian society" and at the same time, no embarrassment in seeking to influence our sphere of activity, to the glory of God and the good of our neighbor.

NOTES

1. Donald Bloesch, *The Evangelical Renaissance* (Grand Rapids: Eerdmans, 1973), 27.
2. Ibid.
3. Cf. Brother Lawrence, *The Practice of the Presence of God* (Springdale, Pa.: Whitaker, 1982) for one of the finest popular treatments of the doctrine of providence.

4. Pat Robertson, *Answers to 200 of Life's Most Probing Questions* (Nashville: Nelson, 1984), 204.

5. Ibid., 271.

6. Ibid., 269.

7. Ibid., 108.

8. Brother Lawrence, *The Practice*, back cover excerpt.

9. George Herbert, *Poets and Prophets, A Selection of Poems by G. Herbert* (Tring: Lion, 1988), 38.

10. Os Guinness, in an interview on The White Horse Inn, a broadcast of CURE, Inc.

11. Cf. Charles S. McCoy and J. Wayne Baker, *Fountainhead of Federalism: Heinrich Bullinger and the Covenantal Tradition* (Louisville: Westminster/John Knox, 1991); Sydney Ahlstrom, "The Puritan Ethic and the Spirit of American Democracy," in *Calvinism and the Political Order*, George Hunt, ed. (Philadelphia: Westminster Press, 1965); Brooks Holifield, *The Covenant Sealed* (New Haven: Yale Univ., 1974); Peter Lillback, "The Binding of God: Calvin's Role in the Development of Covenant Theology" (dissertation, 1985, Westminster Theological Seminary).

12. Robert Dugan, Jr., *Winning the New Civil War: Recapturing America's Values* (Portland: Multnomah, 1991).

13. Ibid., 152–53.

14. Dugan, *America's Values*, 97–102.

15. *Orange County Register*, August 11, 1993 (Metro section, 9).

16. Stephen Carter, *The Culture of Disbelief: How American Law and Politics Trivialize Religious Devotion* (New York/San Francisco: HarperCollins, 1993), 267.

17. *Time* magazine, September 13, 1993, 58.

18. *Chronicle* magazine, April, 1993, 12–13.

10

OUR GREATEST NEED

Today, we no longer believe that humanity needs to be saved from the wrath of God as much as we believe in the salvation of America from a loss of pride and self-esteem.

FORGIVE US OUR DEBTS, even as we forgive our debtors."

The national debt is a matter that should concern every Christian along with every other responsible citizen in America, and although genuine believers may differ widely on how it can be most effectively handled, surely the biblical imperative to be good stewards and pass down blessings instead of curses to our succeeding generations gives much cause for sober reflection. Nevertheless, as important as matters such as the nation's fiscal debt are in the realm of "our daily bread," Jesus raises our eyes in this line to our greatest concern: our debt before God.

We will do anything and everything to suppress the knowledge of God in His holiness. This is precisely what we are told in the opening chapters of Paul's epistle to the Romans. By retaining a knowledge of God, we are reminded of how far we fall short of attaining His approval, His respect, His acceptance. Moderns have learned to live with this problem by either ignoring it (Paul called it "suppressing the truth in unrighteousness") or by redefining the problem in modern language. Men and women are not guilty in any objective sense, but misdirected. God is not angry, just a bit disappointed that we are not realizing our full potential. Even the conservative evangelical churches today tend to downplay the guilt-and-grace message of Christianity in favor of themes more "relevant" (read "acceptable") to proud modern tastes. Yale's H. Richard Neibuhr had liberals in his sights with the following pristine crystallization of modernism, but his summary could equally apply to the message of many evangelicals today: "A God without wrath brought men without sin into a kingdom without judgment through the ministrations of Christ without a cross."[1]

David Walsh reminds us that in his classic, *The Fall*, Albert Camus argues, through his character Clamence, that the modern man and woman has either not found or has refused grace. Therefore, to deal with the guilt he has closed his universe, blocking "the door of the closed universe of which I am the king, the pope, and the judge."[2] We ought not to take modern secularism as any unique threat to Christianity, for it is just this illness that biblical faith has been diagnosing and curing for millennia. The symptoms may be nuanced, but they are in essential agreement with the age-old struggle with God. Knowing we are fallen, guilty, and condemned, we are looking for God as much as a murderer looks for a judge. So instead of facing our dilemma, we judge God. Adam blamed his sin on "the woman *You gave me*." It is not *our* debts, but *His* which concern us, if such matters concern us at all. Never mind *my* petty mistakes: How about Auschwitz, Nagasaki, Serbia —or my niece who died from cancer at twenty-seven? But what we must do as prophets is expose this understandable, but fatal, charade, holding out God's offer of Christ's righteous robe to cover the shame and nakedness we have so desperately tried to hide with modernity's sophisticated fig leaves.

What is more dangerous than the world's diagnosis with this illness is the church's. After all, if the island's only doctor is diseased, what is to become of the rest? What concerns me today is that just as we have forgotten to raise our eyes toward heaven, concerned with God's name and kingdom, we have also forgotten to confess our sinfulness and our need for divine mercy and forgiveness. We seem so busy judging the world that we have forgotten that the church is nothing more than that part of the world that stands under God's forgiveness and renewal. We think that the greatest sins of our day are committed by unbelievers, when in reality the church is in disarray theologically and ethically. I have found it ironic that many of the same brothers and sisters who engage in name-calling against non-Christians and show hostility toward unbelievers who disagree with them are also so resistant to self-criticism in the body of Christ. At the same time that the church is so vocal and sure of itself about what is wrong in society, it silences those who seek to question its own health. Perhaps, like Camus's Clamence, we are so fearful of judgment ourselves that we have attempted to beat God to the punch. We will be the king, pope, and judge.

We cannot expect people to accept Christian morality if they are not at least intellectually persuaded by Christian truth.

But, of course, we are not kings, popes, and judges. We are men and women—justified sinners, whose righteousness is "alien" —that is, not our own, but a gift from God. Whenever I see Christian leaders writing books on the perfect marriage while they are going through a divorce (I know of at least four cases in the last few years), and moral crusaders whose private lives are scandalous, I cannot help but think that much of this feverish activity is an attempt to hide our own weaknesses. By projecting our own sins on the world, we have our sacrificial lambs, but we must come back to the realization that our sins are *our* sins, but were carried by Christ our sacrifice.

CHRISTIANITY WITHOUT A CROSS

Earlier I quoted Nietzsche's remark concerning a European desire to take the fruit of Christendom (its morality) without its root: "One still hopes to get along with a moralism without religious background: but that necessarily leads to nihilism." Now what did he mean by that? Once a generation breaks away from its beliefs, it does not immediately plunge into moral anarchy. It takes some time for Dostoyevski's famous dictum to come true: "If there is no God, everything is permitted." If there is no theology, there can be no morality, Nietzsche and Dostoyevski are saying. After a generation or two passes, those values that were taken as "givens" (the value of life, meaning, truth, beauty, goodness) evaporate and people wonder, appropriately, why they follow certain patterns.

We are witnessing this right now in our own history. We ought not to be surprised that everything is being questioned in the realm of morality, since there is no longer any theological infrastructure undergirding it. Liberals *attacked* orthodox theology, while conservatives largely *ignored* it, so what more could we expect? This generation is simply riding on fumes. We cannot expect people to accept Christian morality if they are not at least intellectually persuaded by Christian truth. The greatest needs we have are theological, and the greatest of these is forgiveness.

Doctrine rather than ethics is at the heart of genuine evangelical faith. It is not that piety or practice is not important, but that it is not central. The cross is central, for it alone saves us.

Modernity starts from the premise that human beings are basically good. Therefore, the most important motif is progress and improvement. As we have seen in the most recent statistics, most evangelicals also start with that sinister premise and conclude, similarly, that the main business is moral improvement. To the extent that Pelagianism (belief in the inherent goodness of man and freedom of his will) reigns in any given age, to that degree will men and women have confidence in movements. Donald Bloesch reminds us, "Evangelical theology affirms against all kinds of Pelagianism and synergism that we are saved not by free will but by free grace. Augustine declared, 'Liberty comes by grace, not grace by liberty.'"[4] The problem is, evangelical theology today has become less evangelical and more modern.

Today, we no longer believe that humanity needs to be saved from the wrath of God as much as we believe in the salvation of America from a loss of pride and self-esteem. We see that objective in terms of moral improvement.

How far this is from the drama we find being played out in Scripture, where Adam's reach for self-deification left the entire race guilty and corrupt, with a will bound to sin, helpless to even lend a hand toward its own salvation. And then, Adam's reach for deification is matched by the Second Adam's willingness to lay aside the pomp of His deity in order to suffer and die for our sins. Here, we do not find a moral crusader who leads us by example to our individual and national salvation, but a redeemer who saves us by suffering our judgment as our substitute. This is why doctrine rather than ethics is at the heart of genuine evangelical faith. It is not that piety or practice is not important, but that it is not central. The cross is central, for it alone saves us. Christ came for sinners, not for the righteous. Good people do not need a Savior.

This was the issue between Jesus and the Pharisees, Paul and the Galatians, Augustine and the Pelagians, and the Reformers and Rome. It is the issue we face today, even in our own churches: Does God alone save, or do we save ourselves with God's help?

Jesus, Paul, Augustine, and the Reformers all emphasized that we could not save ourselves. Of salvation, Jesus said, "With men this is impossible, but with God all things are possible." In fact, our Lord informed the people, "No man can come to me unless the Father draw him" (John 6:44), and He told the Pharisees that their will was not free, but in bondage to sin (John 8:44). Jesus said that He was sent on a mission by His Father to save "all that he has given Me" (John 6:39). One could not even be saved by making a decision, since, as Jesus told His disciples, "You did not choose me; I chose you and appointed you to bear fruit that would last" (John 15:16). Therefore, in the new birth, we are "children born not of natural descent, nor of human decision or a husband's will, but born of God" (John 1:13).

Similarly, the apostle Paul taught that we were born "dead in trespasses and sins" and were "by nature children of wrath" (Ephesians 1:1–3). "The natural man does not accept the things of the Spirit of God; neither can he know them . . ." (1 Corinthians

2:14). "Therefore, it does not depend on man's decision or effort, but on God's mercy" (Romans 9:16). "For while you were dead he made you alive with Christ (by grace you are saved)" (Ephesians 2:5).

Our greatest problem is that we stand under the guilty verdict in heaven, and a day is coming when that appearance in court will make this subject the most acute "felt need" of our entire existence.

This tradition, extending from Christ and His apostles, to Augustine and the Reformers, insists upon the following positions: (1) human helplessness in spiritual things; (2) God's merciful prerogative in choosing whom He will save, apart from any foreseen merit; (3) Christ's substitutionary atonement, which was a legal payment for every transgression of the Law; (4) justification (the judgment of God that we are righteous) based solely on the righteousness of Christ imputed to our account; (5) the supernatural character of the new birth, which is not the result of human willing or running, but is itself the source of both. Protestants, both Lutheran and Reformed, deny that the new birth is the result of the believer's cooperation with divine grace.

Was there ever a creed more alien and yet more necessary for this particular hour?

HOW DO WE RECEIVE GOD'S FORGIVENESS?

If we are to return to the centrality of the cross as the *basis* for our forgiveness, then we must also recover the evangelical understanding of the *means* through which we receive it.

A. The Word

Once again, Bloesch offers a helpful definition: "Preaching is considered the primary means of grace, but not any kind of preaching; the vehicle of God's Spirit is the preaching of the law and gospel—biblical, kerygmatic preaching."[5] We cannot overestimate Bloesch's point here: The Word does not work magically. Nothing happens simply by reading the words off the page. It is a certain kind of proclamation that is a means of grace. It is not preaching "Ten Steps to a Happy Life" from the Book of Proverbs that is a means of grace, but the preaching of the Law and the Gospel.

In an earlier chapter we distinguished the Law and the Gospel, but it deserves a reminder here. When we are seeking favor with God, we often turn to the Scriptures for some help with the "principles" or "steps" of securing it. We are like the rich young ruler: "What is the one thing left for me to do?" But instead of offering helpful hints for happiness and favor with God, the Law convicts, breaks, judges, condemns. It cuts off our hope. Every time we begin to think we have found a way out of this crisis with a holy God, it steps in to show us that we have no way out. We must be judged. Just then, the Gospel steps in and says, "What the Law requires (which is to say, what a holy God requires)—absolute obedience and a perfect record, is precisely what was secured for all believers in Christ through His perfect obedience, death, and resurrection."

Without the preaching of the Law, the Gospel doesn't make any sense. If the wrath of God against sinners is not really an issue, what is the good news? That "God loves you and has a wonderful plan for your life"? That "you can be happier, healthier, and holier in Jesus"? Our greatest problem is not that we are lonely, unhappy, ill, psychologically or emotionally damaged, or "not quite the person we want to be." Our greatest problem is that we stand under the guilty verdict in heaven, and a day is coming when that appearance in court will make this subject the most acute "felt need" of our entire existence. How will we plead? On what basis? Therefore, the greatest news is that we can be justified.

One of the essential points in our evangelical history was that justifying faith required a specific object. Rome insisted that "faith" had God and the Bible in general as its object. In other words, to say "I have faith" meant "I believe in God, the Trinity, and everything contained in the Scriptures." However, the Reformers and their successors argued that the only way a person

217

could be justified (declared righteous) was by looking to Christ as the one who justifies the wicked *as* wicked. If we come to the unbeliever, especially in our day, with any invitation to accept God or Christianity that does not particularly bring this "word" or "announcement," it is not sufficient to elicit saving faith. It will always fall short of its mark. The Puritan Thomas Goodwin remarked:

> Go, take a man that is ungodly, and how will this man ever come to believe in God, unless under this notion, that he is one that justifies the ungodly? . . . It is not believing that God is true, or holy, or just, simply considered in himself, if a man believe these never so strongly, that will justify him not; but to believe on God under this notion, that he is a justifier of the ungodly, this is a man's faith which is accounted to him for righteousness. . . . Now go, take a sinner, he would never have any boldness, never have any confidence, so much as to come to God; he would have no heart to do it; he would be driven off from him, if he did not first look on God as in Christ.

Someone who is aware of his or her own sinfulness will never come to God until he or she receives the announcement that He has made peace. We all know, deep down, that we cannot make the peace, and we are not sure that He is willing—until the Gospel invitation makes that known. That is our mission as a church. No other revelation will speak about God to a sinner without driving the sinner into deeper hiding as he or she hears God's steps in the cool of the day. Not only is justification necessary, therefore, in order to reconcile us to God, but in order to reconcile God to us. Otherwise, "If we consider ourselves under the first covenant [in Adam], all the attributes of God come in upon us with terror. . . . [So] unto us *as sinners* it is God *as gracious*, God as justifying, it is God as in Christ revealed, which is the proper and special object of justifying faith" (italics added).[6]

Does this characterize our preaching today? Or is the diet in sermons, books, tapes, and broadcasts self-help, inspirational, moralistic, political, end-times-ish, or something else other than the preaching of the Law and Gospel—in short, something other than the preaching of Christ and Him crucified? This, of course, does not mean that every sermon must be concerned only with the Atonement and cannot address passages concerned with, say, the character of God, sanctification, election, adoption, or other great truths. But it is to say that the focus of every passage is Christ and His work on our behalf. After all, is it not the case that every spiritual blessing—including our sanctification, election, adoption, is ours only because of our union with Christ? (Ephesians 1:3 ff.).

B. Baptism

In addition to the Word, there are two sacraments. The first, baptism, introduces us to the family of God. While many evangelicals today would disagree over the meaning, mode, and subjects of baptism, there should be no doubt that when we are in doubt and our faith in God's forgiveness is sometimes overwhelmed by our awareness of just how much He has to forgive, we are reminded that God came to us before we came to Him. "We love him because he first loved us" (1 John 4:19). Sealed with the Holy Spirit through baptism, faith, and the Word, we are forgiven people.

C. Communion

Not only have evangelicals (and Christians generally) valued the Word and baptism highly; they also believe that the Lord's Supper is a sacrament. That is, it is a sign and seal through which He gives us what He promises us in the Gospel. "Revivalistic Protestantism has always been in danger of seeking the truth in an inward experience instead of in the Word and sacraments," writes Bloesch.[7] Forgiveness obtained through an experience can just as easily be lost, but God has given us His Word and sacraments as an objective means of giving and strengthening our faith in that promise. Not only do we *hear* God's forgiveness proclaimed in the Word; we *taste, smell,* and *touch* God's forgiveness as He puts it in our hands through the figures of bread and wine. This is not a Roman Catholic notion; it is the traditional evangelical view, much lost to us today.

One of the reasons people seem to experience so little "forgiveness" today is because of the diet of the preaching and the lack of confirmation through the sacraments. In fact, many evangelical churches have abandoned the use of sacraments altogether, which of course means that they no longer fit the evangelical definition. If our greatest need is forgiveness, then our next greatest need is for the faith to receive that forgiveness. And that faith comes by the hearing of the Word and is confirmed and strengthened by the use of the sacraments.

WHAT'S THE AGENDA?

For the last two decades, evangelicals have been picking up the language the liberals were using before them in their Social Gospel. One such word is "agenda." Instead of "doctrine," it's "agenda." We do not wish to waste valuable time and energy thinking about what we believe, even if we are confused. The important thing is that we *do* something.

I am utterly convinced that the world would be instantly attentive if it saw a church on its knees in repentance for its own sins.

But how often, in our conventions and rallies, have we put repentance on the agenda? I do not mean *national* repentance, as though we were the good people calling the bad people back to the fold in order to save America. I mean *personal* repentance. Have we become so self-righteous that we have forgotten our own sins? I was amazed during the scandals of "Pearlygate" in the eighties that so many Christian leaders were defensive, and instead of calling the whole church to repentance (since we know those highly publicized scandals are merely the tip of the iceberg of immorality in our own lives and churches), they attacked the media.

We are the ones who have brought disgrace to the name of God. It is we who have misused God's name, ignored His glory and truth, and sinned against Him in our pride. When I read, "American Christians have the manpower and the money to take back the power bases"[8] I wonder if there is any possibility for the Holy Spirit to break us and cause us to repent, with self-righteousness and self-confident pride topping the list. I am utterly convinced that the world would be instantly attentive if it saw a church on its knees in repentance for its own sins. Imagine what would happen if, next week, instead of a full-page ad in the major newspapers demanding our rights, there appeared an ad with the following lines:

> In recognition of our sins against God and our neighbors, by seeking our own interests and confusing our own aspirations with the will of God, we ask for your forgiveness. Our witness has often been marked by our own greed, power, scandal, self-righteousness, and competitiveness even with each other. We have not modeled the life of God's kingdom, nor have we served our chief purpose in terms of proclaiming the eternal realities which give hope and meaning to our lives here and now. When you came to our churches for bread, too often you were given stones. When you sought water to quench your eternal thirst, we were too busy with secondary pursuits. As we have received God's forgiveness, we ask for yours. And if you want to give us another hearing, we would like to get to know you—regardless of your ideology, politics, beliefs, or values. We may not agree with you, but this time you'll hear something about God and His kingdom. This time, we'll give you bread. We promise.

To be sure, it is not in itself a placebo for getting the ear of our culture, and it may be perceived as a false humility, but surely this ought to be our attitude, and not just our public relations campaign, before a watching but cynical world that so desperately needs to hear what only the church can tell it. Repentance is not merely something to which we must call others; we are all responsible for the evils of our time, as they transcend partisan lines. Vaclav Havel, playwright-dissident, in his inaugural speech as the president of a liberated Czechoslovakia in 1990, after describing the great economic and social crises, declared, "But all this is not even the main problem. . . . We have fallen morally ill *because* we became used to saying one thing and thinking another. We have learned not to believe in anything, to ignore each other, to care only about ourselves" (italics added).[9] This is not a partisan political statement, as Havel indicts everyone on both sides of the ideological divide. Referring to a great Czech Protestant Reformer, Havel also quoted the nation's first president after Czech independence, T. G. Masaryk: "Jesus, not Caesar."[10] May we have the courage to say the same, and believe the same in our current struggle.

CHRIST ALONE!

One of the slogans of the Protestant Reformation, "Christ Alone!" has been a hallmark of evangelical faith and piety for nearly 500 years, as indeed it has characterized faithful Christianity for nearly 2,000 years. That is not because we do not believe in God the Father and God the Holy Spirit, but because, when we are speaking of God's self-revelation and redemption, "there is no other name given in heaven or on earth by which a man can be saved" (Acts 4:12). Christ is the incarnate Word and Redeemer.

But this central affirmation of the Christian religion is undermined by both the left and the right these days. On the left, to actually declare in polite company that only those who place their trust in the atoning sacrifice and present mediation of Christ alone enjoy a saving communion with God is to invite ridicule and scorn for violating the dogma of tolerance. Never mind that it was Jesus Christ Himself who declared, "I told you that you would die in your sins; if you do not believe that I am the one I claim to be, you will indeed die in your sins" (John 8:24). John observes of this incident, "Even as he spoke, many put their faith in him" (v. 30). This has been the "rock" upon which the church has been built since the Messiah was promised to Adam and Eve in Genesis 3. Jesus announced, "I am the way and the truth and the life. No one comes to the Father except through me" (John 14:6), and He went on to say that the Jews could not know the Father unless they knew the Son.

Now, the unbeliever (and here I must include, for accuracy, not for spite, the religious liberal) may respond that this is simply my personal religious conviction, and surely there could be nothing more obvious than the fact that since I am the one making the statement, it is my personal religious conviction. But that does not make such a conviction right or wrong, the religious liberal implying the latter. After all, the belief that Jesus Christ is not necessary for a personal relationship with God is just as much a personal religious conviction. The real question is, therefore, whether it is possible to be a Christian in any meaningful sense apart from this fundamental agreement with the testimony of Christ and His apostles and the unbroken witness of Christians down through the ages. Only if the Bible is no longer our source for what we believe, and only if we are ready to believe that the entire church, for nearly two thousand years, has been fundamentally wrong until the dawn of religious pluralism in the United States, can Christians give up this essential conviction. It is, in short, this conviction which is the chief confession of every Christian.

Liberals often confuse such a confession with political intolerance, as if the belief that God does not hear the prayers of a Jew or Muslim is inherently subversive of public order. This, of course, was the charge of the Romans against the early Christians. And yet, much as orthodox Christians and deists debated each other's religious convictions at America's founding, there is no question that those who maintained this exclusive view of salvation were just as important in the crafting of separation of church and state and the provision of freedom of religion for every citizen. Their deep conviction of salvation through Christ alone hardly impeded Roger Williams and the Baptists, for instance, from engaging in profitable cooperation with Thomas Jefferson, who denied Christ's divinity, as together they built a nation where people were free to worship, or not worship, according to the dictates of conscience.

> *When evangelicals push for prayer in public schools, they are undermining the public proclamation of Christ alone just as surely as their most terrifying "secular humanists."*

In the interest of accuracy, civility, and the discouragement of bigotry, liberals must come to terms with this distinction between religious syncretism, which Christians cannot affirm, and religious tolerance, which Christians must affirm (and, in our history, have had some remarkable success in affirming). An orthodox believer simply cannot say that all religions are equally true or valid. Indeed, the law of non-contradiction would seem to apply to religion as well as other subjects, and I have been in lectures where liberal Christian theologians who tried to harmonize all religions only succeeded in driving the believing Christians, Muslims, and Jews to a united protest at such condescension and trivialization of their beliefs. Ironically, the "civility" was found after such lectures, as we gathered together for a cup of coffee to vent our frustrations at such nonsense, not in the classroom where religious apathy was championed in the interest of tolerance.

But the uniqueness of Christ and of Christianity is undermined by the Right also, in its insistence on a "public faith." Convinced of the myth of "Christian America," many conservative Christians believe that although no specific Christian denomination was constitutionally favored, the nation's "public faith" is generally Christian. In the first part of this century, most would have said that this consensus was generally "Protestant," but the influx of Roman Catholic immigrants and their increasing public significance eventually rendered it impossible to claim a one-to-one correspondence between America and Protestantism. But when one adds the insurgence of millions of new citizens from nearly every part of the globe, representing a matrix of unfamiliar religions, the definition of that "public faith" broadens to "Judeo-Christian." But what happens when Muslims, who are socially conservative, are offended at this exclusivity, and there are now more Muslims than Episcopalians? Perhaps we can expect the next Republican Convention to champion the "traditional monotheistic values upon which this nation was founded" and hear references from the Christian Coalition to its campaign for "theism."

However, for Christians, this simply will not do. It is not *a god* Christians worship, even if this god is distinguished from the religions of polytheism, pantheism, and atheism. Christians worship God as He has revealed Himself in Scripture and in the person and work of Christ. There is no other god, Christians must insist. But the championing of a public theology or "Christian Coalition" that obscures this fact is just as dangerous in its secularism as any challenges from the Left. When evangelicals push for prayer in public schools, for instance, they are undermining the public proclamation of Christ alone just as surely as their most terrifying "secular humanists." That is why the leading orthodox Protestant American theologian of the twenties, J. Gresham Machen, insisted, "The reading of selected passages from the Bible, in which Jews and Catholics and Protestants and others can presumably agree, should not be encouraged, and still less should it be required by law. The real centre of the Bible is redemption; and to create the impression that other things in the Bible contain any hope for humanity apart from that is to contradict the Bible at its root."[11]

That is surely not to say that there cannot be coalitions with non-Christians. But a choice must be made: If a group of Christians wishes to form a coalition for the purpose of influencing the moral, social, and political life of the nation, its members will have to be very clear that they are not building a "Judeo-Christian," "Christian," or religious consensus at all. It is not the place for political groups to create religious coalitions. Rather, such groups will have to be formed along very explicit lines of a cultural agenda which does not affirm or deny the essential creeds of each member in the coalition. To confuse Christianity with Judaism, Islam, or any other religion in the interest of securing cultural victories will prove just as damning for conservatives as for liberals.

Religious liberty rests not on the idea that all religions are equally true or valid. Just as the state cannot make any law ruling that one religion is true over another, it also cannot impose or foster the religious (indeed, devout) dogma that all religions are equally true. Judging such matters is outside the proper jurisdiction of government. Rather, the role of government in all of this is to keep those who disagree theologically from killing each other or trying to impose their creed by force. At present, government has extended its boundaries in this area, as in so many others, now defining its role in terms of preserving the equality of all religions. But those who take their beliefs seriously, Christian or not, must insist that it is the duty of government to preserve the *liberty* of all religions, not their *equality.*

James Madison, for one, anchored his defense of religious liberty not in the belief that orthodox Christianity was no truer than, say, Isis worship, but precisely because he was convinced that Christianity itself required civil liberty for everyone else as well as for itself, since "we cannot deny an equal freedom to those whose minds have not yet yielded to the evidence that has convinced us."[12]

As We Forgive Our Debtors

It is significant that our Lord links God's forgiveness of our sins to our own forgiveness of others. It is not linked in the sense that God conditions His forgiveness on our own, but in the sense that God's forgiveness creates the only real possibility for us to truly forgive our neighbors. Let me explain.

In the Old Testament, prophets often offer "imprecatory prayers," calling down God's judgment. Isaiah declares, "You have abandoned your people, the house of Jacob. They are full of superstitions from the east. . . . So man will be brought low and mankind humbled—*do not forgive them*" (Isaiah 2:9; italics added). Jeremiah cries out against his accusers, "Do not forgive their crimes" (Jeremiah 18:23). The Psalms are full of this sort of thing, as the psalmist calls down God's vengeance on all his oppressors. Such fearful language is only uttered justly by the prophets as they speak for God and foreshadow the final Prophet, Jesus Christ, who, at the end of the age, will judge His enemies and accusers.

In Jesus' day, however, the average man thought he could engage in imprecatory prayers and call down curses upon his enemies. If David did it, why can't we? But, of course, David could do so precisely because he was a forerunner of the Messiah. Just as when he offers his "messianic psalms" that could only refer to Christ and could not even refer to himself (even though they are in the first person), the imprecatory psalms are not a pattern for us, but a foreshadowing of Christ's vengeance on the Day of the Lord.

This is the background, then, for our Lord's insistence that we forgive our enemies. "You have heard that it was said, 'Love your neighbor and hate your enemy.' But I tell you: Love your enemies and pray for those who persecute you, that you may be sons of your Father in heaven" (Matthew 5:43–44). First, in saying, "You have heard that it was said . . ." Jesus is not referring to the Scriptures, for in Scripture only the anointed prophets are allowed to call down curses on their enemies. In fact, through Moses God commanded the people, "Do not seek revenge or bear a grudge against one of your people, but love your neighbor as yourself. I am the Lord" (Leviticus 19:18). What Jesus was referring to was the rabbinical teaching and the common practice that opened the judgment of unbelievers up to everybody. They had their eschatology wrong, thinking that this was the age of judgment, but Jesus made it clear repeatedly that He had come into the world *this* time for salvation, not judgment (John 3:17) and that the true children of God will imitate His patience in waiting until the *second* coming for judgment.

We have already referred to our Lord's rebuke of James and John for wanting to call fire down from heaven on those Samaritans who had not welcomed Jesus. This is the period of common grace, as Jesus adds in our Matthew 5 passage: "He causes his sun to rise on the evil and the good, and sends rain on the righteous and the unrighteous" (v. 45). If a holy God can endure insults, surely unholy Christians can.

In other words, when Jesus tells us to pray, in this same context, "Forgive us our debts as we forgive our debtors," (Matthew 6:12), He is not saying, "For every sin which you do not fully forgive, God will hold one of your own against you," as if we could be saved by our own forgiveness! Rather, He is saying that just as this is the age in which God has decided to forgive *us* when He could just as well have judged us, so we must accept God's common grace and imitate His charity, as "sons of [our] Father in heaven" (5:45). If we, being evil, cannot extend forgiveness to our enemies because of their evil, how was it that we came to believe that God could forgive us?

It is time for judgment to begin in God's house and God's invitation to peace and forgiveness to be extended to the world. As it is, the order is reversed.

Ultimately, God has forgiven our wickedness even to the extent that we do *not* "forgive and forget." Is there anyone in your life you have never really forgiven? Do you harbor absolutely no ill will or grudge against anybody? This is why Jesus adds, "Be perfect, therefore, as your heavenly Father is perfect" (5:48), to drive us to realize that we cannot be forgiven by *trying* to forgive as best that we can, or by *approximating* God's forgiving spirit. Nothing short of perfection will do, and this drives us to realize that we can no more be justified by forgiving others than by perfectly obeying any of the other commandments.

The irony in all of this is that the very despair this creates, when it leads us to embrace God's forgiveness *even for our sin of not forgiving others,* is the portal through which we enter the true freedom to forgive them! When the Law commands me to forgive someone who has wronged me, the first reaction is to intensify my anger. But when the Gospel tells me I am already forgiven, in spite of *my* debts and transgressions against God, then I am free for the first time to forgive even those who will one day be judged by God. On *that* day, we will join the Prophet Jesus in his imprecatory curses. "Therefore judge nothing before the appointed time; wait till the Lord comes. He will bring to light what is hidden in darkness and will expose the motives of men's hearts" (1 Corinthians 4:5). On *that* day, "the saints will judge the world" (1 Corinthians 6:2). For now, we judge in our own assemblies, but we do not judge the world: "I have written you in my letter not to associate with sexually immoral people—not at all meaning the people of this world who are immoral, or the greedy and swindlers, or idolaters. In that case you would have to leave this world," which is precisely the separation Christians suggest from time to time, even while they tolerate scandal in their own ranks. No, Paul says, he is referring to "anyone who *calls* himself a brother," but thinks he can live like a pagan. "What business is it of mine to judge those outside the church? Are you not to judge those inside? God will judge those outside" (1 Corinthians 5:9–13).

In our day, the church resembles Corinth, with its attraction to slick preachers and signs and wonders—an immature church that cares little for doctrine or discipline. Those who know the insides of their own churches today and are familiar with the scandals commonly reported with glee by the secular press can identify with Paul's complaint, "It is actually reported that there is sexual immorality among you, and of a kind that does not occur even among the pagans" (1 Corinthians 5:1). It is time for judgment to begin in God's house and God's invitation to peace and forgiveness to be extended to the world. As it is, the order is reversed.

At the same time, forgiveness is also to be preached to the church. This is not meant to lead the believers back into bondage to fear, but to warn those in the church who are laboring under a false security. We must put our own houses in order, so that the offense is in the message and not in the messengers.

CONCLUSION

So, this is the hour of forgiveness, the Day of Salvation. The Day of Judgment is coming, but God will execute that at the end of history. Is the preaching of the Law and Gospel, repentance and faith, despair and forgiveness, the heart of our public witness? Do we really believe that the greatest need in our land today is for men and women to be reconciled to a holy God through faith in the cross? After all, the Gospel is our only "power base" as a church (Romans 1:12). Is our worship focused on this message, with the Spirit-empowered preaching of the Word and the administration of the sacraments setting the agenda for all areas of church life? If not, let us put that at the top of our list. Let this become the vision for the church as it makes its way into the twenty-first century. Then we will see the glory of God and the power of God turn back the dark curtain of secularism before our very eyes. As the Reformation slogan expressed it, *Post tenebras lux,* "After darkness, light!"

NOTES

1. H. Richard Niebuhr, *The Kingdom of God in America* (New York: Macmillan, 1937), 30.
2. David Walsh, *After Ideology: Recovering the Spiritual Foundations of Freedom* (New York/San Francisco: HarperCollins, 1990), 146.
3. Friederich Nietzche, *Will to Power,* 16.
4. Donald Bloesch, *The Evangelical Renaissance* (Grand Rapids: Eerdmans, 1973), 63.
5. Ibid., 78.
6. Thomas Goodwin, *Works,* vol. 8, 292–93.
7. Bloesch, *Renaissance.*
8. Randall Terry, *Why Does a Nice Guy Like Me Keep Getting Thrown in Jail?* (Lafayette, La.: Huntington House, 1993), 46.
9. In William Safire, ed., *Lend Me Your Ears* (New York: Norton and Norton, 1992), 630.
10. Ibid., 632.
11. J. Gresham Machen, in *Education, Christianity and the State,* John W. Robbins, ed. (Jefferson, Md.: The Trinity Foundation, 1987), 64.
12. James Madison's *Memorial and Remonstrance* (1785).

11

BREAKING THE TEMPTER'S SPELL: WHAT SPIRITUAL WARFARE IS REALLY ABOUT

It is time for us to realize our own helplessness. We are not as strong as we thought we were. We cannot bring in the kingdom or "Christian America" by our zealous works and self-confident unveilings of new crusades.

AND LEAD US NOT INTO TEMPTATION, but deliver us from evil."

Earlier, I referred to Homer's classic, the *Odyssey*, where the hero, sailing past the isle of the Sirens, resists the seductive power of their singing by stopping up his crew's ears and having himself tied to the ship's mast. Our Captain not only was nailed to the cross for our sins; He interceded and still intercedes for us in our temptation. Our Lord not only taught us to ask God to deliver us from temptation in the prayer He taught His disciples. He Himself prayed,

I will remain in the world no longer, but they are still in the world, and I am coming to you. Holy Father, protect them by the power of your name—the name you gave me—so that they may be one as we are one. . . . My prayer is not that you would take them out of the world but that you protect them from the evil one. They are not of the world, even as I am not of it. Sanctify them by the truth; your word is truth. As you have sent me into the world, I have sent them into the world. For them I sanctify myself, that they too may be truly sanctified. (John 17:11, 15–19)

First, Jesus makes it clear that we do not avoid temptation by being removed from the world. Worldliness is just as great a temptation in the well-cloistered, "separated" evangelical subculture, as we have seen. It is not separation *from* the world for which Jesus prays, but separation *in* the world. Second, he prays for our protection from the evil one. This protection does not come through "binding" demons and spirits, nor through pious exercises, but through the *name* of God, the *truth* of God's Word, and the *righteousness* and *holiness* of Christ, our Lord tells us here in John 17. The name of God is protection, not as a magical talisman that we use for authority over evil, sickness, and temptation, but because "everyone who calls on the name of the Lord will be saved" (Romans 10:13); the truth of God's Word is protection, since "faith comes by hearing the Word of God" (Romans 10:17); and the sanctification of Christ is protection, since "he has become for us . . . our righteousness, holiness, and redemption" (1 Corinthians 1:30). Christ sanctified Himself from the world not only as our example, but in order to *be* our sanctification before the Father. Although our progressive sanctification is never complete in this life, we are already holy because we are in Christ. Therefore, the evil one no longer has any authority over us. We are already saints.

It is not separation from *the world for which Jesus prays, but separation* in *the world.*

We find the same witness in Ephesians 6, in the description of our "full armor" against "the devil's schemes" (v. 10). Many today interpret this either in a moralistic direction, where we are supposed to somehow cultivate or come up with each piece in the armor. Others use this text as the call to the troops for political action, even though Paul explicitly says that this is not a war "against flesh and blood, but against the rulers, against the authorities, against the powers of this dark world and against the spiritual forces of evil in the heavenly realms" (v. 12). Still others cast it in a mystical vein, where the spiritual warfare described here is a matter of our binding demons and exercising spiritual authority over the powers of darkness. But Paul makes his point very clear upon closer inspection.

First, Paul says that the purpose of this armor is so that "you may be able to stand your ground," particularly against the insults and accusations of Satan. There is the belt of *truth*, the breastplate of *righteousness*, feet prepared with the *gospel* of peace, the shield of *faith*, the helmet of *salvation*, and the Sword of the Spirit, "which is the Word of God" (vv. 14–17). One readily notices a common theme here. Each piece of the armor has something to do with the objective Gospel. Not one piece of this armor is something we have fashioned. Nowhere in the list, for instance, is "the pistol of piety" or the "boots of a good heart and cheerful attitude." That is not because piety is unimportant, or because our inner experience is insignificant, but because when the enemy comes, he is not coming to "bind" our house or give us generational curses; he is coming to strip us of our faith in the Gospel. He is coming to try to persuade us that we are too sinful, too unholy for Christ to love or to save. We have not advanced enough in the Christian life; we have quenched the Spirit, perhaps we have even committed the unpardonable sin. It is faith that unites us to Christ and all His benefits, so if the devil can take away our confidence in His atoning work, he couldn't care less about wreaking temporal havoc on our family line.

Once again, it all depends on what we think is the greatest problem. If sickness, poverty, political and moral problems, culture wars, and the like are the chief problems, obviously we do not need the kind of armor Paul is talking about here: the Gospel, faith, justification, the Word, and truth. But if the real war is over eternal destiny, these defenses make perfect sense. What are you going to say when Satan brings you doubts about your salvation? Are you going to put the straw of your own imperfect piety or the strength of your heart or activism in the world or in the church in front of the devil's arrows? What you require is the steel breastplate of *Christ's* righteousness. Instead of flimsy experiences, you need truth as the basis for your hope. In other words, Paul says, feed your mind and heart on theology—not as some intellectual game, but for the very survival of your faith in the storms of doubt and despair. As important as the *internal* witness of the Spirit is, Mormons claim a "burning in the bosom" as justification for their hope too, so what you need is the *external* witness of the Spirit working through the Word.

So it is more than coincidence that our Lord follows, "Forgive us our debts . . ." with "And lead us not into temptation, but deliver us from evil." Of course, the devil's assault is not only against our faith, but against our practice, and we are to pray for God's protection not only for our faith in the Gospel, but for our witness before the watching world and our conformity to Christ's image.

In this valley of decision, we can either refuse to accept our helplessness to save ourselves and America, or we can welcome the bad news as an opportunity to take the good news seriously again.

But if we *have* been sidetracked or seduced into the reef of inculturation by the Sirens' song, what can break the spell? If we have succumbed to temptation and given in to evil, how, after receiving forgiveness, do we pull the ship together and set sail again for a safer harbor?

ARE WE WILLING TO ACKNOWLEDGE OUR HELPLESSNESS?

We have already seen how saturated evangelicalism is with the culture's optimistic view of human nature. Helplessness is not something we Americans like to talk about, but it is ever on the mind of the biblical writers and empirically demonstrated in our own lives and in the world. We know we are not all-competent, but we try to pull it off. We are a very proud nation, and even as Christians in America, we are extremely self-confident. For years, I attended the big evangelical conventions where visits by the president of the United States and famous movie stars fed our ambition to keep up with the very worldliness for which we self-righteously condemned the world. Christian leaders announced campaigns for "x" millions of souls by the year 2000, with extravagant media blitzes that, in retrospect, seem to have added no numbers of note to the church. Then, in the next breath, it was said that evangelicals would get America back. It had been stolen from them, but they would retrieve it, and things were couched in this "us/them," "mine/not yours" language we were supposed to have outgrown after the sandbox days.

Little do we realize that by choosing these tactics, we are actually giving secularism a boost up to higher windows of opportunity. We are participating in the power struggle mentality of the Washington lobbies. Instead of being the means to power, this strategy weakens the witness of Christians by reducing Christianity to a competing special interest group. Instead of trying to persuade people of the universal truth claims of Christ, based on the reliability and historicity of His resurrection, we are settling for half-measures. Even if the Christian Right did achieve all of its political and moral aims, we would have to ask, (1) Are these the chief moral concerns of Scripture, or of our particular social group? And, more importantly, (2) Have people been added to the church? Has this produced a greater openness to the Gospel in our culture? But, of course, the Christian Right has not even achieved any one of its major policy objectives, and its hostile rhetoric is only deepening the culture's animosity.

> *Renewal does not begin with society,*
> *but with me; and not with my actions,*
> *but with my mind.*

It is time for us to realize our own helplessness. We are not as strong as we thought we were. We cannot bring in the kingdom or "Christian America" by our zealous works and self-confident unveilings of new crusades. In this valley of decision, we can either refuse to accept our helplessness to save ourselves and America, or we can welcome the bad news as an opportunity to take the good *faith*

news seriously again. I hope we will decide to share David's joy, as he exclaimed, "Now I know that the Lord saves his anointed; he answers him from his holy heaven with the saving power of his right hand. Some trust in chariots, and some in horses, but we trust in the name of the Lord our God. They are brought to their knees and fall, but we rise up and stand firm" (Psalm 19:6–9).

Once we acknowledge our helplessness not only to save ourselves, but to save anybody else, we are ready to be used by God. We cannot create faith, but we can preach the Word and depend on the Spirit of God to create faith. We cannot make the dry bones live, but we can preach to the bones and leave the rest of the business to God.

ARE WE WILLING TO THINK?

The reason the sailors in the *Odyssey* fell, boat after boat, under the seductive powers of the Sirens was that each captain and each crew thought it could resist them. We too have been very confident in our abilities at resisting worldliness and secularism. After all, "we don't dance, drink, smoke, or chew, or go with girls who do," and so while the devil has us congratulating ourselves on avoiding a decoy, he has pulled us into the very reef itself, and we are taking on water. The first step in breaking the tempter's spell, then, is to recognize that we have been seduced as we seek to assess the damage. This means we will have to understand both Scripture and our modern world more thoroughly than we have. Just as it is true that those who do not know their history are doomed to repeat it, it is just as true that those who do not know what it is that shapes the worldview of their time and place will not be able to resist its lies. As it has been said, "You cannot *beware* of that which you are not *aware* of," and before it is a moral or political force, secularism is a spiritual and intellectual system.

If we are to resist the temptation to worldliness, we will have to renew our study of Scripture, not just for devotions, but in order to think differently. "Do not conform any longer to the pattern of this world, but be transformed by the renewing of your mind" (Romans 12:2). Renewal does not begin with society, but with me; and not with my actions, but with my mind. It is the renewing of the *mind*, Paul says, that breaks the grip of secularism. It must not end there, but it cannot begin anywhere else. We need to think differently first, and that is why Paul says elsewhere, "For though we live in the world, we do not wage war as the world does. The weapons we fight with are not the weapons of the world. On the contrary, they have divine power to demolish strongholds. We demolish *arguments* and every pretension that sets itself up against the knowledge of God, and we take every *thought* captive to make it obedient to Christ" (2 Corinthians 10:3–5). In other words, the war in which we are engaged is not a "culture war" in which we use political power to achieve our objectives, but it is a war of arguments. We are to be concerned first with our own capitulation to secularism. We first must make our own thoughts prisoners of Christ. And then we are prepared to engage in discussion and debate, trying to persuade people of our position with good arguments.

Are we willing to think? Are we willing to put the intellectual questions at the top of our agenda and deal with philosophical and theological issues before we engage in particular applications of those beliefs? Or will we try to use political power and economic pressure, giving the impression that what we cannot gain by persuasion we will secure by power?

ARE WE WILLING TO REPUDIATE SECULARISM?

When one asks if we are willing to repudiate secularism, the likely conservative evangelical response is, "What do you mean *repudiate* it? We've been fighting the N.E.A., N.O.W., N.A.R.A.L., People for the American Way, and Clinton." We have greatly misunderstood the nature of secularism and underestimated the reach of its tentacles. For instance, we have seen the dependence of American Christians on modernity for its view of the self, authority, progress, and so on. The church growth movement is rapidly becoming a religious version of Madison Avenue and Broadway. On the same Christian radio station, on the same day, some political activist will be railing against secular humanists, and the next speaker will push Maslow and Jung (humanistic psychologists) on the narcissistic masses with Bible verses wrested from their context. In many cases, in fact, it will be the same person! We cannot preach that Americans are good people who need a moral environment, that self-esteem and self-fulfillment are legitimate Christian obsessions, and a host of other modern heresies and then condemn "secularism."

There is yet another question in all of this. Even if we do untangle ourselves from secularism, can we beat it on its own turf? Many question whether the cultural war can be won by conservatives because, as one has observed, "It is always fought according to the enemy's rules: openness, majority rule, impartiality, notions that are poison to any vital religious tradition claiming to represent the truth."[1] Thus, we actually accelerate defeat (secularization) in the process of attempting victory. This surely falls into the category of "winning the battle, but losing the war." And that is if we actually were to achieve victory in the battles themselves, which, as Carl Henry points out, has not in fact happened: "Moral Majority achieved none of the legislative specifics it endorsed. It therefore raised new questions over whether politically active fundamentalists were now expecting too much from politics in an era when secular humanism has ensnared Western society and is itself deteriorating into raw paganism."[2]

> *Instead of being driven by sociology, marketing, pop-psychology, emotional revivalism, or politics, are we willing to see the great themes of the Christian faith as central to the church's mission and message and the need of the hour?*

It also raises new questions over whether politically active fundamentalists were expecting too much from themselves, since fundamentalism and evangelicalism, as we have seen, are at present too much a part of the problem to be a significant part of the solution. Note Os Guinness's remarks in this regard: "Christendom's ultimate worldling today is not the Christian liberal but the Christian conservative. The contemporary church's prototypical charlatan is not the medieval priest but the modern evangelist."[3] When Karl Marx declared, for instance, in the *Communist Manifesto*, that in modern capitalism "All that is solid melts into air, all that is holy is profaned," he seems to have hit the mark at least on that point. One look at our Christian bumper stickers and T-shirts will bear that out. We are commercial, consumeristic, materialistic, and narcissistic. One trip to the local Christian bookstore will demonstrate the Babylonian captivity of the church to pop-psychology, big business, marketing, and the ethic of "personal peace and affluence."

ARE WE WILLING TO PUT THEOLOGY FIRST AGAIN?

Instead of being driven by sociology, marketing, pop-psychology, emotional revivalism, or politics, are we willing to see the great themes of the Christian faith as central to the church's mission and message and the need of the hour?

In the postmodern context, with all its own problems, there is nevertheless an openness to eternal realities. Although it may be more difficult to claim the universal character of Christian truth, at least society is beginning to open up to many of the forgotten images of childhood. Once more, I am indebted to David Walsh's insights on Dostoyevski. Tolstoy was a utopian moralist who attempted to save humanity through politics, in the name of Christianity. Dostoyevski makes no bones about where he stands in relation to this enterprise, in his work *Under the Rubble*, where "Korsakov explains that without this understanding of the Incarnation and the Resurrection, original sin and the Atonement, even an individual as saintly as Tolstoy could display 'that same old tendency to deify Man, with his inability to resist temptation, that same alluring path of unswerving cast-iron logic, leading ultimately to the Antichrist and the Grand Inquisitor.'"[4] In other words, it does not matter whether it was done in the name of Christianity; Tolstoy was trying to deify man, the irresistible human temptation. "What is missing in the liberal exhortation to simple moral goodness, even as heroically exemplified by the 'Christianity' of Tolstoy, is an awareness of the depth of evil that tugs on the human heart. This lack of awareness fails to recognize the extent to which the thinker's reasoning itself is infected with the disease."[5]

This disease which infected a liberal like Tolstoy also infects conservatives today. Walsh, a Roman Catholic philosopher and political scientist, is closer to a classical evangelical response than most of us today: "The innermost bastion of pride can only be finally dissolved through the acknowledgement that all the goodness we possess is not ours by nature or effort, but entirely by the gift of divine goodness itself. What frees us from the burden of self-perfection is the realization that it is not within our power to achieve. We must be brought to experience our own helplessness in the struggle against evil, in order to discover the reality of grace as the source of transforming goodness and love. It is the distinctly Christian experience of grace, of human helplessness and God's love, that is here identified in Solzhenitsyn as the foundation of order in existence."[6]

And yet, neither Solzhenitsyn nor Walsh goes far enough, it seems to me. The evangelical wants not only to affirm this Augustinian orthodoxy of "grace alone," but he wants to go the further step to argue the point of the Reformation that the liberating power of grace is not found first in its *transformative* character—important as that is, but in its *imputational* character. We not only want to appeal to God's grace as something that *converts* and *improves*, but as something that *declares*. It declares the individual righteous even while he or she is still sinful, even before grace has begun its work of moral transformation. Apart from justification of the sinner before the face of God even *as sinner,* the guilt and just fear of condemnation cannot be dealt with. And until that wall of anxiety can be breached, we will forever make ourselves the ones who must judge God before He gets the chance to judge us.

ARE WE WILLING TO ACCEPT SCRIPTURAL AUTHORITY?

Again, this seems like a silly question to ask evangelicals. After all, many evangelicals even believe in the inerrancy of the original autographs, so is it not a bit odd to ask whether they are willing to accept scriptural authority? Not really.

Just as the full armor includes the Gospel and everything that it brings to the believer, it includes the Word as our only authority. At the time of the Reformation, everybody assumed the trustworthiness of Scripture. Rome, the Reformers, the Anabaptists: Everyone was agreed that the Bible was infallible. The difference was that Rome said that other things were infallible, too, in their *interpretation* of Scripture: councils and popes. Anabaptists often emphasized the "Spirit" over the Word, as if Rome trusted in the word of the pope, Protestants in the word of the Bible, but they trusted in the Spirit who addressed them sometimes in Scripture, and sometimes in other places.

This is why the Reformers came up with the slogan *sola Scriptura*, "only Scripture," because it was not enough to say that the Bible was inspired, infallible, inerrant; it must be sufficient for faith and practice. Today, we not only do not enjoy unanimity on the infallibility of Scripture (not because of modernity's better arguments, but because of its steady, pounding influences); even those who accept its full trustworthiness on paper often do not really see it as sufficient in matters of doctrine and Christian practice. Our real authorities are secular, judging by some of the most popular books being read by pastors these days. We believe that if it is theology, it is in the realm of speculation, but if it is a survey or a sociological study, a political analysis from a professor at a leading university, a psychologist who has developed an entirely new approach to self-esteem, or a business guru giving us his reading of the parables through the medium of a success story, here is truth.

> *We must persuade our contemporaries*
> *that we have as much to say*
> *to the postmodern situation*
> *with our Bibles under our arms.*

Often, I find myself analyzing a particular argument that I know is at odds with the biblical view of God, the self, and so on, but I will uncritically accept it because it "makes sense." But why does it make sense? Because I am being "conformed to the pattern of this world." In other words, it does not make sense because it is more reasonable or logical, but because it fits with the other things I hear from the world. We do not have to actively pursue this worldly orientation. It is there in our mothers' milk, in the air we breathe as we grow up. But we do need to actively pursue transformation of our thinking. There is no standing still in this business. This does not mean that we cannot find great wisdom and even truth in secular philosophies and ideologies, but that when it comes to our final court of appeals, Scripture judges every thought and tests every authority.

Out of their heritage (Russian Orthodoxy), Solzhenitsyn and Dostoyevski anchor their hope in the authority of an eternal, transcendent church embodied in the Russian civilization. But as evangelicals, we must anchor it in an eternal, transcendent Word, to which the whole church bears (or ought to bear) witness. Ironically, when these writers appeal to a transcendent *church*, after coming through the fires of disillusionment with modernity, they are hailed as "postmodern," whereas those who appeal to a transcendent *Word* above the church are often forced by the new academic establishment to wear the shibboleth of disdain, "premodern," like a scarlet letter, however much one may have experienced the same disenchantments and repudiated the same myths. But we must persuade our contemporaries that we have as much to say to the postmodern situation with our Bibles under our arms. This is the burden of the present generation of evangelicals who must be faithful to Scripture *and* to the mission field to which God has called us in His gracious providence.

NOTES

1. Donald Bloesch, *The Evangelical Renaissance* (Grand Rapids: Eerdmans, 1973), 35; citing Fleming, 15.
2. Carl Henry, in *Evangelical Essentials* (Grand Rapids: Zondervan, 1991), 23.
3. Os Guinness, "Mission in the Face of Modernity," in *The Gospel in the Modern World*, edited by Martyn Eden and David Wells (Leicester, England: IVP, 1991), 86.
4. David Walsh, *After Ideology: Recovering the Spiritual Foundations of Freedom* (New York/San Francisco: HarperCollins, 1990), 205.
5. Ibid., 165.
6. Ibid.

12

WHOSE KINGDOM, POWER, AND GLORY?

We are in desperate need of recovering our eternal per-
spective—raising our eyes toward heaven, so that our
sanity may be restored and so that God's kingdom,
power, and glory might once again occupy the attention
of the church and the culture.

SO FAR, OUR LORD, in such simple profundity, has given us a brief, but pregnant, statement of theology, a prescription for secularism in the form of a prayer—raising our eyes toward heaven. We have access to the one true God, creator of heaven and earth, because, through the saving sacrifice and mediation of Christ, we have been made sons of God and co-heirs of Christ. Paul put it this way: "Blessed be the God and Father of our Lord Jesus Christ, who has blessed us with all spiritual blessings in him," heading the list with election, adoption, redemption, faith, and sealing, with the Holy Spirit given as "a deposit guaranteeing our inheritance until the redemption of those who are God's possession—to the praise of his glory" (Ephesians 1:3–14).

Therefore, we can call God "Father": "For you did not receive a spirit that makes you a slave again to fear, but you received the Spirit of sonship. And by Him we cry, "Abba, Father" (Romans 8:15). Nevertheless, He is our Father *in heaven*, and this spans the gulf between God and us, the Creator and the creature. Beyond the matter of our sinfulness, our mere creatureliness puts a distance between God and us, just as even the greatest masterpiece of Rembrandt is still not Rembrandt. As we raise our eyes toward heaven, where the anchor of our hope still holds, where Christ the Advocate intercedes for us and where we ourselves are seated with Him, all earthly hopes, relationships, and inheritances obtain their proper, sane appraisal and perspective. They do not vaporize, as in mysticism; rather, they come into even sharper focus.

The doxology, "For thine is the kingdom, the power, and the glory forever. Amen," appears in later manuscripts and may well not have been a part of the original prayer. Regardless, it summarizes the prayer, and we have no reason to judge it contrary to Scripture even if there is a chance that it is not, in fact, such.

IT BELONGS TO GOD, AND HE IS BUILDING IT

The word from which we get "secular" is the Latin *saeculum*, taken from the Greek *aion*, meaning "age." In context, it refers to what Paul in the New Testament called "this present evil age" (Galatians 1:4), in distinction to "the age to come" (Ephesians 1:21; cf. Hebrews 6:5). Historically, Christians have walked this tightrope between the "already" and the "not yet," meaning that the kingdom is present, and yet it has not been fully consummated; there is, therefore, a tension. Of course, the claims of eternity drive the believer toward sanctification, and no one is a purely private individual. As we are changed, we seek to change our environment. And yet, we cannot get too carried away with this process of transformation, since we realize that the day of final judgment is left to Christ at the end of history. Thus, *secularization* is the process of either downplaying the significance or even existence of God and His reign in this world right now through Jesus Christ, or of affirming that reign as embodied in a particular set of secular goals, values, and ideals. In other words, not only does the so-called "secular humanist" secularize society when trying to remove any mention of God or religion from public institutions; the evangelical Christian also secularizes society when God becomes Uncle Sam to the tenth power and Christianity merely serves to lend credibility to an already approved set of political, economic, and social policies that have absolutely no clear sanction in Scripture itself.

Secularism, therefore, in biblical terms, is being conformed to the pattern of this world's way of thinking, by looking to secular authorities (politics, marketing, polls, psychology, sociology) to define the Christian faith and worldview, instead of being transformed by the renewing of our mind through the transcendent revelation of God (Romans 12:2). To become secularized is to become so attached (curved in, bent over) to "this present evil age" that the things of "the age to come" are ignored or pushed off to the side. And yet, this is precisely what is done today every week, by liberals and conservatives, sometimes in different ways, but with the same effect: secularization. The subject is us, not God; theology isn't "practical"—we want "application," "relevance," and so forth. When Christians say this, regardless of how warm their piety or affective their zeal, they are saying that the things which belong to this present evil age are the really important matters, and in their secularity they are incapable of understanding the thrust of the New Testament epistles, written as they were to those who, though actively engaged in the common civic, social, and cultural tasks of their unbelieving neighbors, had a profound sense that they were aliens; the confidence in "the things to come" fueled their activity in this world, in this present age.

> *Let us trace God's steps for a moment,*
> *as He made it clear to His people that*
> *the kingdom belonged to Him, and it*
> *was He who would build it by His will*
> *and power, for His glory and honor.*

As a footnote, it probably is worth noting that the distinction between "this present evil age" and "the age to come" does not set earth against heaven, time against eternity, matter against spirit. Rather, in the age to come, the earth itself receives its liberation from bondage to decay; time and eternity kiss, as time measures bliss rather than death and suffering; the body is resurrected to share equally with the soul in the joy of salvation. This is why orthodox Christians can be positively involved in the world, living world-affirming, world-embracing lives, and yet not give in to the naive utopianism of ideology. Just as the biblical realism in doctrines such as the Fall and redemption keeps us from either perfectionism (because of the former) or apathetic despair (because of the latter) in our own lives as Christians, so too the world-embracing redemption secured by Christ calls us to recover our role in creation as stewards. And yet, as the Reformation confessions put it, even the best works of the best Christian in this life are stained with sin, so there can be no nation that can boast in its goodness or powers to save. To work today, in the light of the age to come, provides sanity in a world of disappointments. To work today, as if we could bring about the age to come, is sure to end up only secularizing the Christian hope.

Let us trace God's steps for a moment, as He made it clear to His people that the kingdom belonged to Him, and it was He who would build it by His will and power, for His glory and honor.

Although God withheld from King David the privilege of building the temple, David was able to get the ball rolling for his son, Solomon, to whom this privileged task was given. After the officers and leaders of the families volunteered their labor and consecrated themselves to the task, David offered the following doxology (1 Chronicles 29:10–13), which closely parallels the Lord's Prayer:

> Praise be to you, O Lord,
> God of our father Israel,
> from everlasting to everlasting.
> Yours, O Lord, is the greatness and the power
> and the glory and the majesty and the splendor,
> for everything in heaven and earth is yours.
> Yours, O Lord, is the kingdom;
> you are exalted as head over all.
> Wealth and honor come from you;
> you are the ruler of all things.
> In your hands are strength and power
> to exalt and give strength to all.
> Now, our God, we give you thanks,
> and praise your glorious name.

David

Even by petitioning God for "our daily bread," we are acknowledging that "everything in heaven and earth" is the Lord's. By confessing our sins to God we are acknowledging that that which is wrong is judged so for no other reason than that it is declared to be so by God. By petitioning Him for forgiveness, we acknowledge that He alone is the judge and the justifier of the ungodly, and by asking Him to keep us from evil, we are acknowledging that He alone is our Sanctifier and Defense against the creature who has made it his sole objective to undermine the glory of God and the faith of the elect. In short, prayer should always be a "declaration of dependence," as much in regard to things earthly as things heavenly.

When we come to the doxology (from *doxa*, "to glorify or praise correctly"), we are, so to speak, wrapping up our box of petitions in suitable paper, recognizing that the *source* of every good gift is God; the *ground* of every good gift is the righteousness of Christ; the *instrument* or means of obtaining every good gift is faith in the Gospel, and the *goal* of every good gift is the glory of God and advancement of His kingdom in this world. The doxology alone should measure our theology, prayers, and activity in the church and in the world, to determine whether they are fit for a heavenly audience.

THINE IS THE KINGDOM

David learned the hard way that the kingdom of God is just that—*God's* kingdom. When it came time to give Solomon the charge to build the temple, David confessed, "My son, I had it in my heart to build a house for the Name of the Lord my God. But this word of the Lord came to me: 'You have shed much blood and have fought many wars. You are not to build a house for my Name, because you have shed much blood on the earth in my sight. But you will have a son who will be a man of peace and rest, and I will give him rest from all his enemies on every side. . . . He will be my son, and I will be his father. And I will establish the throne of his kingdom over Israel forever'" (1 Chronicles 22:6–10). Ultimately, this "son" was not even Solomon, but Jesus Christ, the Son of David and Prince of Peace. David never was "the man," but he foreshadowed Him. Israel never was David's kingdom.

247

As we have seen, Israel was, like Eden, the union of church and state, a "theocracy" through which God Himself directly spoke, judged, and acted out the unfolding purposes of redemptive history on the stage of Israel. The kingdom of God was Israel, not merely as a spiritual people (i.e., believers in the promise), but as a nation; not merely a spiritual land, but earthly real estate. Nevertheless, in the new covenant, the kingdom takes on an entirely spiritual character, where the Jews and Gentiles are brought together through the peace of Christ's sacrifice. "Understand, then, that those who believe are children of Abraham. The Scripture foresaw that God would justify the Gentiles by faith, and announced the gospel in advance to Abraham: 'All nations will be blessed through you.' So those who have faith are blessed along with Abraham, the man of faith" (Galatians 3:7–9). "In other words, it is not the natural children who are God's children, but it is the children of the promise who are regarded as Abraham's offspring" (Romans 9:8). The designation of Israel as "a kingdom of priests and a holy nation" (Exodus 19:6) is now applied to the New Testament church, composed of all Abraham's children, Jew and Gentile (1 Peter 2:9). In fact, Paul tells the Galatian church, composed of Jews and Gentiles both, that they are "the Israel of God" (Galatians 6:16).

> *To the extent that we believe that the source of the kingdom is power or marketing, it is to that extent that our message and methods will be concerned not with "our Father in heaven," but with "our Audience on earth."*

The Kingdom's Authority and Reign

Therefore, the kingdom of God is specifically defined as the reign of Christ as prophet, priest, and king, and it is advanced through the preaching of the Word, accompanied by the Holy Spirit, and by the administration of the sacraments of baptism and the Lord's Supper. It is not a kingdom that derives its source from human authority, nor does it depend on any worldly factor for its success. It is the kingdom of God that creates the people of God, not vice versa. The kingdom comes upon us as a fog, or as the wind (John 3:8), and sweeps us into it. Or to use the analogy Jesus uses in this passage in John 3:8, it is to be born a second time, to die to one identity ("in Adam") only to be raised to a new one ("in Christ"). Thus, as the Spirit blows, with His Word going before Him through His Spirit-filled messengers (all believers), a new community is created; heaven comes to earth and the kingdom of God spreads its shade across the nations.

The writer to the Hebrews makes it clear that the physical land and nation of Israel were not the ultimate promise but a mere shadow of what was to be. Even after the people were led into the "promised land": "They did not receive the things promised; they only saw them and welcomed them from a distance. And they admitted that they were aliens and strangers on earth." Even in the Holy Land of Israel? "People who say such things show that they are looking for a country of their own." But they were in their own country. Not really, argues the writer to the Hebrews: "If they had been thinking of the country they had left, they would have had the opportunity to return. Instead, they were longing for a better country—a heavenly one. Therefore God is not ashamed to be called their God, for he has prepared a city for them" (Hebrews 11:13–16). This is so vital for our understanding of the kingdom, because most Christians today tie the kingdom to a socio-political and geographical place on earth—either Jerusalem, or Washington, or both. But *"thine* is the kingdom." The kingdom belongs to God, not to man. It is not the possession of any nation or people, but the gracious gift for all believers: "For he has rescued us from the dominion of darkness [paralleled by Israel's exodus from Egypt] and brought us into the kingdom of the Son he loves [the true promised land], in whom we have redemption, the forgiveness of sin" (Colossians 1:13).

He Owns Even "Secular" Kingdoms

God's sovereign rule through providence is implied here. For instance, not only did David learn that God owned Israel; the pagan King Nebuchadnezzar learned that God owned Persia too! While he was boasting about the kingdom he had built as a testimony to his glory and splendor, God made Nebuchadnezzar insane. The king shared meals with the animals and was drenched with dew each morning; his nails grew like claws, and his hair like feathers. It is not at all far-fetched to see how self-intoxication can so upset one's balance and perspective that insanity is inevitable. As Paul said of those who exchange the glory of God for the "glory" of created things, "Seeking to be wise, they became fools" (Romans 1:22). How many modern examples do we have of the neuroses associated with self-intoxification?

Nevertheless, Nebuchadnezzar learned that his kingdom really belonged to someone else. One wonders if the church today needs to learn this lesson again: that the kingdom is created by, sustained by, and exists for God and His glory. To the extent that we shift the focus of the kingdom from God to man, to that extent it will simply become a social institution. To the extent that we believe that the *source* of the kingdom is power (i.e., economic or political crusades) or marketing (i.e., principles of business success), it is to that extent that our message and methods will be concerned not with "our Father in heaven," but with "our Audience on earth." And for those who think that the *nature* of the kingdom is temporal and earthly, their activity will be more concerned with imposing their own will on society in pursuit of the "Christian nation" idea of the kingdom. The new apostles will be the founding fathers, regardless of the fact that many of them were open critics of orthodox Christianity. The new gospel will be salvation of the chosen nation by moral clean-up and social legislation. Or, for those who think more in the vein of the church growth movement, the Spirit-empowered preaching of the transcendent Word will be replaced with down-to-earth, practical pep talks, and the administration of the sacraments will be replaced with any number of new practices selected not for their divinely ordained purpose of confirming the Gospel, but according to their usefulness in entertaining and inspiring. Evangelism will be edged out by self-oriented programs designed to make us a bit more comfortable with this world. To reinforce this, the congregation at worship will become the audience at play. The music will be happy and as down-to-earth as shampoo jingles, and it will focus on me and my personal experience rather than on God and His work in Christ.

If the reader considers such remarks far-fetched, notice how nearly the following declaration from one of the leaders of the Christian Right parallels Nebuchadnezzar's boast, "Is this not the great Babylon which I have built?"—substituting America, of course, for Babylon:

> If we are indeed God's people and we are the most important things in the universe, then He has endowed us with enormous potential that we haven't even begun to develop. . . . Carried to its end, Jesus' mandate [to move mountains] says people of faith can literally control planets, because, after all, people—not stars and planets—are the stuff of eternity. . . . The greatness of mankind is found in the dignity we achieve with God. When we see the accomplishments of Christian civilization, we have to recognize that those achievements have been nothing short of awesome.[1]

I'm not suggesting any direct correspondence between pagan kings and Christian leaders. The question I'd like to propose is, Are we a bit more concerned with our own kingdom power and glory in America than with the kingdom of God? Contrasting Americans with "jungle dwellers," this author lists the products of modernity as if they were sacred expressions of Christian faith and, at a time when even the once-triumphalistic, Enlightenment secularists are wondering if Babel (civilization) can save humanity, after all, this writer seems to think it still can, as we reflect on "how our culture has helped to reshape the destiny of man."[2] Religion is *useful* for social progress: "We have been saying for a long time that religion is good for people, but there is conclusive scientific proof that it is beneficial not just for your soul but for body and mind as well."[3] Therefore, in keeping with the Enlightenment criterion for religion (its *usefulness*, not its *truthfulness*), Robertson and other leaders seek, however unwittingly, to keep this secular experiment (is it too strong to call it the Babylonian dream?) alive. And not only does the world have America to thank. "Thanks to the Christian Coalition," Robertson boasts, "they now have a champion. They have computers. They have money and mailing lists, and they have the power to call politicians to account for their votes. . . . This has never happened before in America. Christian people have never had as sophisticated an organization as they have now."[4] It would seem that America has

251

even exceeded Israel's claim to being God's chosen nation. And notice, it is not even the works of the law that make American Christians so "blessed" by God; it is the marvels of money, technology, and well-organized teams. After comparing America to Israel and attempting to demonstrate that the former has inherited the promises of blessedness from the latter, Robertson writes,

> As we review the history of the United States, it is clear that every one of those promises made to ancient Israel has come true here as well. There has never been in the history of the world any nation more powerful, more free, or more generously endowed with physical possessions. The song "America, The Beautiful" sums it up. . . . We have had more wealth than the richest of all empires. We have had more military might than any colossus. We have risen above the nations of the earth.[5]

And why? Because of God's *unmerited favor*? That is a confusing question. On one hand, Robertson insists that it is not because we are more intelligent or superior, and yet, he writes, "It happened because those men and women who founded this land made a solemn covenant that they would be the people of God and that this would be a Christian nation. God in turn has watched over our land—*shed his grace on us,* as the song says [although one wonders how grace can be deserved]. He has prospered our endeavors. He has given victory to our forces in battle. He has kept us safe from storm and pestilence, and our material wealth has grown exponentially."[6] Even though Robertson maintains very fine definitions of God's saving grace in Christ, is this message clear in a movement that confuses the national blessing of Israel's obedience with America?

Nebuchadnezzar's boast haunts, "Is this not the great Babylon which I have built?" How far is this really from Israel's trust in the things her hands had made (Isaiah 17:7)?

Far from inhibiting us from activity and reducing us to quietists, the realization that it is *God's* kingdom is the most exciting vision imaginable. We are part of a supernatural program that outlasts the dictators, anarchies, crusades, wars, plagues, and revolutions of history. Even in this fallen world, gripped by the here and now, we are part of a transcendent, eternal family that is growing through our witness! This makes us eager participants in the affairs of this world, but not in any triumphalistic or self-confident sense: "'Not by might, not by power, but by my Spirit,' says the Lord" (Zechariah 4:6).

THINE IS THE POWER

If there is to be reformation and revival in our time, there must be a recovery of the doctrine of God's sovereignty. Here, a few points are in order.

First, God is sovereign in creation. Everything that we see around us exists not as a cosmic mistake (as in Gnosticism, embraced by much of modern science, wherein nature and matter are evil and must be either controlled or escaped by the mind), but as the activity of a self-determining, self-existent, self-sustaining God who could just as easily have chosen not to create. God created everything, including matter, nature, culture, and work. It is all under His sovereign regency because He is its author.

---

*Although human beings are held
responsible for their actions,
God's sovereignty governs history,
from the falling of a bird to
the rising of an empire.*

Second, God is sovereign in providence. Unlike the "watchmaker" of deism who created the world, wound it up, and left it to natural laws, the biblical God is just as active in nature as in supernature, in the mundane and common as in the spectacular and miraculous. Although the kingdoms of this world are not yet, in God's plan, *observably* ruled by God, even the most wicked of nations is under God's sovereign rule, whether it acknowledges it or not. We are reminded of Pharaoh: "For this very purpose *I* raised you up," God declared concerning the Egyptian tyrant who held God's people captive, "'that I might display my power in you and that my name might be proclaimed in all the earth.' Therefore God has mercy on whom he wants to have mercy, and he hardens whom he wants to harden"(Romans 9:17–18, quoting Exodus 9:16).

We recall the realization of the Babylonian king Nebuchadnezzar, "His dominion is an eternal dominion; his kingdom endures from generation to generation. *All the peoples of the earth are regarded as nothing. He does as he pleases with the powers of heaven and the peoples of the earth. No one can hold back his hand or say to him: 'What have you done?'*"(Daniel 4:34–35). Thus, even these wicked rulers who held the Jews in slavery were tools through whom God executed His plan.

The same is true of God's people even now. "Everyone must submit himself to the governing authorities," Paul told the Roman Christians, "*for there is no authority except that which God has established. The authorities that exist have been established by God.*" In fact, the ruler is "God's servant to do you good" (Romans 13:1–4). This makes sense if Paul were referring to a godly ruler, but at this time, Nero was emperor (54–68 A.D.). The Jews were expelled from Rome because of "disturbances" that were attributed to "one Chrestus," or "Christ." Although it is possible that Paul's letter was written before Nero began his reign of terror over the Christians, persecution was certainly in the background of these early Christians. That makes Paul's remarks all the more extraordinary. Like Pharaoh and Nebuchadnezzar, Nero too was raised up by God in order to further the divine plan.

There is, therefore, no power—however cruel, unjust, and wicked, that is beyond God's sovereign will. Nothing happens apart from God's decree (Ephesians 1:11), and even the outcome of a roll of the dice is determined by God (Proverbs 16:33). Although human beings are held responsible for their actions (for they really are their actions, carried out voluntarily and freely), God's sovereignty governs history, from the falling of a bird to the rising of an empire.

Third, God is sovereign in salvation. This one is particularly disturbing to us. We Americans especially have difficulty coming to terms with a God who has control over our temporal and eternal destinies. The romantic cry of the human spirit, ever since the Fall, has been, "I am the master of my fate, the captain of my soul" (William Henley, *Invictus*). And yet, God's sovereignty does not end with birds and empires.

Jesus taught God's sovereignty in salvation with utmost clarity (cf. John chapters 6, 10, 17; 15:16, etc.). Scores of texts could be adduced to support this rich biblical teaching, but two will suffice. As Paul was explaining why God's plans had not failed simply because the Jewish nation was not saved, he referred to the fact that God has always been saving a remnant. After all, did God not promise Abraham that it was through his seed that all nations would be blessed? And yet, He chose Isaac and rejected Ishmael. "Not only that, but Rebekah's children had one and the same father, our father Isaac. Yet, before the twins were born or had done anything good or bad—in order that God's purpose in election might stand: not by works, but by him who calls—she was told, 'The older will serve the younger.' Just as it is written: 'Jacob I loved, but Esau I hated.'" Paul knows what we are thinking and anticipates our response:

> What then shall we say? Is God unjust? Not at all! For he says to Moses, "I will have mercy on whom I have mercy, and I will have compassion on whom I have compassion." It does not, therefore, depend on man's decision or effort, but on God's mercy. . . . Therefore God has mercy on whom he wants to have mercy, and he hardens whom he wants to harden. One of you will say to me: "Then why does God still blame us? For who resists his will?" But who are you, O man, to talk to God? Shall what is formed say to him who formed it, "Why did you make me like this?" [Isaiah 29:16; 45:9] Does not the potter have the right to make out of the same lump of clay some pottery for noble purposes and some for common use? What if God, choosing to show his wrath and make his power known, bore with great patience the objects of his wrath —prepared for destruction? What if he did this to make the riches of his glory known to the objects of his mercy, whom he prepared in advance for glory—even us, whom he also called, not only from the Jews but also from the Gentiles? (Romans 9:14–16, 18–24)

Likewise, in Ephesians, the apostle declares,

> Praise be to the God and Father of our Lord Jesus Christ, who has blessed us in the heavenly realms with every spiritual blessing in Christ. For he chose us in him before the creation of the world to be holy and blameless in his sight. In love he predestined us to be adopted as his sons through Jesus Christ, in accordance with his pleasure and will—to the praise of his glorious grace, which he has freely given us in the One he loves. . . . In him we were also chosen, having been predestined according to the plan of him who

works out everything in conformity with the purpose of his will (Ephesians 1:3–6, 11).

God is, therefore, sovereign in our salvation, in that He has chosen us even before we chose Him; in that He has redeemed us, while we were still enemies; in that He "made us alive with Christ even when we were dead in transgressions" (Ephesians 2:5); in that He justified us through faith even though we remain sinful throughout the whole course of our life; and in that the very faith through which we are justified is itself the gift of God, and not the contribution of our own "free will." Furthermore, God's sovereignty in salvation is amply demonstrated in His ability to preserve us in that faith He gave us to the very end (Philippians 1:6), in spite of our unfaithfulness (2 Timothy 2:13).

Far from leaving us in despair, this message gives us lasting comfort:

> And those he predestined, he also called; those he called, he also justified; those he justified, he also glorified. What, then, shall we say in response to this? If God is for us, who can be against us? . . . Who will bring any charge against those whom God has chosen? It is God who justifies. Who is he that condemns? . . . For I am convinced that neither death nor life, neither angels nor demons, neither the present nor the future, nor any powers, neither height nor depth, nor anything else in all creation, will be able to separate us from the love of God that is in Christ Jesus our Lord (Romans 8:30–31, 33, 38–39).

No wonder this wonder of God's power led Paul to his doxology, in praise of God's glory:

> Oh, the depth of the riches of the
> wisdom and knowledge of God!
> How unsearchable his judgments,
> and his paths beyond tracing out!
> "Who has known the mind of the Lord?
> Or who has been his counselor?
> Who has ever given to God,
> that God should repay him?"
> For from him and through him and to
> him are all things.

> To him be the glory forever!
> Amen. (Romans 11:33–36)

Finally, God is sovereign in the consummation. As we look around the world today, there is little reason to hope that this earth will one day mirror God's glory. The end of suffering, violence, poverty, war, immorality, pollution, decay, frustration, injustice: It sounds too good to be true, and we are weary of broken promises.

The Reformation did not set out to change culture, but to restore the Gospel and the God-centered message of Scripture. And yet, that recovery itself led to the flowering of science, democracy, public education, economic progress, and civil liberties wherever it was planted.

And yet, God never promised the restoration of all things within history, as modernity has. Modernity, indeed, *has* failed on its promise. Science has not brought lasting peace and eternal answers; technology has not solved the world's problems; politics has driven armies to more genocides in the name of progress and utopia than in any other period of human history. But God's promise, though off in the distance, is certified by the fact that the age-old promises of a Messiah *have* already been fulfilled in history. As there were impatient scoffers then, so there are now and will be until Christ returns. Nevertheless, the apostle Paul counsels patience:

> We know that the whole creation has been groaning as in the pains of childbirth right up to the present time. Not only so, but we ourselves, who have the firstfruits of the Spirit, groan inwardly as we wait eagerly for our adoption as sons, the redemption of our bodies. For in this hope we were saved. But hope that is seen is no hope at all. Who hopes for what he already has? But if we hope for what we do not yet have, we wait for it patiently (Romans 8:22–25).

Notice that this text reminds us that we already have the *first-fruits* of the Spirit; that is, He has been given to us as a pledge or down-payment (Ephesians 1:14). And yet, this is not the fullness of our redemption. We are not truly redeemed until our bodies share in this salvation, just as the earth is not truly redeemed until that time. But we wait for this material redemption patiently.

Like the Gnostics of old, we often think of God as the author of redemption *from* matter, not the creator and savior of matter. But the Scriptures make it clear that God sent Christ not only to redeem individuals, but to redeem the whole creation (Romans 8:22–25). The earth will not be destroyed, as many of us heard growing up, but it will be restored by a divine act just as definitive as creation itself (Revelation 21).

THINE IS THE GLORY

At a time when the church and its clergy had accorded to themselves the worldly pomp and glory, the Protestant Reformation proclaimed, *Soli Deo gloria!* ("To God *alone* be glory!"). If human beings are saved entirely because of the grace of God and through no merit on the human side, surely all of the glory went to God. He had saved us entirely by Himself, without our help. What a ground for worship! This is the outlook that motivated a whole generation of artists, scientists, educators, writers, and common men and women in all walks of life to live for someone and something beyond themselves and their own happiness. Columbia University historian Eugene F. Rice observes that the Reformation brings us face-to-face with "the gulf between the secular imagination of the twentieth century and the sixteenth century's intoxication with the majesty of God. We can only exercise historical sympathy to try to understand how it was that many of the most sensitive intelligences of a whole epoch found a supreme, a total, liberty in the abandonment of human weakness to the omnipotence of God."[7] The "cultural elite" were God-centered, and the effect was enormous.

The Reformation did not set out to change culture, but to restore the Gospel and the God-centered message of Scripture. And yet, that recovery itself led to the flowering of science, democracy, public education, economic progress, and civil liberties wherever it was planted. First things were first. The eyes were raised to heaven, and sanity was restored for millions across Europe.

The glory has left the church because the Gospel has left the church—or has been dismissed.

Names of individuals and institutions such as Bach, Handel, Rembrandt, Dürer, Cranach, Mendelssohn, Donne, Herbert, Milton, Spenser, Raleigh, Drake, Leibniz, Newton, Harvard, Dartmouth, Yale, Princeton, Brown, the Royal Society, the French Academy of Painting, and many others could attest to the enormous significance of the Reformation message in every sphere of culture. It was not a program of "culture wars" and taking over "power bases," but of becoming the brightest and best to the glory of God, finding ways of positively contributing to a culture that would never, this side of the second advent, be perfected, but could be seasoned and enlightened. It was Bach who signed his compositions *Soli Deo Gloria*, and it is this slogan that still graces the old buildings in the great cities of northern Europe even after its message has been abandoned. Perhaps, if God granted us another Reformation, the same could be said of our era, as we embark on a new millennium. But our orientation must change.

Are we living at a time when the kingdom, power, and glory of God are championed? Or, instead of the glory of God, is the glory of self our occupation? Judging by the average Christian bestseller list, the latter. All this business about God's kingdom, power, and glory might run counter to a church that is so worldly that believers are actually encouraged to become, almost as an act of piety, "lovers of themselves, lovers of money, boastful, proud . . . , lovers of pleasure rather than lovers of God" (2 Timothy 3:1–5). We even have high priests of the new gospel, who, like the medieval champions of the kingdom, power, and glory of man resist any notion that robs man of his pretended glory. Robert Schuller, for instance, declares that "The Reformation erred in its insistence that theology be God-centered rather than man-centered" and said that its notion of sin is "insulting to the human being."[8] Nevertheless, he still considers himself evangelical and reformed, and, tragically, many believe him, since his message is now in the evangelical mainstream, and many pastors learn to imitate him at his very popular Institute for Church Growth.

The glory has left the church because the Gospel has left the church—or has been dismissed. It is not because God has been "ejected" from the public schools, but because His name, His kingdom, His power, and His glory have been replaced with our own agendas, priorities, goals, and self-glorifying interests in the church. With the exception of a few Renaissance mystics, who rhapsodized about the glory of self,[9] even the Reformers never faced the obsession with self with which we are inundated in our day. Surely, we must recover the God-centered focus of our forebears. After all, if secularism is a philosophy of life with self at the center, the church must bend its knees with the world in repentance.

CONCLUSION

Whose kingdom are we building? Boston University social scientist Peter Berger makes this sharp observation:

> Strong eruptions of religious faith have always been marked by the appearance of people with firm, unapologetic, often uncompromising convictions—that is, by types that are the very opposite from those presently engaged in the various "relevance" operations. . . . Put simply: Ages of faith are not marked by "dialogue" but by proclamation.[10]

Have we become so "down-to-earth" that we have snapped our chord connecting us to the heavenly realities? Are we so "with it" and "relevant" that we are simply echoing popular culture and are, therefore, irrelevant? And is the goal of this kingdom we are building God's glory? Whatever goals we might consider worthwhile (providing a sense of community and fellowship, assisting families in building good, solid homes, improving the moral and spiritual climate of the country, meeting "felt needs," or even building big churches) are a distraction, in competition with God Himself. And, like David and Nebuchadnezzar, anyone can be humbled. Yes, even Americans. We are in desperate need of recovering our eternal perspective—raising our eyes toward heaven, so that our sanity may be restored and so that God's kingdom, power, and glory might once again occupy the attention of the church and the culture.

NOTES

1. Pat Robertson, *The Turning Tide: The Fall of Liberalism and the Rise of Common Sense* (Dallas: Word, 1993), 266–67.

2. Ibid., 152.

3. Ibid., 277.

4. Ibid., 286.

5. Ibid., 293.

6. Ibid., 294.

7. Eugene F. Rice, *The Foundations of Early Modern Europe* (New York: W. W. Norton, 1970), 136.

8. Robert Schuller, *Self-Esteem: The New Reformation* (Waco: Word, 1982), 65.

9. Viz., Giovanni Pico della Mirandola's *Oration on the Dignity of Man*, part of which reads as if God were addressing man: "You, who are confined by no limits, shall determine for yourself your own nature, in accordance with your own free will, in whose hand I have placed you. I have set you at the centre of the world. . . . And if, content with the lot of no created being, he withdraws into the centre of his own oneness, his spirit, made one with God in the solitary darkness of the Father, which is above all things, will surpass all things."

10. Quoted by Donald Bloesch, *The Evangelical Renaissance* (Grand Rapids: Eerdmans, 1973), 12.

13

AMERICA:
MISSION FIELD
OR BATTLEFIELD?

We are going to have to realize that America is a mission field, not a battlefield. We are not going to take America back—America is lost!

I UNDERSTAND THAT THE RATINGS went through the roof on a recent "Oprah Winfrey Show" that featured Michael Jackson as special guest. As I thought about that, the decline of Western civilization began to come into sharper focus, and I wondered, "What would happen if the apostle Paul were on a modern talk show? What would he say?" Of course, it was just a thought—and not a good one; I was, after all, inspired by a bit of news concerning day-time television.

But, of course, the apostle Paul did make it onto the first century's equivalent of a TV talk show. Acts 17 records the story: Paul had been left in Athens while Timothy and Silas went elsewhere. An evangelist at the core of his being, he was looking for opportunities to build bridges with the people he was sure he would have the opportunity to meet.

The question I want to ask as we take a closer look at this famous appearance is this: Do we see the world out there as a mission field, or as a battlefield? The answer makes all the difference in the way we approach the world around us.

When missionaries get on their planes, they board realizing that they are starting from scratch. They are not going in an effort to engage in a culture war. They are going to reach people with the Gospel of Jesus Christ. They know that if, for instance, polygamous cultures are going to change, it will only be after the culture embraces the Gospel of Jesus Christ and realizes their obedience to their redeeming king, as a result of God's saving work. Let's look at Paul's audience, his speech, and then his approach.

THE AUDIENCE

Paul's audience is made up primarily of two philosophical sects, both of which continue to characterize contemporary thought, even though the labels are changed. The first were the Epicureans. These followers of Epicurus (341–270 B.C.) were basically deists, who narrowed religion to that which is rationally conceivable and calculated to give the most bang for the buck in terms of happiness. These were the ancient rationalists. They believed there were gods, but these gods were so removed that they played no active part in everyday life, as such. They were the ancient secularists, indifferent to religion and to the gods: "Eat, drink, and be merry; but we ourselves are at the center of the universe, and we are autonomous creatures. We must chart our own course."

The Stoics were at the other end of the spectrum from the Epicureans. Zeno was their founder (340–265 B.C.) and his followers were pantheists: While God was far removed from the Epicurean world, here He was part of it. God was part of the trees and the rocks, animals, and oceans. Furthermore, the Stoics believed that by transcending emotion and passion, they could create world harmony and peace. This is the New Age movement of the Ancient World (with important differences, of course), focusing on the unity of human beings and ferns! The Stoics were also fatalists, because they did not believe in a personal God but in sheer determinism.

What the two groups held in common was a love for the latest ideas. Acts records that they did nothing but spend their time at the Areopagus, sitting around debating the latest ideas. Paul had already been talking to members of this debating society about

Jesus and the Resurrection, so it was the hot topic. I can't imagine that it would have been a hot topic if he had simply asserted it. He was arguing it, probably passionately, and that meant that he probably had *reasons* in favor of the Resurrection. His reasons were compelling enough for these people to invite Paul to the theater-in-the-round for further discussion. So, suddenly Paul's ideas were not put off in a corner where religion is so often sent, or put off in a temple, but he was brought to the secular center of town where philosophy and the latest ideas where debated.

THE SPEECH

Paul's speech is very interesting: Basically, he goes through the points expressed in our Apostles' Creed. He starts out, "I believe in God the Father Almighty, Maker of heaven and earth." And it's a good place to start, because, first of all, they were not even theists; they required a basic understanding of God Himself before they could understand Jesus and the Resurrection. So Paul represents God as the Creator, sovereign ruler, and the Father of all creation.

Interestingly, this is the main point of confrontation, and it is not a "felt need." Paul did not walk into town and take a survey of topics that they would like to talk about at the Areopagus. Instead, Paul let a good case stand on its own. You can create in a person a need he never knew he had. Even apart from the Holy Spirit, you can create (purely intellectually) in a person's mind a rational need that makes sense. (Of course, only the Holy Spirit can take that out of an intellectual cast and give one a real felt need for it.) The point of confrontation is idolatry.

Bridge-building

Paul reaches out, and the bridge he builds is not necessarily a positive bridge. He is talking about idolatry as a *bad* idea, though he does call the people "extremely religious." He is using "religious" in two senses here: One is positive, as we normally use it, and the other meaning is "superstitious." This is not really what most philosophers want to hear! And yet, Paul attacked them for being too religious. It was not only true; it was a brilliant tactic. As we noted earlier, Nietzsche said that when Christian dogma

falls apart there will be a rain of gods. G. K. Chesterton said that
when men stop believing in the one, true God, it's not that they
don't believe in anything, but that they believe in everything and
anything. And here, Paul was telling "sophisticated" rationalists
that they were quite a superstitious lot!

> _We must refocus our own preaching,
> teaching, and reading on recovering an
> understanding of God's character._

How do _we_ stand on this point? Robert Bellah and his asso-
ciates in _Habits of the Heart_ mention "Sheila-ism." Sheila says, "I
don't really go to church, I kind of have church in my home. I
believe in God; it's kind of that little voice inside me." And so,
Bellah aptly concludes, "that means that there are approximately
256 million religions in America, one for each of us."[1]
We have had a proliferation of deities every bit as much a
forest of idols as Athens was when Paul found it. But isn't that
acceptable as long as we are religious? President Bush, speaking at
the National Religious Broadcasters' convention, announced,
"America is the most religious nation on earth," and he received a
standing ovation. Think of prayer in public schools—it does not
matter what god we worship. As Eisenhower said, you have to
have religion at the bottom of civil society; without it there's no
morality. "You have to have religion," he said, "and I don't care
which one it is." As long as we have school prayer, does it matter
if a Mormon does it, or a Buddhist? We would like a Christian
prayer in there, if possible, but we don't need to pray in the name
of Christ.

The Content of the Message

The word "god" has no content in America anymore, no
more content than it had for the Athenians. We must recover the
doctrine of God in our society, to fill the category of the "unknown god" with his content as Paul did with the Athenians. People have no idea who God is. "By 'God' most Americans refer to a
general sense of good and happiness in the world," according to

266

The Day America Told the Truth.[2] Ask the average Christian to define the biblical portrait of God, and he or she will find it difficult. Most can tell you about their experiences with God, but the objective content of the doctrine of God has been lost. We must refocus our own preaching, teaching, and reading on recovering an understanding of God's character.

What does Paul do to present his biblical doctrine of God? First, he tells the Athenians that the biblical God is creator of all things, visible and invisible. This is not something that either the Epicureans or the Stoics wanted to hear. They were united in believing that the realm of matter was evil, the realm of spirit good. The best thing one could possibly do was meditate and get outside of this world and matter, to break through to a spiritual state where one could focus on heaven and "the spiritual" realm and experience the sublime. Paul says God created everything, including the matter they considered evil.

Not only does the biblical doctrine state that God is creator, but also that He is Lord. Again, pagan dualism insisted that there is a part of creation that is good, created by the good god; and another region that is evil, ruled by a bad god or by demonic forces. Here Paul asserts that God is sovereign over everything, not just good, but even evil! God is not only sovereign over the realm of spirit, but over matter as well. We often take the pagan view, in that we agree God is sovereign over the realm of heavenly things, so that when we talk about religion and spiritual things we are "talking about God now." But when we talk about art, politics, culture, or science, then we are not talking about God. How different the dualistic approach is from the founders of modern science, who came out of the Reformation, insisting that science was the "second book of God." The Bible tells us why we are here, and science shows us the intricacy of that creation and explains things the Bible leaves to its discovery. These things are complimentary because there is one creator and one Lord over both. Instead, we often think that God is Lord over religion, so in order for us to go into music, it must be "Christian" music. And we distinguish between "Christian service" and secular work, because we do not really believe that God is the Lord over all areas of life and that His sovereignty extends beyond religion.

The true God does not sit around in temples, Paul says, waiting for someone to offer incense to Him or light a candle for Him. He is active, engaged, interested in every aspect of the world He created. Paul says He gives all men life and breath and everything else. In other words, Paul is telling them, you cannot confine God to religion.

And then there is the unity of the race. From one man, one historical Adam, God made an entire race. He has predetermined their times, their existence, their residences, and everything else about their lives. The Epicureans here are confronted with the personal God who is not removed from human life. It is interesting that many people see predestination as a doctrine that attempts to show the distance between us and God. But here Paul uses the doctrine to show how close God is to us.

Arminianism is halfway to Epicureanism, or secularism, because it's halfway to the point of saying that God is removed from the process of salvation. If God is my copilot, or partner, with whom I cooperate in the process of salvation, we are halfway to removing God from the picture. And I maintain that if it was good enough for the apostle Paul to preach God's sovereignty over all of life, it is good enough for us to bring back to a culture that is deistic on one side, and New Age-ish on the other.

God is also the Father. "From one man he made every nation of men that they should inhabit the whole earth, and he has determined the time set for them and the exact places where they should live. God did this so that men would seek him and perhaps reach out for him and find him, though he is not far from each one of us. For in him we live, and move, and have our being, as some of your own poets have said." Karl Barth called man "the pilgrim." God addresses us from the Scriptures as pilgrims. Even if we grew up in a wonderful, warm family environment, we are still alone and alienated and disturbed because we are pilgrims. Away from God we are always alone, even in a crowd. Paul is telling the Greeks, you are not alone, for God is so close to you right now that you could reach out and touch Him by faith.

But Paul is not buying into Stoicism either. He isn't saying that God was part of nature, because he has just established the sovereignty of the God who determines history, but is not a part of history. He is the Father of the race, not in the usual sense where you have the universal fatherhood of God, the universal brotherhood of man, and the neighborhood of Boston, but He is the universal Father of the race in that we are created in His image, and no other creature bears His image. There is a limited sense in which God is the universal Father of all.

We must be careful here, because that sense is not, of course, that of adoption for all people. Calvin asked if we should begin with the knowledge of God or the knowledge of ourselves. It doesn't matter which we start with, he concluded, because you can't talk about man without eventually talking about God. Man depends on God to have any meaning for his existence and to have any self-definition. Again, Paul is emphasizing against the Epicureans God's involvement and His nearness. It is foolish, Paul is telling them, to worship even the very delicate, brilliant imaginations of our own hands and minds. How many times have we heard, "My idea of God is . . ." But the world is not concerned about our idea of God. The world is concerned about God's idea of God, and we believe that God has revealed Himself in Scripture (both Old and New Testaments), so that any other God is an idol. And Paul is saying that as revelation unfolds, we are responsible for our decision in that moment. No, Abraham did not believe in the Trinity, but he would have if it had been revealed to him. There is a progress, an unfolding, to redemption. When we stand in a particular place in time, we are responsible for the degree to which God has revealed Himself up to that time. That is why Paul says, "In the past, God overlooked such ignorance, but now he commands all men everywhere to repent." It is not enough to have their own idea of God, they must have God's idea of God. We should not be encouraged to see people offering public prayers, attending prayer breakfasts, talking about "god" and saying they believe in "god" unless it is the God of biblical revelation about whom they are speaking.

And finally, Paul comes to the heart of the matter: Who is Christ? It is time to repent. That is what Paul tells them in the Areopagus: In spite of God's nearness and involvement with every detail of your lives, you still do not acknowledge Him.

A lot of people like to hold a positive view of general revelation, as though, somehow, people can become Christians as Buddhists. Many evangelical leaders are moving in the direction of what Roman Catholic theologian Karl Rahner calls the "anony-mous Christian," the Christian who does not know he is a Chris-tian. In fact, he can even be an atheist, says one evangelical leader, but as long as he does good things, he shows that he really is a Christian.[3]

That is a positive view of general revelation. But Paul dem-onstrates, in Romans chapters one and two, that general revela-tion only has enough power to convict us of our crimes; it does not have the power to lead us to salvation. That is why Paul says, You have to believe my revelation. This is revelation I'm bringing you. You will not get this from a beautiful night at the pops concert or from reflecting on the beauty of nature. You will not get this from viewing the Mona Lisa or from reason. You are only going to get this from revelation, which is outside of you. Whatever lenience God has shown in the past, as far as the content necessary for saving faith, now He requires all men and women to reject their idols and worship the only Way, Truth, and Life. "There is no other name under heaven, by which men may be saved."

Now, this is not very seeker-sensitive. We often think of our own situation as unique. Today, we think that pluralism is a new problem, asking, "What do we do about all these people who aren't Christians?" But this problem is encountered every time a missionary goes to a foreign land, where Christianity has never been taken or hasn't been present for centuries. Every time mis-sionaries have boarded their ships or planes, they have had to deal with the fact that these people did not get up that morning believ-ing that they would go to hell unless they accepted Christ. It is no different for us, and that is hard for us to say. We turn the situa-tion from a mission field into a battlefield when we say, "But it shouldn't be like that in America, where we've had the Gospel, from which we've sent so many missionaries." To think that America would be the object of Korean and African Christian missions, which it is now, is a source of incredible humiliation for us. It is an issue of pride, ultimately. We are going to have to realize that America is a mission field, not a battlefield. We are not going to take America back—America is lost! America at its very foundation is exactly where the Athenians were in the Are-opagus, worshiping the unknown god alongside all the idols they had time to worship.

The Confirmation of the Resurrection

It is time to trust Christ, the incarnate Son of God, Paul tells them. The Resurrection is the event which completes the work of redemption. God has proved this by raising Christ from the dead. Christ was crucified for our sins and raised for our justification. And finally, Paul says, He is the life everlasting. As I said, Paul is going through the whole Apostles' Creed, even though it was not in its present form until around the eighth century. The Creed is a great outline of the content of the Christian faith.

Paul says there is judgment at the end of time that is secured by judgment within time. At the Cross, God issued His verdict: He who believes in My Son has eternal life, and he who does not believe in Him is condemned already. God judged every believer's sin at the Cross, buried it in Christ's tomb, and conquered it in Christ's resurrection. To reject God's judgment of Christ in my place, within history, is to confirm God's judgment of me in my own place at the end of history. That is why Paul is using the Resurrection here as the confirmation of the believer's justification and the unbeliever's judgment. If somebody is raised from the dead and says He is coming back the next time, not to save, but to judge, that is a pretty reliable word.

> *Direct confrontation is what our secular contemporaries are looking for from us—not pronouncements, not dicta, but engagement, dialogue, discussion, persuasive arguments.*

Our whole faith depends on historical facts—historical facts that are just as real as the events of the Civil War. Paul told the Corinthians that if Christ was not physically raised from the dead, then Christians are, of all people, really pitiable—they have been duped. Christianity is not valuable because it helps people, though it does. It is not really valuable because it motivates them to do nice things, or because it gives them exciting experiences, but because it is true and it makes sense of the whole meaning of history.

The Resurrection gives weight to this moment we are living in time. It defines the whole purpose of our lives, the whole meaning of human history and human existence. The coming judgment, says Paul, is going to be according to strict justice; either through the imputation of Christ's righteousness which renders us absolutely perfect before Him, or through the perfect standards we think we can live up to. He says those who live by the law will be judged by the law; those who do not have the law will be judged by the law written on their hearts.

We have lost the fine art of persuasion, argument, and proclamation.

How about Paul's reception? It was mixed. Some jeered. It was not fireworks, but it was evangelism. It was apologetics, and the kingdom of God was advancing in that moment in time. Ironically, today we are willing to get jeered for our stand on moral and political issues, but we are so ashamed of being jeered for the Gospel that we will take out the offensive parts. Some were intrigued by Paul: "We would like to hear you speak on this subject later." Direct confrontation (not mean-spirited debates without humility or charity, but stimulating engagement) is what our secular contemporaries are looking for from us—not pronouncements, not dicta, but engagement, dialogue, discussion, persuasive arguments. This must be our effective evangelistic strategy. Our arguments have to be good. Even then, arguments cannot save or convert, but they can become tools in the hands of the Holy Spirit.

PAUL'S MISSION

Is it power or persuasion? Is our mission as Christians, and was Paul's mission as an apostle, one of persuasion or one of power? Notice that here, Paul does not appeal to power. He has not tried to close the Areopagus down for a city-wide boycott because of the nude statues. He does not put posters up around town inviting people to attend a public burning of idols. He doesn't even engage in "power evangelism," chasing demons or binding forces. Although he was an apostle and confirmed the Gospel through signs and wonders, Paul refuses to distract them from the real issue, which is ultimately a war of persuasion—a war of ideas and convictions.

We have to recover the fine art of persuasion. Paul had been *"proclaiming* Jesus and the resurrection," *"arguing* daily in the open marketplace." Don't you love these phrases? Not in the religious places only, but in the open marketplace. The marketplace in those days, unlike our supermarkets today, was a place not only for the marketing of fruit and vegetables, but of ideas. It was the natural place where people debated philosophy and politics and religion. There is no "Christian ghetto" approach, where Paul pinned up posters and said, "Please come to our church for an evangelistic meeting." He expected Christianity to win—not merely in the safety of the four walls of the church, but in the public square. Paul met unbelief on its own turf.

In Acts 18, where Paul goes to Corinth, we read, "Every Sabbath, Paul used to speak in the synagogue, trying to *persuade* both Jews and Greeks." Look at those words: "proclaiming," "arguing," "persuading." These words have dropped out of the evangelical vocabulary when it comes to missions. Missions elsewhere, yes; but not missions here at home. We have lost the fine art of persuasion, argument, and proclamation. Notice Paul's use of secular literature. He quotes Aratus, Cleanthes' "Hymn to Zeus." Why didn't he just read the Bible? Because these pagan poets had some truth that matched what Paul was saying. No doubt, Paul enjoyed reading it, and it also built a bridge to those to whom he was to minister.

Paul was genuinely impressed with this capital of ancient culture, idolatry and all. We cannot persuade people to embrace Christianity until we appreciate the strength of that which keeps them from embracing it. Until we understand the attraction of the idols, we will never know what arguments will persuade people away from them. Furthermore, there is much for a Christian to appreciate in pagan culture—its art, architecture, and medicine (anesthesia is nice). There is much in pagan culture that is not directly influenced by Christianity that nevertheless has much to elicit our value and appreciation, and God is even Lord over that. Those advances continue because of the goodness of God's hand. Paul gains his audience's attention by appealing to that which is familiar to them, not by that which is familiar to Paul himself, reaching beyond the core of literature which interests him most, the Torah. He reaches out to them by taking the trouble and the time to get to know and understand their culture.

These things are obvious to many missionaries, but we do not think of ourselves as missionaries in America, but as soldiers on the American battlefield, and that is our problem. We speak "Christian-eze" because that's comfortable to us. We have a whole empire of Christian books, tapes, TV, and radio with a tiny fraction of non-Christians ever tuning in (happily). Are we really doing it for the world, or are we doing it for ourselves? If we really did put the Gospel first, and if saving souls were as important as we say it is, we would push aside all obstacles and dig in to try to understand our culture as best we can. Instead of putting our culture off and fighting it (while taking its worldliness on board), we would be trying to persuade unbelievers of the Resurrection of Jesus Christ, while serving a positive, constructive purpose in society, at the post to which God has called us.

FIVE THESES FOR MOVING BEYOND CULTURE WARS

(1) We must recover the proclamation of God's character.

Like the Athenians, Americans are worshiping the "unknown god"; like Paul, we must begin with the character of God before the rest of the Christian message can make any sense. We cannot be excited about polls showing that 98 percent of the American people believe in "god," nor do we want to encourage people to go on believing in (or praying to) this unknown deity any longer. Our first mission is to fill in the blanks. In other words, it is an educational task with our own people: teaching them the character of the God we worship as Christians.

(2) We must recover the proclamation of Christ's person and work.

Methodist theologian William Willimon points up the centrality of this issue:

The modern church has been willing to use everyone's language but its own. In conservative contexts, gospel speech is traded for dogmatic assertion and moralism, for self-help psychologies and narcotic mantras. In more liberal speech, talk tiptoes around the outrage of Christian discourse and ends up as an innocuous, though urbane, affirmation of the ruling order. Unable to preach Christ and him crucified, we preach humanity and it improved. . . . By the time most of us finish qualifying the scandal of Christian speech, very little can be said by the preacher that can't be heard elsewhere.[4]

(3) We must recover the art of persuasion.

The reason that America is so secularized today is not because of public policy, but because of public belief. We must win arguments, not just cases. We must be willing and ready to give everyone an answer as never before, and this means that we will have to become better listeners—humbler, and more (dare I use this much-abused term?) tolerant of other people's points of view. We do not have to agree, but we do have to understand; otherwise, there can be no persuasion.

One of the reasons secularism became such a powerful force was that theological proclamation was not central in the church's witness; but another reason is that the public witness of the church ceased to be concerned with arguments and withdrew into its own inner spirituality. There were a few exceptions, of course, but they were lonely. One thinks, in this country, of "Old Princeton," with Hodge, Warfield, and Machen. Fiercely resisting modern liberalism, they nevertheless knew the strength of their opponents. In fact, they had studied with and under many of the leading fathers of modern liberalism. Even as cynical an agnostic as Walter Lippman concluded concerning Machen's defense of orthodoxy:

Fortunately, this case has been stated in a little book called Christianity and Liberalism by a man who is both a scholar and a gentleman. The author is Professor J. Gresham Machen of the Princeton Theological Seminary. It is an admirable book. For its acumen, for its saliency, and for its wit this cool and stringent defense of orthodox Protestantism is, I think, the best popular argument produced by either side in the current controversy. We shall do well to listen to Dr. Machen.

The American journalist, who founded the *New Republic* and provided many of the insights for Wilson's Fourteen Points and

League of Nations, added, "The liberals have yet to answer Dr. Machen. . . ."[5]

And do scholars today believe that Machen has been answered yet in any satisfying manner? Yale humanities professor and arguably America's most distinguished literary critic, Harold Bloom, doesn't seem to think so. This insightful Jewish intellectual characterizes American religion as "Gnostic." The tendency to deify the American self and divorce oneself from tradition, history, the intellect, and so on, unites diverse religious communities in America. And yet, Machen pops up again in the discussion, as Bloom contrasts his intellectual defense of orthodox Christianity with the Gnosticism of modern evangelicals, fundamentalists, and New Agers. Conservatives, he says, in their "reductive anti-intellectualism," are heirs of the "crusade against the mind, and not the legatees of Gresham Machen." Surrounded by unflattering descriptions of fundamentalists, Machen stands out in Bloom's mind. The title "Know-Nothings" should apply to fundamentalists, Bloom argues.

> It is especially applicable because they know nothing at all, including the Bible, which they carry about but appear never to have read. Real Fundamentalists would find their archetype in the formidable J. Gresham Machen, a remarkable Presbyterian New Testament scholar at Princeton, who published a vehement defense of traditional Christianity in 1923, with the aggressive title, *Christianity and Liberalism*. I have just read my way through this, with distaste and discomfort but with reluctant and growing admiration for Machen's mind. I have never seen a stronger case made for the argument that institutional Christianity must regard cultural liberalism as an enemy to faith.[6]

Bloom has just as little time for the moderate and liberal versions as for the fundamentalists. But Machen stands out. His arguments were *persuasive*. His opponents were every bit as harsh and derogatory as secularists are today against conservatives, but instead of matching slander with slander and competing in the business of name-calling, Machen looked for better arguments. The world may not *believe* better arguments, but it just might listen to a church that searches for them.

276

At the Scopes Trial, fundamentalism went in the direction of anti-cultural and anti-intellectual bigotry. Although evangelicals have tried to recover from that legacy, the persuasive power evident in Warfield and Machen is largely missing today. We must recover that robust Reformation orthodoxy that makes sense of things, and then listen to the best contemporary arguments and criticisms, and only then put together our best case possible.

(4) We must recover an interest in our culture *and* our creed.
T. S. Eliot said,

> Just as the supposed intellectuals who regard theology as a special study with which they need not concern themselves, while at the same time the theologians observe the same indifference to literature and art as special studies which do not concern them, so the masses regard both fields as territories of which they have no reason to be ashamed of remaining in complete ignorance. Accordingly, the more serious authors have a limited and even provincial audience, and the more popular authors write for an uncritical and illiterate mob today.[7]

That is what we are seeing, not only in the secular world, but in the evangelical culture as well. If Christians are going to participate in "culture," they will have to read something beyond Christian versions of the most popular books in the larger world.

Paul knew both his audience on earth (demonstrated by his grasp of its literature) and his Audience in heaven (demonstrated by his grasp of Scripture). We must strive for nothing less.

This is a very exciting period for the meeting of orthodox Christianity and postmodernity. One example of a modern liberal who has embraced a "postmodern orthodoxy" is Thomas Oden:

Neck deep in the quick sands of modernity, the postmodern mind is now struggling to set itself free. Some of these postmoderns have happened onto classical Christianity and experienced themselves as having been suddenly lifted out of these quicksands onto firmer ground. They have then sought to understand the incredible energy and delivering power of Christianity, and, in the process of returning to the classical texts of ancient Christian tradition and Scripture, have begun to discover that the orthodox core of classical Christianity constitutes a powerful, viable critique of modern consciousness. . . .

So there is a sense in which liberalism, neoorthodoxy, and fundamentalism are all surprisingly more like each other than any of them is like orthodoxy in tone and spirit. For, although they all had different responses to modernity, they are all more deeply enmeshed in the spirit of modernity than postmoderns, who have learned by many difficult routes that modernity is only a fleeting stage of human consciousness on which Christianity must not bet all its chips.[8]

Princeton philosopher Diogenes Allen adds, "There is therefore no need for Christians to continue to be defensive. Just as Socrates did in ancient Greece, we have a mission: to challenge the supposition that the status of the universe and our place in it have already been settled by science and philosophy. . . . In a postmodern world Christianity is intellectually relevant."[9]

> *Culture is not shaped by politics, but vice versa. Family values are intrinsically religious values and derive from religious convictions.*

Of course, postmodernism is itself a secular experiment, like modernism, and there are fatal reefs below, but if we know both our own faith (Scripture and its best interpreters through the centuries) and the basic presuppositions of the culture in our day, we can chart our course into the open seas of mission and opportunity. Paul knew both his audience on earth (demonstrated by his grasp of its literature) and his Audience in heaven (demonstrated by his grasp of Scripture). We must strive for nothing less.

Furthermore, we must come to terms with this basic fact: Culture is not shaped by politics, but vice versa. Family values are intrinsically religious values and derive from religious convictions. We cannot expect those who do not hold Christian convictions to accept the values those convictions convey, nor can we be surprised when the values of secularism follow the triumph of secularization in society generally. In an article in *The Wall Street Journal*, Jewish conservative Irving Kristol brought this point home:

> It is one thing to deplore abortion, or to believe there is something inherently wrong, even sinful, about it. But it is quite another thing to demand that the secular authorities enforce a theologically defined "right to life" policy. This policy is politically unacceptable to the majority of the electorate, however ambivalent their feelings. It is also unenforceable as new abortifacients come on the market. The lack of popular sanction is revealed by the fact that the rate of abortion among Catholic women is no lower than the national average. The rate of abortion among Republican women —after the necessary statistical adjustments are made for social class—is no lower than Democratic women.

Republican women

Does this mean that we do not seek the end to abortion through political means? I, for one, do not draw that conclusion. The movement to abolish slavery was fueled by Christian concerns, but there was a sufficient consensus among Christians and non-Christians alike, after a great deal of labor in persuasion, to secure a political victory. If one concludes that abortion is the taking of an innocent life, as I do, it is surely not beyond the role of the state to protect such life by force. Nevertheless, we should take Kristol's point seriously and ask ourselves if by pouring all of our money and energies into political solutions alone, we have ignored the deeper cultural crisis which renders abortion and similar acts of moral anarchy socially acceptable even among Catholics and evangelicals who are supposed to prize life the highest. Reflecting on the approach of Orthodox Jews in Israel, Kristol concludes:

> The Orthodox strategy now is to attack abortion by making Jews in Israel more Orthodox, not simply anti-abortion. Might it not be a good idea for Christians in the U.S. to pursue a parallel strategy,

instead of fostering the illusion that we are a "Christian nation" when we are not even a nation of observant Christians? Last spring, I found myself at the commencement exercises of Yeshiva University in New York. Yeshiva is a "modern Orthodox" institution. That is to say, the students pursue secular studies (and secular careers) along with religious ones and to the naked eye are not different from students at any other university. But the naked eye does not see all. These 500 boisterous young men and women in the graduating class observe the Jewish dietary laws, respect the Sabbath, know their Bible and prayerbook, and can chatter with one another in Hebrew as easily as in English. And as I watched them celebrate the occasion with their families—taking photos, shouting greetings, embracing family members—I was aware of something else. How utterly ridiculous it would have been to have a politician or a publicist give them a commencement address on "family values." . . .

The moral of this little anecdote is that, if you are serious about "family values," you have to begin by understanding that they are not secular values. Most Americans do believe in family values, but they find it close to impossible to protect or insulate young people from the secular authorities, whether political, educational or cultural. . . . In his convention speech, Pat Buchanan referred to the "culture wars." I regret to inform him that those wars are over, and the left has won. Conservative cultural critics exist and I am one such and we work hard, with occasional success, at damage control. But the left today completely dominates the educational establishment, the entertainment industry, the universities, the media. One of these days the tide will turn. In the meanwhile, however, there is no point in trying to inject "family values" into these institutions. They will debase and corrupt the very idea while pretending to celebrate it.[10]

These are difficult words for us to accept, but they should not send us into a tailspin of defeatism and despondence. Rather, they should send us back to our first calling as Christian parents, parishioners, pastors, teachers, and workers. They should challenge us to recover our own homes from the clutches of secularization. We must ask ourselves whether we are doing all that we can to teach our children the Scriptures and whether we are passing down to them a body of well-defined beliefs and a coherent worldview. If a teenager comes to his father or mother after a day of indoctrination in "tolerance" (i.e., religious and intellectual apathy) and asks, "How do you know Christianity is true and everyone who doesn't believe it is going to hell?" is the average Christian parent prepared to give him an answer? If not, God will not ask the school principal to give an account for that child; He will ask the child's parents. Imagine what kind of a church we would have inherited if the early Christians had left their children's moral, spiritual, and intellectual training up to the state! Our children are being baptized in the fire of secularism, and we cannot lock them up in their rooms or hide them from these realities. Even if they are in private Christian schools, they are never immune to secularization, as we are seeing the triumph of secularization (the downplaying of God and theology) in the churches themselves. It is a recovery of the Christian faith within the church itself, not the imposition of Christian values over a hostile society, that holds the only possibility for meaningful change.

Do we pray with our children? Do we have a regular method of instructing them in the great themes of Scripture? I don't mean throwing up a quick greeting and reading some promise taken out of context, but thorough instruction. The Protestant Reformation was passed on to the succeeding generations through the same ways that the faith has always been passed down: through catechetical instruction. In the early church, it was *The Didache* or Manual of Teaching, and the Reformation revived this method of mass education in the home and the church through its many catechisms (Luther's catechisms, the Heidelberg Catechism, the Westminster catechisms). These time-tested manuals are ideal for morning and evening devotions, and their enduring significance is measured by the fact that they are still published, used, and available at bookstores.

Now is the time to make sure our own houses are in order, beginning with ourselves, our families, and our churches. This is not to abandon the world or our place in it, but to retrench ourselves in order to have something meaningful to give to the world and pass on to the next generation. After all, we cannot pass our Christian experiences down to the next generation, but we can pass on the Christian message.

The eighteenth-century American theologian, pastor, evangelist, and missionary, Jonathan Edwards, with Whitefield and Tennant, was a leader of the Great Awakening. Not only had he inherited the great truths of Scripture from his forebears; he passed them down himself. Gathering for family holidays at the Edwards home, one could find senators, justices, writers, and even the future vice president of the United States, Aaron Burr. The president of Yale, Timothy Dwight, was Edwards' grandson, Edwards himself the president of Princeton (then the College of New Jersey). American historians find it impossible to tell the story of our nation's intellectual history without recurring references to this towering figure and his influence over theology, philosophy, education, and missions. His children and disciples launched the movement to abolish slavery. In fact, his son's tract, *The Impolicy of the Slave Trade and Slavery* (1791) was very influential, as was that of his closest disciple, Samuel Hopkins, who distributed a pamphlet to the members of the Continental Congress in 1776, pointing out the hypocrisy of overthrowing British tyranny while institutionalizing slavery of Africans.

A generation that knows or remembers nothing more than a religious experience has already fallen under the spell of secularism, even if supposedly insulated by Christian institutions.

One also remembers the influence of the Presbyterian minister, John Witherspoon, president of the College of New Jersey (Princeton), who, in addition to signing the Declaration of Independence, trained a good number of the fledgling nation's new leaders, including James Madison. There was a general impression, even among deists who were openly hostile to supernatural religion, that although biblical Christianity offended their moral sensitivities, some of the nation's keenest and worthiest thinkers were numbered among the orthodox. There was a time, then, in our evangelical past when evangelism, missions, education, science, art, culture, theology, and life were considered protagonists in the common struggle to glorify God and enjoy Him forever.

I do not relate these stories in order to suggest that only important families count, but rather to point out that in history those who really transform society are often not those who carry placards and boycott corporations, but those who are willing to dedicate their total energies and resources to the welfare of their children. No more poignantly does this come into focus than in a conversation I had with a friend who lamented his son's antagonism toward the faith. I asked him, "Do you spend much time with him?" knowing that this friend was involved in Operation Rescue and had been arrested a number of times, spending many nights in jail away from home. "Not really," he confessed. "I've hardly seen him lately." But more often, it's for less high-minded motives that we weaken our family life. Our children often grow up watching us say one thing at church about protecting "family values" and then pursue materialism, power, position, and pure self-interest Monday through Friday. If we want to produce a positive cultural influence, it will not come through politics, but through dynasties of faith.

When was the last time we had a really good conversation about the great Christian truths with our children? This is, at last, a more critical question than asking when was the last time we marched, protested, or boycotted.

Again, that is not to say that there is no place for public protests, but rather to insist that if we are really to recover our sanity in this increasingly pagan environment and become "salt" and "light" once more, we will have to pour our energies into re-educating ourselves in the basics of the Christian faith, develop a deep and lasting sense of meaning and purpose, understanding the fundamental arguments for our faith, and then pass these down to the next generation. A generation that knows or remembers nothing more than a religious experience has already fallen under the spell of secularism, even if supposedly insulated by Christian institutions. As Kristol argued above, it is time to make American Christians more orthodox, and not just anti-abortion; to pour our energy and resources into building solid Christian homes and grounding people in "the deep truths" of the Word (1 Timothy 3:9), instead of trying to get secularists to embrace the values which run counter to their creed. Surely orthodoxy does not stop with the intellect, but it does begin there. Ours is a religion of a Book, with pages, words, doctrines. Our source is the *Word* of God, not the *Feeling* of God or the *Experience* of God or the *Imitation* of God; it is a message that is entirely one-directional. It is

God addressing us; it is not a dialogue, but a monologue. God's communication with us in His Word must shape our feelings, experiences, and practice, not vice versa.

But what happens when the missionaries themselves become cannibals, all the while crying down cannibalism? Ironically, the church has made peace with the very culture upon which it has declared war. The church embraces the culture's secular notions of human nature, the meaning of life, self-fulfillment, and so on, while eschewing the values such a human-centered orientation inevitably produces. As we have seen, with Christians and non-Christians neck and neck in actual practice of the secular creed, reformation must begin in the church, and ecclesial reformation itself must begin with the recovery, not of ethics, but of theology. Reverse that priority, and a church ceases to be in truth Christian.

(5) We must be the ones to accommodate our language—not our message, but our language.

We are doing the opposite: We accommodate our message but not the language. We still speak Christian-eze; we still talk about being "blessed" and "anointed" and use other Christian language that nobody understands outside of the evangelical world. We live in our own spiritual ghetto, divorced from the real world, and yet, we are accommodating the message to the world. We market the Gospel to the world and its felt needs while failing to interact with the culture on its own terms. I am suggesting—as indeed I think Paul's example suggests—that we need to do the reverse. The biblical approach is "in the world, but not of it," not "of the world but not in it."

CONCLUSION

Recently at my bank, the teller said to me, "You know, I notice you keep depositing these checks that say 'Christians United for Reformation.' What exactly do you mean by 'Reformation'?"

I answered quickly, so as not to anger the mob behind me in line, "Well, we are trying to get the church back to the business of dealing with the big spiritual issues."

He said, "When I saw 'Reformation' I assumed you were against movies and TV and everything. Aren't you talking about moral reformation?"

"No," I replied, "it's not a moral reformation that we are talking about."

"You're kidding," he responded. Still baffled, he asked, "Well, are you a part of the religious right?"

"No. Our issues are not moral or political."

"Well, what is your position regarding gays in the military?"

"We don't have a position on gays in the military."

"You mean, you're a Christian organization, you want a reformation, and you don't have a position on gays in the military?"

"No, we don't. It's not about Christ or restoring the Gospel."

Now the line seemed very long and fidgety. He said, "You know what, you can call my [homosexual] lifestyle an abomination—"

"—I do," I interrupted, both of us grinning at the response.

"You can call it an abomination if you give me the right to co-exist with you."

"Why shouldn't I give you the right to co-exist? I expect the right to co-exist, and I am a sinner too. The only difference between us is not our guilt and corruption, but in how those two problems have been solved."

Then he asked for more information about our work and its message. "I will hear you later on this," was the clear message. Since then, I have taken him information and tapes, and he has even expressed an interest in the possibility of attending church.

But what if I happened to attend a church where he could likely hear the pastor announce that there was going to be a march later in the month to oppose "those radical feminists, homosexuals, and other perverts who are corrupting our wonderful nation"? I am not saying that it is not the church's place to condemn homosexuality; clearly it is. But the church's condemnation is spiritual, not political; it warns of a heavenly sword, not an earthly one. Furthermore, it offers a heavenly truce for anyone who is willing to put down the arms and embrace God as Father through the blood of Christ. At last, conversion accomplishes what coercion could never secure.

We can handle our situation in America in one of two ways. We can see it as a mission field, or as a battlefield, but our decision will determine our witness for decades to come. God grant us the wisdom and grace to make the correct choice.

NOTES

1. Robert Bellah et al., *Habits of the Heart* (New York: Harper & Row, 1985), 221.
2. J. Patterson and Kim, *The Day America Told the Truth* (New York: Plume/Penguin, 1992), 201.
3. Clark Pinnock, *A Wideness in God's Mercy* (Grand Rapids: Zondervan, 1992), 100, 112, 158, 160.
4. William Willimon, *Peculiar Speech: Preaching to the Baptized* (Grand Rapids: Eerdmans, 1992), 9.
5. Walter Lippman, *Preface to Morals* (Macmillan, 1929), 32–33.
6. Harold Bloom, *The American Religion: The Emergence of the Post-Christian Nation* (Simon and Schuster, 1992), 228–29.
7. T. S. Eliot, *Christianity and Culture*, (New York: Harcourt, Brace and Co., 1949), 32.
8. Thomas Oden, *After Modernity . . . What?* (Grand Rapids: Zondervan, 1990), 60, 66.
9. Frederic Burnham, ed., *Postmodern Theology* (New York: Harper, 1989), 23, 25.
10. Irving Kristol, "Family Values—Not a Political Issue," *The Wall Street Journal*, 7 December 1992.

AFTERWORD

In his concluding chapter to *Christianity & Liberalism,* written almost seventy years ago, J. Gresham Machen summed up the situation quite clearly for us:

> There are congregations, even in the present age of conflict, that are really gathered around the table of the crucified Lord; there are pastors that are pastors indeed. But such congregations, in many cities, are difficult to find. Weary with the conflicts of the world, one goes into the Church to seek refreshment for the soul. And what does one find? Alas, too often, one finds only the turmoil of the world. The preacher comes forward, not out of a secret place of meditation and power, not with the authority of God's word permeating his message, not with human wisdom pushed far into the background by the glory of the Cross, but with human opinions about the social problems of the hour or easy solutions of the vast problem of sin. Such is the sermon. And then perhaps the service is closed by one of those hymns breathing out the angry passions of 1861, which are to be found in the back parts of the hymnals. Thus the warfare of the world has entered even into the house of God, And sad indeed is the heart of the man who has come seeking peace.

> Is there no refuge from strife? Is there no place of refreshing where a man can prepare for the battle of life? Is there no place where two or three can gather in Jesus' name, to forget for the moment all those things that divide nation from nation and race from race, to forget human pride, to forget the passions of war, to forget the puzzling problems of industrial strife, and to unite in overflowing gratitude at the foot of the Cross? If there be such a place, then that is the house of God and that the gate of heaven. And from under the threshold of that house will go forth a river that will revive the weary world.

Moody Press, a ministry of the Moody Bible Institute,
is designed for education, evangelization, and edification.
If we may assist you in knowing more about Christ
and the Christian life, please write us without obligation:
Moody Press, c/o MLM, Chicago, Illinois 60610.

For more information concerning the mission and activities of
Christians United for Reformation (CURE),
address correspondence to

CURE
2221 E. Winston Rd., Suite K
Anaheim, CA 92806
(800) 956-2644